Be. Lead. Innovate.

The Leadership Framework to Build Capacity and Measure What
Truly Matters

Reda Othman & Suzanne Shippee

A1dvancement LLC was founded by Dr. Reda Othman to equip leaders with tools for personal, professional, and organizational growth. This publication reflects that mission and is released under his direction.

ISBNs
Print: 979-8-9997220-1-0

eBook (Kindle): 979-8-9997220-0-3

Printed in the United States of America

For additional resources and leadership tools, visit:
https://www.othmansleadership.com/

Contents

For Ribi, Carmen, and Layan, the three lights that guide me home
no matter where leadership takes me.
– Reda

To Nate, whose patience has been the quiet encouragement behind
every word, and whose love makes even the heaviest work lighter.
– Suzanne

To the Builders of Better Futures

This book is written for the leader in everyone. It calls to those with a desire to serve others and shape outcomes that endure. Use it as a trusted guide and reference for continuous growth, reminding yourself that leadership isn't about having all the answers, but about how you can **Be** authentic, **Lead** with intention, and **Innovate** for lasting impact.

Why we wrote this book

I (Reda) belong to the K–12 community, but my view of leadership shifted profoundly during my doctoral studies. In my very first course, *The Reflective and Visionary Leader: Theory and Practice*, I experienced a transformation in how I understood leadership. The theories and practices came alive, not just through the readings, but through the voices of my colleagues, who shared rich and deeply personal experiences from their own schools and organizations. Around that same time, I was introduced to the Myers-Briggs assessment. For me, it was more than a tool. It gave language to struggles carried quietly for years. I had been aware of blind spots in my leadership, but I could not name or understand them, nor the psychological reasons behind certain behaviors. The clarity I gained from the assessment was so powerful that I made the decision to become certified, so I could help others unlock the same awareness. From there, the journey accelerated. More courses, certifications, and eventually, the creation of *Othman's Leadership Podcast*. After three separate conversations with colleagues, each of them pointed out something I had not fully recognized in myself: I was gathering resources and insights from across fields, not just education, but leadership research, organizational development, and beyond. What I had taken for granted, they named. And in that naming came the purpose of this book: to bring resources together in one place, accessible to leaders stepping into new roles or wishing to grow in their current positions.

The achievement of *Be. Lead. Innovate.* was never meant to be a solo effort. One of the most important insights I carried forward from my Myers-Briggs journey is that each of us brings unique strengths and shortcomings to our interactions. To bring this vision to life, I knew I needed a partner, a trusted collaborator who could balance my perspective and share in the mission. That is when I reached out to my friend, Suzanne, someone I deeply respect and whose commitment to leadership development matches my own. What drew me to Suzanne as a co-author was the extraordinary breadth of her leadership experience. She has led with equal skill in corporate settings, university classrooms, and a variety of K–12 experiences , always blending strategic thinking with people-centered leadership. From managing multimillion-dollar budgets and pioneering large-scale organizational initiatives, to shaping teacher preparation programs and developing intercultural training, Suzanne has a rare ability to connect vision with execution. She brings both the rigor of business and the heart of education, and it is that combination that makes this book more than just my perspective. Her strengths in program development, talent selection, and values-based learning deepen and balance the work, ensuring that *Be. Lead. Innovate.* is not only a resource, but a guide leaders can trust across industries. What began as a personal project quickly became a shared vision - to create a book that offers principles, tools, and real stories to navigate the complex leadership journey. It is offered in the hope of shaping lasting impact, within schools and anywhere leadership is called upon.

Introduction

Although this book is written with the K–12 community in mind, its focus is not limited to education. At its heart, this book is about leadership, the practice of guiding people, making decisions that matter, and leaving an impact that extends far beyond your immediate role. Whether you are leading a school, a business, a nonprofit, or a team within a larger organization, the principles here apply. Leadership is universal, and the skills it requires are transferable across fields. The school hallway, the corporate office, and the boardroom all demand the same core ability to bring out the best in people while meeting the needs of the organization.

All stories on these pages are based on real experiences. They come from our own journeys, and from leaders who shared their experiences through Othman's Leadership Podcast. To honor confidentiality, some names and details have been adjusted, but the lessons carry the weight of reality and the benefit of hindsight.

The design of this book is intentional. Each chapter is structured to maximize both depth and usability, giving you enough substance to grow in a specific skill without overwhelming you. To achieve that, we wove together several complementary elements:

- **A Story**: because leadership is most powerful when you can see it in action. For example, a story of coaching a struggling teacher or navigating conflict with a colleague illustrates the principle better than abstract theory ever could.

- **Principles**: research-based truths distilled into clear takeaways. Each principle includes step-by-step guidance on how to apply it and examples that show what it looks like in practice.

- **Tools and Frameworks**: proven, research-backed models that leaders across industries have relied on for decades. These are not abstract "how-tos," but evidence-based approaches with a track record of impact, like the After Action Review (AAR) from the U.S. Military or Design Thinking, popularized by leading universities and now central to innovation worldwide. Their inclusion here gives you access to methods that have shaped results in sectors far beyond education.

- **Strategy in a Sketch**: a visual tool or diagram to help you see the concept at a glance and remember it when you need it most.

- **From One Leader to Another**: distilled insights from podcast conversations with leaders across industries. These are powerful, field-tested lessons from respected practitioners, giving you a front-row seat to wisdom you would otherwise only gain through years of experience.

- **Make It Yours**: reflection prompts that invite you to apply the learning directly to your context. They are designed to help you build skill by practicing, adapting, and owning the principles in your day-to-day leadership.

These pieces were not chosen at random. They are carefully curated to speak to both the head and the heart, to nourish you with knowledge, application, and reflection. Each stands on its own, but together they create a balanced diet that strengthens the reader from beginning to end.

We also considered how the material could be presented in a way that is readable, flexible, and adaptable to your needs. Time is limited, challenges are urgent, and development often happens in the margins of busy schedules. For that reason, we designed this book so you will find fundamental concepts repeated and enhanced in various contexts, and you can choose the chapter most relevant to you at the time of reading. If collaboration is the skill you want to strengthen, turn to that chapter. If you are wrestling with stress or burnout, begin there. If your next challenge is data storytelling, skip ahead to that section. The chapters are self-contained but interconnected, so whether you move linearly or selectively, you will still walk away with tools you can put into practice immediately.

Most importantly, this book is not theory for theory's sake. Everything in these pages has been tested in classrooms, in schools, in organizations, and in coaching conversations. You will find research, but you will also find practice. You will hear stories of missteps as well as successes. You will discover not just what leadership is supposed to look like, but what it often feels like when you are in the middle of it. That honesty matters, because real growth happens when ideas meet reality.

Our hope is that you will not only read these words but use them. Choose a chapter. Try a tool. Reflect on a question. Bring an insight into your next meeting or conversation. Leadership is a skill built over time, and every practice, no matter how small, adds up. This book is here to guide you as you take those steps toward being, leading, and innovating with impact.

Voices That Shaped This Book

I wish to express my sincere appreciation to the leaders who joined me on *Othman's Leadership Podcast.* Thank you for your courage and generosity in offering practical wisdom. You may never meet the readers of this book, but your insights will ripple through their schools, teams, and communities.

Every principle shared is sharpened by your lived experience, and your voices transform this book from a single perspective into a supportive partnership. In the dedicated "From One Leader to Another" section, each chapter carries your voice forward. May you see in these pages the far-reaching potential of your contributions.

Part One

BE

Explore the inner work of leadership and how habits, mindsets, and disciplines determine the influence you wield and the impact you create.

1

Be Yourself

How will Self-Awareness Help Others Trust You?

60% of people say they struggle to answer the question, "Who am I?"

YouGov Survey, 2020

This Person Doesn't Know What They Want

It was hiring season at a large urban school, and the leadership team was knee-deep in resumes. The team had posted three open roles: a math teacher, a behavior interventionist, and an instructional coach. Different responsibilities. Different skill sets. Different impact.

As they sorted through applicants, one name came up not once, but three times. Same person. Same resume. Three different positions.

At first, Principal Brown assumed it was a clerical mistake. But as they opened each application, it became clear: this person had intentionally applied to all three roles. Each cover letter had a slightly different tone, but none stood out. They were generic. Polished, maybe, but not anchored in a clear sense of direction. It felt like someone trying to be whatever the school wanted, without offering a strong sense of who they actually were.

The leadership team paused. They weren't just assessing qualifications, they were sensing something deeper. After a moment of silence, the principal summed it up in one sentence that stuck with the whole team, "This person doesn't know what they want." It wasn't harsh. It was honest. And it became the reason they didn't move the candidate forward. It wasn't because they lacked experience, but because they lacked clarity.

Dr. Brown later reflected, "If someone isn't grounded in who they are or where they can thrive, how can we trust they'll fit here and lead others well?"

That moment reminded her of something she had seen again and again. Whether in interviews, team meetings, or coaching conversations: People have more faith in you when you know yourself. When your choices match your identity. When your words align with your direction. Self-awareness is where trust begins.

PRINCIPLES

Principle 1: Own Your Story, Don't Rent It

Think of a chameleon. It changes colors for several reasons but the most important is for safety. Many leaders do the same. They act in different ways depending on who they want to impress or how much is at stake. But there's a cost. Over time, they forget what their true color was. When fitting in becomes a default, authenticity becomes a stranger. As Brené Brown (2021) explains, acceptance doesn't come from adapting who we are, it results from having the courage to show up fully. And before we can be that version of ourselves in public, we need to be that person in private. It begins with one question: What story am I telling about myself and is it even mine?

Schwartz, Gomes, and McCarthy (2010) describes identity as a reflection of the stories we repeat to ourselves. But too often, those stories aren't authored, they're absorbed. Passed down from family, shaped by rejection, or hardened through years of comparison, we start believing things like, "I'm not enough," or "If I show who I really am, I'll be rejected." These internal scripts run quietly in the background, influencing our choices, confidence, and sense of worth. According to psychologist Daniel Goleman (1995), emotional memory is stored deep in the brain's wiring, often activating before we even realize it, especially when we've been shaped by fear or shame. That's why many leaders don't realize they're editing themselves; their brain has already rehearsed the performance before they even enter the room. And research from Carol Dweck (2006) shows that individuals with a fixed mindset often define their identity through the lens of others' expectations, equating authenticity with risk.

So what does it take to change the narrative? It starts by reflecting on these three things:

1. Spot the Script: What belief seems to be guiding how I am thinking or acting right now?

2. Trace the Voice: Whose approval or expectation might be behind it?

3. Reclaim the Pen: What truth can I name instead that reflects my values, not my fears?

Write your new story in one or two sentences. Speak it to yourself before a tough meeting, an important conversation, or any moment when the instinct to conceal yourself returns.

Authenticity begins with self-awareness. And the leadership we trust most isn't the kind that tries to impress us, it's the kind that feels grounded, whole, and real. So, the next time you feel yourself pretending, pause and ask, "Am I trying to be who others say I should be, or am I being authentic?" That's the moment you take back your story and lead from it.

Principle 2: Lead Because You Are Capable

Many leaders wait to take action until they feel more prepared, confident, or "ready." True leadership starts with recognizing that you are already capable. Act with the skills, values, and perspective you have now. Stop demeaning yourself, focus on your strengths, and lead decisively. Growth comes through action, not perfection. This idea, anchored in the work of Louise Hay (1984), challenges the belief that worth is something we must earn. As she once wrote, criticizing ourselves doesn't create change, self-approval does.

But self-worth without self-awareness is conceit. Goleman (1995) explains that emotional self-awareness is a key pillar of emotional intelligence. He defines self-awareness as the ability to recognize what we're feeling as we're feeling it. Without this awareness, emotions take the wheel. But when we can name them, e.g., anger, shame, jealousy, we shift activity to the brain's neocortex, creating space for a thoughtful response rather than a knee-jerk reaction. It's less about controlling our emotions and more about identifying them with clarity for an appropriate response.

This same principle is echoed in *The Secret*, where Rhonda Byrne (2006) describes feelings as internal feedback systems, messengers that tell us when we're aligned with or drifting away from our values. The goal is not to avoid discomfort, but to notice them as a cue. Am I out of sync with who I am and want to be? What is the root cause of this reaction?

So how do you practice this? Start small. At least once a day, pause and check in:

1. What emotion am I feeling right now?
2. Where do I feel it in my body?

3. What might this emotion be trying to teach or protect?

4. How would I respond differently if I believed I was already enough?

You don't need to fix anything in that moment. You just need to notice. That noticing becomes the pivot point from reactivity to reflection, from shame to steadiness.

Leadership isn't about proving your value. It's about leading from it. The moment you stop chasing worth and start observing your internal world, you become more grounded and trustworthy.

Principle 3: Stop, Drop, Roll On

When we can't identify what we're feeling, it becomes difficult to understand our stress, disappointment, or shame. Without the words to name these emotions, they can cloud our thinking and drive our reactions. As Brown (2021) writes, "Language is our portal to meaning-making, connection, healing, learning, and self-aware-ness." Simply put, the ability to name our reality is an essential life skill.

Lieberman (2013) explains through neuroscience research that labeling an emotion moves us from reactivity to regulation. When we give a feeling a name, we shift brain activity from the amygdala (the panic zone) to the prefrontal cortex (the reasoning zone). And that shift matters because leaders who can recognize their emotions as they happen are more likely to respond with clarity than react with confusion. It's the difference between snapping at a colleague and pausing to say, "I'm feeling overwhelmed right now, and I need a minute."

But naming is only step one. The next step is determining how that emotion is causing you to hide your true self from others. It's time to shed the mask we've learned to wear to protect our-selves. That mask might look like perfectionism, people-pleasing, over-achieving, or detachment. These aren't flaws, they're adaptations. We've learned them to fit in, stay safe, or get ahead. But if we're not careful, those same masks become walls. And what started as protection ends up limiting connection.

Simon Sinek (2009) helps us understand this through his concept of alignment: your WHY (values), HOW (behaviors), and WHAT (presence) should tell the same story. That's what authenticity really means, not oversharing or putting your emotions on display, but leading with insight and integrity.

Here's a daily practice to keep you aligned:

1. Name the Feeling: What's actually going on under the surface?

2. Spot the Mask: What role do I step into when I feel unsafe or unseen?

3. Choose the Integrity Move: What would it look like to be true to myself while still being considerate of others?

Naming emotions and dropping the mask are powerful practices that encourage self-awareness and encourage you to ask if your behavior is protecting, preventing, or promoting your real self. And as Brown (2021) reminds us, "Clear is kind." When you boldly express your values, emotions, and expectations with clarity, you inspire trust, ignite momentum, and lead yourself and others toward meaningful, positive change.

Principle 4: Look Inside and Out

Effective leadership requires self-awareness and awareness of others. To lead with clarity and confidence, you must pay attention to your morals, motivations, and behaviors, as well as how your actions are perceived and experienced by those around you. Focusing on only one perspective gives an incomplete understanding and limits your impact. Organizational psychologist Tasha Eurich (2017) defines this as the difference between internal self-awareness and external self-awareness.

Internal awareness is knowing your values, triggers, aspirations, and emotional patterns. It's your compass. Internal self-awareness keeps you grounded. It gives you clarity in moments of confusion and confidence when the pressure rises. But without it, you may find yourself playing roles to gain approval, abandoning the very values you want to model.

At the same time, external self-awareness doesn't mean chasing feedback or performing for praise. It means tuning in. How does my energy affect the room? How is my tone interpreted by this team? External awareness is understanding how your behavior affects others. It's the reflection of those around you and it's important.

Goleman (1995) found that individuals who cultivate both types of awareness, along with emotional regulation, are not just more empathetic, but more effective. They don't ignore how they feel or how others feel but use that information to course-correct in real time, leading with both honesty and care.

Evaluate yourself:

1. Inner Check: What value am I acting from right now? Is this reaction aligned with who I want to be?

2. Outer Check: How might my words or body language be interpreted? What emotional residue am I leaving in the room?

3. Adapt with Integrity: What shift could I make that honors both my truth and my impact?

When internal and external self-awareness work together, your actions are coordinated. You become the kind of leader who knows what is important and profitable for you and others.

So before your next meeting, decision, or conversation, pause and ask yourself: "What am I bringing into this space and how will others experience it?" When both mirrors are clean, leadership becomes both personal and relational.

FROM ONE LEADER TO ANOTHER

Suzanne Shippee

Retired Regional Sales Manager, Director of Clinical Experiences, and Coordinator of English Learning
  As heard on Othman's Leadership Podcast, Episode 24

From Imitation to Impact

When I (Reda) sat down with Suzanne Shippee, I expected to hear stories about strategy, structure, and leadership wins. And while those certainly came up, what stood out most was her candor about the inner work of leadership, the kind that doesn't show up on organizational charts or performance dashboards.

Early in her leadership journey, Shippee found herself grappling with a challenge many rising leaders face: how to lead with credibility while still staying true to herself. She spoke about a mentor she admired who was polished, reserved, and formal. Naturally, she assumed that to be respected, she needed to emulate that same style. So she did. But in a very short period of time, she noticed something was off. "It didn't feel right," she told me. "And worse, it started to strain one of my key relationships at work...That's just not me."

That realization became a turning point. "I learned that leadership isn't about performing someone else's version of success. It's about honoring your own values and voice." As someone who's naturally animated, enthusiastic, and relational, Shippee began embracing those qualities rather than editing them out. The shift was subtle, but powerful. Her team responded with their own energy and enjoyment of the work they accomplished together.

Shippee continually seeks to ground her thoughts and actions in a purpose greater than herself. She starts her day with a morning quiet time to prepare spiritually and emotionally, and ends with evening physical exercise and mental reflection to destress and refresh. A good, hard look at the positives and negatives of the day gives her a new perspective for continual improvement. "Taking responsibility models the honesty I want for my team," she said, explaining how those daily practices help her lead with humility, not defensiveness.

Shippee offered another powerful insight into authentic leadership, this time, around delegation. Shippee admits that it doesn't come naturally to give up control but she's learned that the benefits outweigh the costs. Autonomy succeeds where micromanaging doesn't. "I set the goals and the timeframe," she explained, "and then I let the individual use their personalities, talents, and methods to reach them." The result? "They've enjoyed it more because they have the freedom to work in a way that suits them, and we still meet all objectives."

Shippee's leadership philosophy is rooted in honesty, integrity, and authenticity. As she proved, imitation might be the highest form of flattery, but real leadership begins when you trust your own voice.

STRATEGY IN A SKETCH

The Myers-Briggs Personality Framework helps leaders understand how people perceive the world, make decisions, and interact with others. It reveals patterns that often explain tension, miscommunication, or missed opportunities. At its core, the framework sheds light on preferences, moves beyond labels and asks, "How does my style impact others? When conflict arises, do I double down on my preferred approach, or adjust to foster collaboration and achieve results?" This framework matters most when it moves us from self-awareness to self-adjustment.

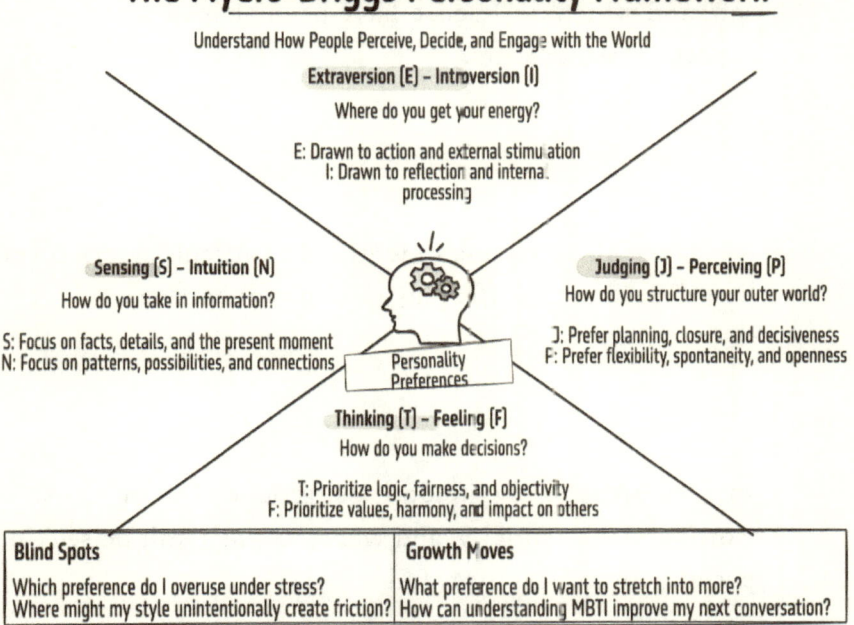

The Myers-Briggs Personality Framework

Understand How People Perceive, Decide, and Engage with the World

Extraversion (E) – Introversion (I)

Where do you get your energy?

E: Drawn to action and external stimulation
I: Drawn to reflection and internal processing

Sensing (S) – Intuition (N)

How do you take in information?

S: Focus on facts, details, and the present moment
N: Focus on patterns, possibilities, and connections

Judging (J) – Perceiving (P)

How do you structure your outer world?

J: Prefer planning, closure, and decisiveness
F: Prefer flexibility, spontaneity, and openness

Personality Preferences

Thinking (T) – Feeling (F)

How do you make decisions?

T: Prioritize logic, fairness, and objectivity
F: Prioritize values, harmony, and impact on others

Blind Spots	Growth Moves
Which preference do I overuse under stress?	What preference do I want to stretch into more?
Where might my style unintentionally create friction?	How can understanding MBTI improve my next conversation?

With acknowledgment to The Myers-Briggs Company, exclusive publisher of the official MBTI® assessment since 1975

MAKE IT YOURS

- Which aspects of my identity feel aligned with my authentic self, and which do I sense have been shaped more by the expectations of others?

- When was the last time I identified a difficult emotion and how did naming it affect my response or behavior?

- In what areas of my life do I feel grounded in my sense of worth and authenticity, and where might I still be seeking permission to lead as my full self?

2

Be Courageous

How can you Provide Feedback That Fuels Growth?

Constructive feedback is a gift. It helps people grow, builds trust, and improves performance.

Sheila Heen

The Observation

Ms. Carter had been teaching eighth grade English for nearly a decade. Her classroom walls were lined with student essays, literary quotes, and motivational posters in soft pastels. She took pride in the environment she'd cultivated, a place where students felt safe, known, and occasionally even inspired.

So when she saw the calendar invite from her principal, Mr. Gomez, for her formal evaluation, she didn't worry. If anything, she was ready to shine.

That morning, she kicked off a lesson on Of Mice and Men with a warm-up about dreams and dignity. Her students were a bit rowdy, but she moved through the lesson with her usual energy, asking thoughtful questions and weaving in student voices.

The next day, she met with Mr. Gomez for the post-observation conference. He started with compliments about her rapport with students and the creative structure of her lesson. But then, gently, he shifted: "I did notice that some students weren't fully engaged. A few seemed unsure of what the objective was. Have you considered using clearer success criteria or structured check-ins?"

Ms. Carter smiled tightly and nodded. But her stomach sank.

Success criteria? Unclear objective? She'd literally written the goal on the board and circled it. She'd spent hours planning that lesson. Did he not see the student who stayed after class to ask more about the theme of loneliness? Or the boy who never participates, raising his hand?

The rest of the conversation passed in a blur. She left the room feeling defensive and wounded. Over lunch, she vented to a colleague, "He's nitpicking. He has no idea what it's really like in that room."

For the next few weeks, she avoided Mr. Gomez in the hallway. She replayed his feedback in her mind, not as constructive, but as criticism. And the more she dwelled on it, the more she felt unappreciated.

It wasn't until a quiet moment over spring break while she was revisiting her lesson plans and sipping coffee in a café that something shifted. She looked again at the feedback. Without the sting of the moment, it read differently. Clearer success criteria. More structured check-ins. Not a dismissal of her talents, just a suggestion to deepen her impact. It wasn't personal. It was professional. And maybe, just maybe, it was an opportunity to grow. She learned that just like giving feedback, receiving feedback well is a skill, one that can be learned and practiced.

PRINCIPLES

Principle 1: Use Feedback As Input, Not Identity

Feedback can feel deeply personal. A missed expectation or a simple comment can punch like a judgment on who we are, not just what we did. But what if feedback wasn't about your identity, but your direction? Imagine hearing your GPS say "recalculating route." You don't panic. You don't spiral into shame. You adjust. Feedback works the same way, it's not a verdict, it's a signal.

Douglas Stone and Sheila Heen (2014) in *Thanks for the Feedback* describe how feedback often prompts what they call "identity triggers," those internal alarms that make us feel exposed, off-balance, or under attack. But learning to receive feedback well starts with reframing it. Instead of asking, "Is this feedback true?" try asking, "What part of this might help me grow?" This shift moves us from defense to development. From threat to choice.

This mindset is what the authors call a growth identity, a belief that feedback, even when it stings, is still just data. It's someone's perspective, shaped by emotion, context, and interpretation, not absolute truth. You don't have to agree with all of it to learn from some of it.

Marshall Rosenberg's in *Nonviolent Communication* (2015) reinforces this idea. He teaches us to separate feelings from evaluations, and evaluations from needs. When we hear "You're not leading effectively," the instinct might be to feel shame or anger. But a more beneficial translation might sound like, "This person likely has a need for more clarity, structure, or collaboration and they're expressing that through feedback." That lens softens the blow and opens the door for dialogue instead of defensiveness.

Try this three-step practice the next time feedback catches you off guard:

1. Pause the Story: What reaction or identity trigger is surfacing for me?

2. Mine the Message: What useful insight might be underneath the delivery?

3. Respond with Intention: What clarifying question or grounded response could keep this about learning, not defending?

Receiving feedback doesn't mean agreeing with everything. It means being open enough to reflect and confident enough to choose what you carry forward. Leadership requires that kind of filter: one that's strong enough to protect your sense of self, but open enough to let truth in.

Principle 2: Endorse The Advantages

Trying to drive on a dark night with headlights off is like working without constructive feedback. It can lead to uncertainty, second-guessing yourself, and silent frustration. Now imagine turning on your brightest lights and blinding oncoming traffic. No one wants that inconsiderate behavior when driving or receiving feedback. Leadership is about finding the balance: enough light to help others grow, but not so much that it stuns them. This is the discipline of clarity and the true courage behind giving valuable feedback.

We often avoid giving feedback because we fear damaging relationships or being misunderstood. But as Ken Blanchard and Spencer Johnson (2015) remind us in *The New One Minute Manager*, great leaders look at it as a positive occasion. They don't wait for quarterly reviews but choose to catch people doing something right and offer feedback that is specific, timely, and sincere. Avoiding or delaying feedback doesn't just miss the moment, it misses the opportunity for relationship building and career growth.

Marshall Rosenberg's *Nonviolent Communication* model (2015) sharpens this idea further. Effective feedback isn't about judgment, it's about consideration. It begins with observation, not accusation, names the emotion, articulates a need, and ends with a respectful request. Notice the difference between, "You're careless with deadlines" versus "Your report came in late and meeting timelines matters to our goals. What measures can you adopt to ensure a timely report next month?" One blames, the other builds.

Giving feedback should send a message that says, I care enough to tell you the truth and I trust you enough to handle it. According to Stone and Heen (2014), most feedback falls flat not because we don't know what to say, but because we don't know how to say it in a way that people can actually hear. The key? Start with one specific behavior. Make your intention clear. Keep your tone grounded. And deliver it with the goal to support, not correct.

Here's a simple rhythm to practice:

1. Spot It: What moment or behavior stood out to you?

2. Say It: What's the clearest, kindest way to name it?

3. Support It: What action or resource can help them take the next step?

Leadership involves telling the truth in a way that preserves dignity. Because clarity isn't cruelty, it's care. And when you combine directness with respect, feedback stops feeling like a spotlight on failure and starts becoming a guide toward possibility.

So the next time you feel the urge to hold back, pause and ask: "Is my silence helping this person grow or just protecting my own comfort?" Then say the thing that matters. Say it clearly. Say it kindly. That's courage in action.

Principle 3: Start with Curiosity, Not Correction

Effective feedback starts with curiosity, not control. When leaders approach others with understanding rather than trying to correct or assert authority, they create space for growth. This mindset improves conversations, strengthens trust, fosters learning, and transforms relationships.

In *Crucial Conversations*, Patterson et al. (2002) highlight that our emotional responses are often shaped by the stories we tell ourselves about others. We jump to conclusions like, "They just didn't care," or "They weren't prepared," when in fact, we may not have the full picture. The authors urge leaders to "Master Their Stories" by pausing to ask, "What might I be missing?" That single moment of curiosity often determines whether a feedback conversation leads to reflection or aversion.

Douglas Stone and Sheila Heen (2014) reinforce this idea in *Thanks for the Feedback*. They found that one of the most common breakdowns in feedback is assuming we already know why someone acted the way they did. But asking a question like, "What was your intention here?" or "How did you experience this?" often reveals new insights that shift the entire tone of the exchange. These small questions can unlock deeper understanding, disarm tension, and build connection.

Marshall Rosenberg's *Nonviolent Communication* (2015) provides a practical map where feedback follows a rhythm of observation, feeling, need, and request. For example: "When I noticed the slides were incomplete, I was concerned because I need one day to practice the presentation. Next time, why don't we review the situation one week before, and again three days before the due date?" This style models empathy without lowering standards. It's not about sugarcoating. It's about staying connected while being direct.

Here's a practice to reframe feedback:

1. Notice Your Narrative: What assumptions am I bringing into this conversation?

2. Lead with Inquiry: What question could open space instead of closing it?

3. Anchor in Empathy: How can I express my concern without casting blame?

Leadership rooted in discovery isn't soft, it's strategic. It requires self-regulation, a genuine interest in the other person's perspective, and a belief that most people want to do well. When we ask before we assume, we turn feedback into a co-created experience. We move from, "Here's what you did wrong," to "Let's make sense of this together." And that's when real growth begins.

Principle 4: Be Brave Enough to Go First

Sometimes, feedback may not be evaluative at all. It may just be a matter of sharing information that helps. In groups, sharing can feel uncomfortable, which is why most people wait until one person is brave enough to go first. When no one speaks up, the unspoken rule becomes, "don't take the chance." As the authors of *Crucial Confrontations* explain, the longer we withhold constructive feedback, the more we normalize avoidance and the harder it becomes for others to break the silence (Patterson et al., 2004). The first voice doesn't just offer insight, it changes what's possible in the room.

A simple story brings this to life. During a virtual staff meeting, a principal spent seven minutes speaking under the assumption everyone could see what he could see. Seventy educators stayed silent, watching with apprehension and confusion. Eventually, one colleague gently asked, "Excuse me, are you sharing your screen?" His surprise was immediate and so was his question: "Why didn't anyone say something sooner?" Another staff member admitted,

"I was building up the courage." That one sentence captures what so many of us feel. We know something's off but we hesitate. We wait. And in that waiting, we miss the chance to create a climate of cooperation and camaraderie.

According to Stone and Heen (2014), the hardest part of feedback isn't finding the words, it's managing the emotional risk. But when someone speaks first, even with a small observation, it lowers the threat level for everyone else. It sets a new tone, one where care and truth can coexist.

Think of speaking up like opening a window in a stuffy room. It might disrupt the stillness, but it brings in fresh air needed for everyone. As Blanchard and Johnson (2015) remind us, effective feedback doesn't have to be flawless. It just has to be timely. The sooner we say the small thing, the less weight it carries, and the easier it is for others to join the conversation.

Here's a practice to build this habit:

1. Notice the Pause: When you sense something's off but no one is speaking, that's your cue.

2. Choose Clarity with Care: Ask yourself, "How can I say this gently and clearly?"

3. Set the Tone, Not the Standard: When it's obvious that a voice is needed to open the conversation, don't let the pursuit of perfect phrasing hold you back.

Courage in feedback can often simply include being first to share. When you break the silence with care, you're not just offering feedback, you're giving permission to others to do the same. You're saying, "It's safe to speak the truth here." And that's when cultures begin to shift.

FROM ONE LEADER TO ANOTHER

Joaquin Reyes

Learning Solutions Consultant, Santander Bank; iPEC Certified Coach
   As heard on Othman's Leadership Podcast, Episode 20

Call Them Forward

Joaquin Reyes learned his earliest lessons in leadership behind a popcorn counter. As a young supervisor at a movie theater, he noticed that new hires were constantly being corrected but never shown what "good" actually looked like. "The junior managers would say the stand wasn't clean enough," he recalled, "but no one defined what clean meant." That disconnect sparked a deeper realization for Reyes. Feedback that only calls out problems but doesn't clarify expectations sets people up to fail. It's not just about identifying gaps; it's about coaching people to close them.

That mindset followed him into the training world, where he began using the SBI model - Situation, Behavior, Impact - to ground his feedback in observation, not judgment. "When we say things like 'you were unprofessional,' it doesn't help," Joaquin explained. "But when we say, 'Yesterday during the meeting, you interrupted someone mid-sentence, and they didn't speak again,' that creates clarity." Specificity doesn't soften the feedback, it gives it impact. As he put it: "If we want people to grow, we have to show them what that looks like."

Another experience that shaped his philosophy came when a leader gave him feedback without ever looking up. "I was standing there, and he didn't even raise his eyes from the desk," Reyes said. That moment stuck with him, not because of what was said, but because of how it was said. "If you're not emotionally present, you're not ready to give feedback," he reflected. For him, giving feedback isn't just about delivering a message, it's about showing up with intention, presence, and respect for the other person.

Reyes believes that feedback works best when it emphasizes a person's strengths while addressing their actions. "You have to reinforce the person's identity and then talk about the behavior," he said. He shared a story about a top performer in training who kept dominating the discussion and silencing others. Instead of chastising the person, he affirmed their confidence and experience and added, "Have you noticed that when you speak first, others stop sharing?" That moment didn't shut the person down, it invited them in. "People need to feel seen before they'll listen," he said.

In every context, from popcorn counters to corporate board-rooms, Joaquin has learned that feedback is not a transaction; it's a trust-building moment. When you offer it with clarity, care, and belief in the person's potential, you're not fixing them, you're help-ing them grow into who they already have the capacity to be.

STRATEGY IN A SKETCH

Giving effective feedback is difficult. That's where the Situa-tion-Behavior-Impact model (SBI) comes in. It gives you a simple structure to deliver feedback that's clear, direct, and fair, without triggering defensiveness or shame.

Most feedback fails because it's vague ("You're not being a team player") or emotional ("I'm angry with you"). SBI forces you to slow down and separate facts from frustration, and anchor your message in what happened, not how you felt. It's an extremely useful frame-work when tensions mount and stakes are high. Sketch it out ahead of time to center yourself and use it to deliver praise just as much as to critique. Pro tip: Don't skip the "impact" step. That's the moment the other person hears why it matters, and why it's worth changing.

SBI Tool

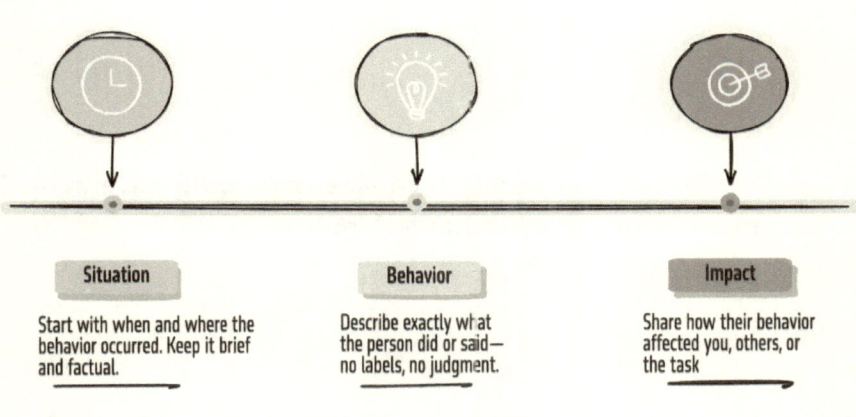

Situation

Start with when and where the behavior occurred. Keep it brief and factual.

Behavior

Describe exactly what the person did or said— no labels, no judgment.

Impact

Share how their behavior affected you, others, or the task

Adapted from the Center for Creative Leadership's guide, Feedback That Works (2017)

MAKE IT YOURS

- How do I typically respond when I receive feedback? Which of the above strategies could help me respond more effectively?

- When have I withheld feedback that could have helped someone grow? What stopped me?

- How will I change the feedback approach I use to emphasize strengths and encourage growth?

3

Be Understood

How Can You Communicate Your Message with Impact?

A brilliant idea that no one understands is no better than silence.

David Ogilvy

If They Can't Understand It, It Doesn't Matter

One of the most promising professional communities I (Reda) have ever been part of was a small district-wide team tasked with rethinking how we supported teachers. The mission was to improve instruction and learning outcomes across schools. What made the work special wasn't just the goal, it was the tone. Our lead facilitator was one of the most open and collaborative leaders I've worked with. She welcomed feedback and even changed our meeting flow to include a "collaborative agenda," where anyone could contribute items for discussion.

When my turn came, I added something I felt deeply passionate about: knowledge management. I had been reflecting on how much wisdom was being created inside our schools, but how little of it was being captured or shared. I imagined a living system, something that would gather, organize, and distribute ideas and resources so teachers wouldn't have to reinvent the wheel every year.

I was given the floor. I began to speak. And after three minutes... I crashed.

My thoughts spilled out, disconnected, abstract, and overly complex. I saw puzzled faces. Then came a wave of clarifying questions, which only made me more flustered. I knew exactly what I meant but no one else did. The follow-up questions illuminated the confusion. "Wait, are you talking about a software platform or a meeting format?" "Is this a plan we'd pilot or just a suggestion for now?" The sequence of my message was off. I had mixed big ideas with details and assumptions without guiding people through the logic.

I had been contemplating this exchange for weeks and now was utterly disappointed in my inability to convey the idea I believed could help teachers across the district.

Six weeks later, we had another meeting. This time, I came back prepared. I had spent time learning about communication frameworks, especially the Pyramid Principle, and realized just how much I had obscured the point. So I restructured my message and started with three big ideas: what knowledge management is, how it could help us accomplish our shared goal faster and more efficiently, and what we'd need to implement it. I built upward from there.

And this time, the response was different. One participant leaned in and said, "Now this is something we can actually test. I can see where we'd start." Heads nodded. Questions were about how we could accomplish it, not what it was. We finally had momentum. That experience taught me that even a great idea holds little value if it cannot be clearly understood by others.

PRINCIPLES

Principle 1: Discover Relevance

Communication only matters when it connects with the audience. Leading with your own agenda, without understanding what others care about, limits impact. The most effective communicators focus first on what matters to those they are speaking to, ensuring their message is relevant, engaging, and meaningful.

Nilofer Merchant (2011) describes great communicators as part strategist, part anthropologist. They study their audience's values, pressures, and pain points, then shape their message to resonate. It's not manipulation, it's alignment. Whether you're introducing a new policy, pitching an idea, or giving feedback, people tune in when they hear themselves reflected. "We need to cut costs," is better received when worded differently: "To protect the programs our students rely on, we'll need to reduce spending by 10%." Same message, but connected to their concerns.

This principle is embedded in Chip and Dan Heath's SUCCESs model in *Made to Stick* (2007), especially the pillars of Emotion and Credibility. People remember messages that connect to what they care about and believe messages when they feel real and relatable. That's why analogies, metaphors, and stories are powerful tools. A teacher explaining standards-based grading might say, "Think of it like leveling up in a video game, each unit builds toward mastery." That framing invites something relatable and positive.

Here's a communication strategy to apply this habit:

1. Listen First: What does your audience value, fear, or need clarity on?

2. Frame for Relevance: Lead with the impact that matters to them, not just the information you want to share.

3. Anchor with Connection: Use examples or analogies that feel familiar and affirming.

Meeting people in their context builds trust. It signals, "I understand you before I ask you to understand me." When individuals feel seen and acknowledged, they're more open to engaging with new or challenging ideas.

Principle 2: Listen to Understand

Communication is like a bridge, it only works when both sides are firmly anchored. No matter how strong the structure, it can't hold if one end is unstable. Real connection and purpose are achieved when both sides are secure and engaged. That's why the best communicators begin not with persuasion, but with interest. They listen first.

This idea echoes across leadership wisdom. Rosenberg (2015), in *Nonviolent Communication*, explains that empathy, not logic, is what opens people up to dialogue. When others feel genuinely heard, they're far more likely to listen in return. Stephen Covey said it simply, "Seek first to understand, then to be understood." Listening in leadership involves more than just hearing words; it requires reflecting, clarifying, and noticing what's not being said.

Practicing this kind of active listening means asking open-ended questions and mirroring what you hear. For example, in a tense conversation, instead of reacting with a defense or fix, you might pause and say, "It sounds like you're feeling overwhelmed because the timeline feels unrealistic. Did I get that right?" That moment of validation doesn't just calm the emotion, it helps uncover the real issue beneath the surface. It also signals that you're not here to win, you're here to work together.

Nilofer Merchant (2011) reinforced this in a Harvard Business Review article. She says that if we want our ideas to be heard, we must first build a bridge of relevance and connection. Listening, she argues, earns us the right to contribute meaningfully.

Try this listening framework before offering feedback:

- Pause to Reflect: What's this person really trying to express?

- Check for Accuracy: Paraphrase their words back. Ask, "Did I get that right?"

- Make Room Before You Respond: Wait to speak until they feel understood.

Leaders who listen like this don't lose authority, they gain influence. When people feel heard, they become more receptive, not just to your message, but to your leadership.

Principle 3: Start with the Core, Then Cut the Clutter

Have you ever tuned into a radio station and only heard static? There may be a valuable message, but the interference makes it hard to receive. When leaders communicate in the midst of distractions, important ideas risk being lost in the noise. Words pile up, meaning gets buried, and people walk away confused or disengaged. Clarity is a crucial communication skill. Every message you send is shaping trust, alignment, and action. And the most effective messages begin with a single, sharp focus.

Chip and Dan Heath (2007) call this principle Simplicity. But simplicity doesn't mean dumbing down, it means narrowing in. "To strip an idea down to its core, we must be masters of exclusion," they write. Leaders often try to say everything at once, hoping to cover all bases. But the result is usually the opposite; messages that seem significant fail to resonate. The goal is not to summarize everything, it's to identify the one thing your audience must remember and act on.

Actor and science communicator Harvard Catalyst (2024) offers a simple guideline: make no more than three points, explain tough ideas three ways, and repeat your main point three times. Why?

Because human memory is limited. If your listeners can't remember what you said, they can't act on it. And leadership is always a call to action.

Here's how to practice this:

1. Find Your Core: Before any meeting, message, or memo, ask yourself: What is the one essential point I need them to walk away with

2. Trim the Excess: Eliminate qualifiers, jargon, and stacked ideas. Say it like a headline, not a dissertation.

3. Anchor It: Use a metaphor, image, or familiar example that brings the message to life.

Instead of saying, "I wanted to touch base regarding the potential need to reschedule due to some possible conflicts with several members of our leadership team," say: "Let's reschedule the meeting to ensure full participation." It's faster. It's clearer. And it gets the job done. The Heath brothers say it best: Don't bury the lead.

Deliver your core message with clarity. Focus on a single, well-stated idea, cut unnecessary detail, and communicate with purpose. When your message is clear, it drives understanding, engagement, and action.

FROM ONE LEADER TO ANOTHER

Dr. Rebecca Staton-Reinstein

CEO of Advantage Leadership | Author of 30 Days to Building a Strategic Plan
   As heard on Othman's Leadership Podcast, Episode TBD

Know What They Need Before You Speak

When Dr. Rebecca Staton-Reinstein was invited to speak at an elementary school about one of her favorite books, she thought it would be easy. But as she sat down to prepare for a room full of fourth and fifth graders, she realized she couldn't just show up and "talk." She needed to rethink everything. "I had to figure out what message I wanted to get across, and how to say it in language they would understand," she recalled. That meant simplifying the language, checking the grade level through readability tools, and working through multiple drafts to land the message in a way that would connect. "I worked on it probably as hard as I worked on any paid gig I ever had," she admitted. "I really had to apply every single thing I've ever learned about communicating and getting the message across." It wasn't about what she wanted to say, it was about what they needed to hear.

That mindset shapes how Staton-Reinstein approaches every audience, whether it's children, business leaders, or community members. "It's not about you, it's about them," she said. She teaches speakers and leaders to start with a few essential questions: Who is the audience? What are they expecting? How do I want them to feel, think, or act by the time I'm done? That orientation reshapes the preparation process, not as a download of information, but as a moment of service. "Too many people still think speaking is about looking smart," she noted. "But real communication is about helping people receive what they need."

Staton-Reinstein keeps her message design grounded in clarity. "You should speak at about an eighth-grade level, regardless of who's in front of you," she advised. Her reasoning is simple: the more complex your words, the harder it is for people to grasp and remember your message. That doesn't mean dumbing it down but means stripping away ego. She's seen senior leaders sabotage their impact by using jargon or assuming everyone already understands their perspective. "You can't assume comprehension, you have to check for it," she said.

Even with all her preparation, Staton-Reinstein knows that communication can go sideways when the speaker isn't aware of their own habits. One of her most honest admissions came when she reflected on her tone. "I come off as the authority," she shared. "It's probably the hardest habit I've ever tried to break." She's learned to monitor how she shows up, not just what she says. That includes adjusting her body language, opening up space for dialogue, and using humor to disarm tension. "When you walk into a room thinking 'I have all the answers,' people shut down," she said. "But if you come in with curiosity, they lean in."

Staton-Reinstein's message is clear: speaking with impact doesn't start with slides or scripts, it starts with understanding your audience. The most effective communicators don't just prepare their message, they prepare themselves. They ask, listen, adjust, and deliver with purpose, knowing that clarity and impact require intention. As Staton-Reinstein modeled in her narrative, understanding your audience is the first step to earning their understanding.

STRATEGY IN A SKETCH

Developed by Barbara Minto during her work at McKinsey, the Pyramid Principle is a method for structuring ideas from the top down, starting with your conclusion and then layering in supporting arguments. It's grounded in the psychology of how people process information. We understand best when we see the "why" first, followed by the "how."

The Pyramid Principle

Structure your message so people don't have to work to understand your point

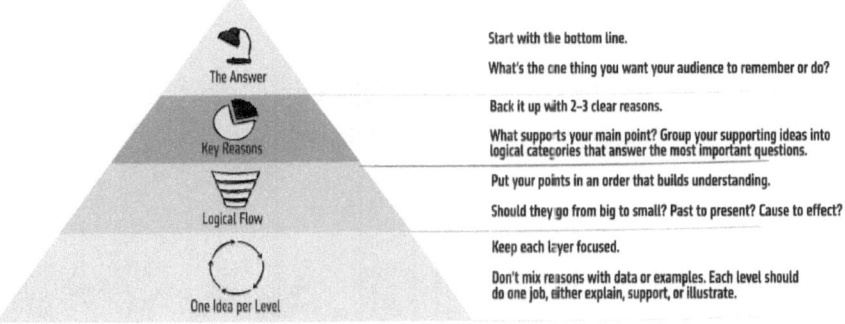

The Answer
Start with the bottom line.
What's the one thing you want your audience to remember or do?

Key Reasons
Back it up with 2–3 clear reasons.
What supports your main point? Group your supporting ideas into logical categories that answer the most important questions.

Logical Flow
Put your points in an order that builds understanding.
Should they go from big to small? Past to present? Cause to effect?

One Idea per Level
Keep each layer focused.
Don't mix reasons with data or examples. Each level should do one job, either explain, support, or illustrate.

Based on Barbara Minto's framework in The Pyramid Principle (2009).

MAKE IT YOURS

- When preparing presentations, do I spend time learning the concerns and needs of the audience?

- Can I simplify my intended message to just one clear sentence?

- How might I use the Pyramid Principle to bring clarity to an upcoming presentation or meeting?

4

Be Disciplined

What Can Help You When Motivation Fades?

Successful people do what unsuccessful people are not willing to do.

Jim Rohn

One Word That Changed Everything

It was a typical Friday afternoon, but Mr. Jones felt more weary than usual. The week had been grueling. He was juggling a full-time teaching job while trying to make headway on doctoral research. He finished his last class and was ready to head home, yearning for a break. As he glanced at his desk, a nagging thought crossed his mind. A critical research task remained incomplete. He knew that leaving it undone would weigh on him all weekend, yet he felt utterly unmotivated to tackle it. His energy was depleted, and he longed for the comfort of home.

Just then, Mr. Geddis, a respected English teacher, walked by his classroom door and wished him a good weekend as he headed toward the exit. Something about his calm demeanor and years of wisdom prompted the question, "Mr. Geddis, what do you do when you know you have a necessary task to complete, but you just can't seem to find the motivation?"

He paused and smiled knowingly. His response was simple yet profound: "Discipline."

That one simple word lingered in the air grew the wings of inspiration. Mr. Jones took the advice to heart and began working on the task. The first few minutes were the hardest, but the sense of relief and accomplishment when finished was undeniable.

When he finally headed home, Mr. Jones felt like a burden had been lifted. The task was no longer looming over the weekend, and he was free to enjoy his family without the weight of unfinished work. That day, he learned a valuable lesson: discipline is not about waiting for motivation to strike, it's about showing up and doing what's necessary, even when it's hard.

Sometimes, wisdom comes in the form of a single word. That day, it was "discipline," and it became a guiding principle for many challenges to come. "Self-discipline is the ability to do what you should do, when you should do it, whether you feel like it or not." Tracy (2010, quoting Elbert Hubbard)

PRINCIPLES

Principle 1: Take One Step, Then the Next

Think of crossing a bridge in the fog. It's important that you reach the other side but you can't see it. You're not even sure how long the bridge is. But you take a step. Then another, until you finally make it. That's what self-discipline looks like. It is the courage to keep moving forward and doing what's required to accomplish the task.

Ryan Holiday (2014), in *The Obstacle Is the Way*, writes a glaringly obvious statement that is often difficult to follow, "You've got to start, to go anywhere." Discipline isn't about waiting for the perfect moment or mood, it's about moving in the right direction, putting one foot in front of the other. Again. And again. In *Discipline Is Destiny* (2022), Holiday explains: "You don't have to always be amazing. You do always have to show up." It's not about intensity. It's about consistency. Lou Gehrig's 2,130 consecutive games weren't driven by hype, they were fueled by habit. His greatness was forged in a pattern of commitment, not simply adrenaline.

Brian Tracy (2011), in *No Excuses*, offers the same truth in tactical terms: big goals are simply a series of small, daily steps. "Winners take the first step," he reminds us. The trick is not waiting to feel ready but to act, then adjust. You don't build discipline by trying to push through everything at once. You build it by doing what matters most, especially when it's inconvenient or unglamorous.

Neuroscientist Anna Lembke (2021) adds a biological lens in *Dopamine Nation*. Our brains are wired to chase quick rewards, not long-term effort. But over time, acts of delayed gratification, like choosing not to scroll mindlessly on a mobile phone, reshape our neural pathways and increase our tolerance for discomfort. That's the foundation of resilience.

Try this micro-practice for building discipline:

1. Shrink the Goal: What's the smallest next action that moves you forward?

2. Anchor It: Tie that action to something that already happens daily (e.g., after coffee, before bed).

3. Repeat Relentlessly: Don't aim for perfection, aim for completion.

Discipline isn't sexy. It's not loud. But it's what moves you forward when inspiration fades. So the next time you feel overwhelmed, unmotivated, or behind, pause and ask: "What's the next right thing I can do?" Then do it.

Principle 2: Be Hard on Habits, Gentle on Yourself

Picture a gardener tending her plot. She waters consistently, pulls weeds regularly, and adjusts when the weather changes. She doesn't scold the plants when they don't bloom overnight. That's how discipline should work. It's about the process. You build strong systems, but meet yourself with patience when the results take time. This is the leadership mindset: be firm with your habits, and gentle on yourself.

Tracy (2011), in *No Excuses*, says, "Each time you push yourself to do the right thing, even when you don't feel like it, you boost your confidence." But that push doesn't require pressure or punishment, it requires structure. Creating routines like focus hours, weekly planning, or evening reflection minimizes decision fatigue and builds momentum. Instead of relying on daily willpower, you rely on systems you've designed in advance.

Ryan Holiday (2022) echoes this in *Discipline Is Destiny*, noting that consistency, not intensity, is the real superpower. Toni Morrison carved out early mornings to write before teaching. Lou Gehrig played through discomfort because he respected the power of showing up. The common thread? They protected their habits, knowing that small accomplishments lead to great success.

Lembke (2021) helps us see the biological side. She explains that small, repeated actions paired with grace after failure, rewire our reward systems. When we replace harsh self-criticism with structure and mindfulness, we reduce our dependence on fleeting motivation. We stop treating every dip in performance as a flaw and start treating it as data.

Here's how to apply it:

1. Build Systems That Guide You: Anchor habits to existing routines and use cues (e.g., "After I pour coffee, I plan my top task.")

2. Expect Imperfection: When you miss a day, don't spiral. Just restart. The goal is rhythm, not streaks.

3. Separate Worth from Output: You are not your checklist. Growth happens behind the scenes, too.

So next time you feel off track, don't ask, "What's wrong with me?" Ask instead, "What habit needs adjusting and how can I reset without shame?" That question builds real discipline that is rooted in high standards, but anchored in self-respect.

Principle 3: Let the Pain Shape You, Let Purpose Guide You

Pain is inevitable but not all pain is equal. Some pain weakens us. Some sharpens us. The difference is whether it's tied to purpose. Discipline isn't just about doing hard things, it's about choosing meaningful pain over meaningless pleasure. Like a sculptor carving stone, chipping away what's unnecessary results in something beautiful when guided by vision, not impulse.

Lembke (2021) explains that leaning into controlled discomfort, whether it's focused work, cold exposure, or emotional restraint, can rebalance the brain's reward system. "Pressing on the pain side of the balance," she writes, "can lead to its opposite, pleasure." This discomfort isn't punishment. It's preparation. And it rewires us for long-term satisfaction, not short-term gratification.

Holiday (2022) shows how disciplined figures like Queen Elizabeth II and John F. Kennedy embraced hardship in service of something larger. They understood that pain, when rooted in mission, becomes fuel. In *The Obstacle Is the Way* (2014), Holiday proposes that discipline deepens when we stop resisting adversity and start shaping ourselves through it.

Tracy (2011) gives us the question every leader should ask when unmotivated: "What's the price I'm willing to pay to live the life I want?" That question doesn't eliminate the pain. It dignifies it. Whether it's waking early to finish a report, resisting the urge to argue, or preparing thoroughly for a tough conversation, discipline becomes less about toughness and more about alignment. Your why holds the discomfort in place.

Try this approach when discomfort shows up:

1. Name the Cost: What short-term discomfort is this action asking of me?

2. Link to Purpose: How does this connect to a goal, value, or bigger reason I care about?

3. Reframe the Pain: Instead of "This is hard," try "This is helping me become the person I want to be."

Think of pain like a chisel. In chaos, it breaks things. In the hands of purpose, it refines. The leaders who last aren't those who avoid discomfort, they're the ones who decide what it's for. They don't just endure. They evolve. So when things get hard, ask yourself: "Is this pain pushing me forward, or pulling me away?" Then follow the one that builds you.

FROM ONE LEADER TO ANOTHER

Kevin Palache

Independent Associate at the LegalShield Corporate
  As heard on Othman's Leadership Podcast, Episode TBD

Build the Discipline to Keep Showing Up

Kevin Palache doesn't glamorize discipline. He defines it, borrowing the words of Brian Tracy, as "doing what you need to do, when you need to do it, whether you feel like it or not." It's not about self-deception. "Discipline isn't a motivational feeling. It's a muscle," he explained. Whether you're talking about "health, business, relationships, or finances," Palache believes the long-term outcomes in any area come down to one thing: your habits. "If you don't discipline yourself, life will discipline you. Your doctor will. Your bank account will. Your future self will."

He paused during the conversation and quoted Jim Rohn: "Discipline weighs ounces. Regret weighs tons." Kevin knows the weight of regret firsthand. In college, he ran track and showed early signs of potential. But he didn't follow through. "I didn't show up to practice consistently. I cut corners," he admitted. "I was talented, but I wasn't disciplined, and that caught up to me." He lost his spot on the team. That moment stayed with him, long after graduation. "It wasn't about my ability. It was about my consistency."

Years later, that loss turned into a lesson and a personal framework to keep his discipline sharp. For Palache, it all comes down to three anchors: calendar, tracking, and accountability.

Calendar. "I live by my calendar," he said. "Everything important, calls, reading time, gym time, rest, it's all blocked." He schedules his life in 15-minute increments. It may sound intense, but for him, it's freedom. "Make your calendar your boss or your coach," he advises. "If it's not on there, it doesn't exist."

Tracking. Palache keeps a daily log of actions: books read, presentations delivered, habits completed. It's his way of confronting reality without judgment. "You can't change what you don't track," he said, referencing The Compound Effect by Darren Hardy. Most people guess their way through the week, but Palache wants the data. "Your numbers will tell you the truth, even when you don't want to hear it."

Accountability. Every weekday by noon, Palache checks in with a trusted partner using the acronym PAVE: Personal development, Activity, Vision, Events. "It's not just about having someone to report to. It's about having someone who cares enough to follow up if I don't show up," he said. That quiet form of pressure helps him follow through when motivation fades. "Discipline is easier when you're not doing it alone."

But what happens when you fall off? Palache had to rebuild momentum after losing consistency in 2020. The pandemic shook his routines, stalled his business, and left him in a slump. "I stopped doing what I knew worked," he admitted. But instead of spiraling, he returned to his anchors: small habits, virtual events, and a revised daily rhythm. "You don't have to be perfect. You just have to be consistent again."

Palache's message is simple, but significant: "Whether I'm hitting my goal or not, I'm still doing the work. People don't follow what you say, they follow what you show them." Discipline, for him, is about alignment, not force. "Your situation doesn't have to define you," he said. "But your habits will."

To any leader struggling to find their rhythm again, Palache leaves no room for excuses: "Ask for help. Get a coach. Restart your tracker.

Block 15 minutes." Kevin Palache teaches that discipline is about building systems that keep you aligned when willpower runs out.

STRATEGY IN A SKETCH

The If–Then Tool, developed by psychologist Peter Gollwitzer, is a framework for turning good intentions into reliable action. Its purpose is simple: pre-decide what you will do when a predictable challenge arises. Instead of relying on willpower or reacting in the heat of the moment, you anchor your behavior to a clear condition. For example, a teacher might say: If a parent raises a concern angrily, then I will first acknowledge their emotion before moving to problem-solving. Or consider leadership upward: If my supervisor, whom I often find difficult, assigns me unexpected work, then I will clarify priorities respectfully before agreeing. Even with students, the tool works: If my class returns restless from lunch, then I will begin with a two-minute breathing exercise before diving into math problems. The brain is wired to recognize cues; the "if" serves as the trigger, and the "then" becomes the automatic response. Leaders who practice this avoid inconsistency and decision fatigue—they act in alignment with their values even when pressure is high.

Try this:

Think of one moment you consistently struggle with. Now finish the sentence:

"If _____ happens, then I will _____." That's your discipline cue.

"If-Then" Tool

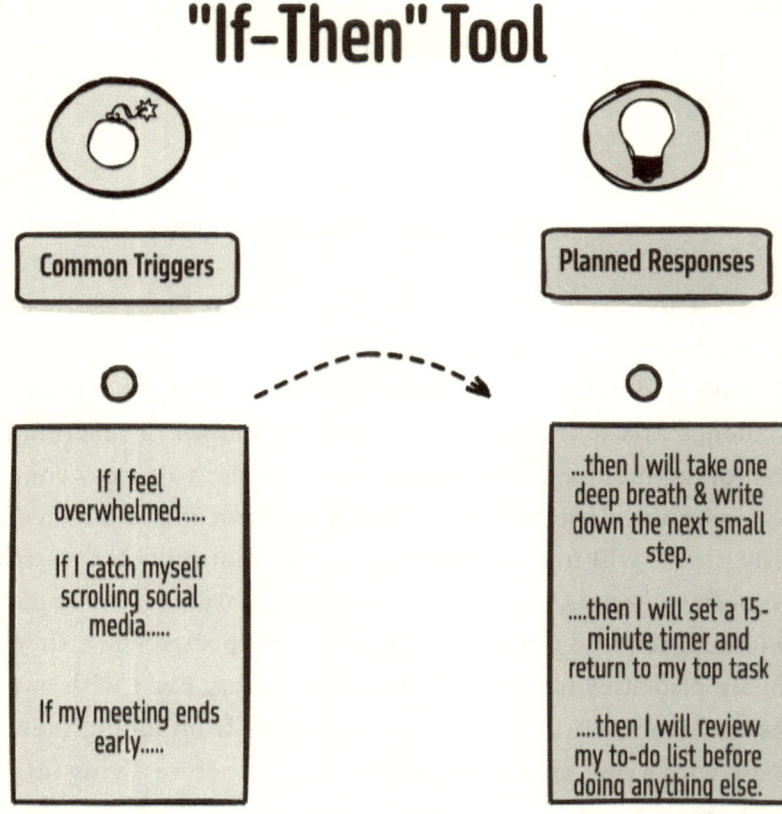

Common Triggers

Planned Responses

If I feel overwhelmed.....

If I catch myself scrolling social media.....

If my meeting ends early.....

...then I will take one deep breath & write down the next small step.

....then I will set a 15-minute timer and return to my top task

....then I will review my to-do list before doing anything else.

Based from Gollwitzer's research (1999).

MAKE IT YOURS

- What routines and habits can I develop to help move me toward accomplishing my goals?

- What triggers my procrastination or interrupts my progress? How can I break that pattern?

- What prioritized action steps and timeline can I outline to ensure steady progress toward completing my current responsibilities?

5

Be Tuned In

Does Your Emotional Intelligence Elevate Interactions?

The most important thing in communication is hearing what isn't said.

Peter Drucker

She Missed The Beat

At Brookfield Middle School, the staff had weathered a lot together, including curriculum changes, shifting mandates, and the ups and downs of adolescent energy. They weren't just colleagues; they were a team. So when a new principal, Dr. Collins, was hired midyear, teachers were hopeful. She came with glowing references, a warm smile, and an open-door policy. She was organized, responsive, and clearly cared. She made herself visible in classrooms, sent regular updates, and often offered help before anyone asked. On paper, she was doing everything right. But something was amiss.

In staff meetings, Dr. Collins often spoke at length without leaving space for dialogue. When teachers raised concerns, she'd glance at her phone and respond with solutions before fully hearing the problem. If someone hesitated or asked for time to reflect, she'd push forward anyway, filling silences, redirecting conversation, or following up with emails that staff was unsure how to interpret.

To her, leadership was about forging ahead. But to the staff, it felt very different. "She doesn't read the room," one teacher said quietly after a meeting. "It's like she's peddling fast and doesn't realize the traffic all around her."

Over time, the tone in the building shifted. Fewer teachers voiced concerns during meetings. Side conversations before and after became more guarded. People stopped bringing ideas forward. Dr. Collins's announcements were met with polite nods, but little real engagement. Even her well-meant gestures of birthday cards and shout-outs felt disconnected, like someone trying to lead without truly understanding who they were leading. What unfolded was not open resistance, but quiet disengagement. When leaders fail to listen and connect, they risk losing the very trust and energy that move a community forward.

PRINCIPLES

Principle 1: Tune In With Questions

The foundation of strong relationships is built on paying attention to the people and situations around you. Goleman (1995) titled this type of consciousness as "emotional intelligence." Goleman identified five learnable skills that shape how we manage ourselves and interact with others:

1. Self-awareness, or understanding our emotions, values, and impact on others

2. Self-regulation, the ability to manage impulses and stay composed under pressure

3. Motivation, which is the inner drive to achieve for the sake of excellence

4. Empathy, the capacity to understand and care about what others are feeling

5. Social skill, which allows us to build trust, navigate relationships, and influence with authenticity.

Goleman (1995) also notes that empathy is the foundation of social awareness. It is the ability to sense others' feelings and perspectives and respond appropriately. Leaders high in this skill build better collaboration, resolve conflict faster, and foster deeper engagement. They don't just listen to respond, they listen to understand.

Rosenberg (2015), in Nonviolent Communication, echoes this by teaching that empathy is "a respectful understanding of what others are experiencing." This doesn't mean fixing, agreeing, or analyzing. It means receiving and making space for someone else's internal world without rushing to solve it. In leadership, that space can be rare but when it's there, people feel valued.

In *Emotional Agility*, Susan David (2016) reinforces that real connection happens when people feel emotionally safe. And emotional safety grows when leaders mirror back what they hear, validate emotions, and resist the urge to quickly correct. A moment of reflective listening like this: "It sounds like you're feeling frustrated because the timeline keeps shifting. Is that right?" can defuse tension and invite clarity.

To build this habit:

1. Focus Fully. In your next conversation, put away distrac-

tions and give your full attention with eye contact and active listening.

2. Mirror and Check. Reflect back what you heard. Use words like, "It sounds like..." or "I'm hearing that..." Then check for accuracy.

3. Ask a Question. Before offering a solution, ask, "What feels most important to you right now?" or "What would support look like here?"

Empathetic listening reduces defensiveness, builds trust, and creates space for honest feedback. And the bonus? When people feel heard, they become more open to hearing you. So before you speak, advise, or redirect, ask one more question. Leadership is not a monologue. It's a dialogue. And it begins with tuning in.

Principle 2: Use Emotions as Data, Not Directives

Sometimes, we encounter or express volatile emotions. A sharp email gets sent. A meeting goes sideways. We react, others react, or both. But what if you considered using emotion as a data point, a very important data point to analyze?

Goleman (1995), in Emotional Intelligence, explains that emotions are fast-moving signals, often triggered before logic can catch up. When the brain perceives a threat, the amygdala sends out an alarm that can override our rational brain in what's called an "emotional hijack." In those moments, we don't think, we defend. The key isn't to suppress the emotion, but to spot it, name it, and understand what it's pointing to.

This insight is echoed by David (2016) who writes that emotions are "data, not directives." Anger may signal a violated value. Fear may be protecting something you care about. Sadness may point to loss. But when we avoid these feelings or blindly act on them, we lose the opportunity to lead instead of being led by our emotions. Naming an emotion shifts brain activity from the amygdala to the prefrontal cortex, increasing our capacity for reason and reflection. That pause is everything, and gives you access to better choices.

To put this into practice:

1. Catch the Signal. Notice when your body tightens, your tone sharpens, or your thoughts race. Notice the same in others. These are cues.

2. Name It, Don't Numb It. Use precise language to identify your feelings or to check the emotions of others. (*Atlas of the Heart* by Brené Brown offers a strong vocabulary list.)

3. Ask What It's Pointing To. What value is this emotion protecting? What need might be unmet?

Emotions aren't problems. They're patterns trying to tell us something. The most emotionally intelligent leaders don't deny their feelings or the feelings of others, they decode them. They pause, get curious, and then choose how to move forward.

Principle 3: Decelerate

Imagine trying to steer a car while flooring the gas pedal. That's what leadership looks like without emotional regulation. You may know where you're going, but you leave damage along the way. Self-regulation reminds you to slow down and brake when necessary. It's what keeps you and the others around you safe.

Goleman (1995) describes self-regulation as the ability to control or redirect disruptive impulses and moods. Leaders who can regulate rather than suppress emotions project steadiness, even when facing pressure, disappointment, or provocation. They model emotional safety for others by managing their own internal barometer.

David (2016) writes that "between stimulus and response, there is a space, and in that space is our power to choose." But most of us move too quickly. We react from habit, not intention. Reactivity often feels like control in the moment, but it can leave connection, and often trust, damaged in its wake.

Pausing even for a few seconds can help deactivate the fight-or-flight response and re-engage the reasoning part of the brain. The organization, Six Seconds, a global nonprofit dedicated to emotional intelligence, calls this short pause the "amygdala reset," a brief moment that interrupts emotional reactivity and creates space for wiser action (Six Seconds, n.d.).

Here's a practical way to apply this:

1. Feel It Without Feeding It. Notice the emotion building (tight shoulders, racing heart, rising tone). Label it silently.

2. Create a Micro-Pause. Take one full breath before speaking or responding. Even a short pause slows the nervous system.

3. Reframe Before You Respond. Ask questions like these: "What outcome do I want from this moment?" or "What value do I want to lead with right now?"

Self-regulation is strength under control. It's what separates reacting thoughtlessly from responding appropriately. It allows you to hold your ground without losing your grace. And over time, it builds the kind of emotional credibility that makes people feel safe in your presence, even in the middle of conflict. A thoughtful pause before responding can change more than the moment. It can change the relationship.

Principle 4: Move From Reaction To Recovery

Every leader has a trigger story, something someone says, a tone someone uses, a moment that flips an internal switch. You feel your jaw clench. Your mind races. Your default response kicks in. It's fast, familiar, and usually unhelpful. But emotional intelligence doesn't demand we eliminate our triggers. It asks us to know them and grow our range of possible responses.

Goleman (1995) reminds us that when we're triggered, the brain's amygdala takes over in a split-second "hijack," flooding us with emotion and narrowing our ability to choose. What we say or do next often reflects old habits, not wise leadership. But emotional intelligence expands our understanding of what triggers us and why.

David (2016) writes that the goal is not to avoid difficult emotions but to face them with curiosity and compassion. "Emotions are teachers," she explains. They point to what we value and where we're vulnerable. A strong reaction isn't a flaw. It's feedback. When we explore that feedback, we gain insight and access to various responses that override reflexive conditioning.

One powerful practice comes from the MBTI Step II framework, which explores emotional range and flexibility. Leaders who learn their natural tendency to internalize or externalize emotion, take time or act quickly, can identify where they need refinement. Range is the ability to choose a new pattern, especially under pressure.

To practice this principle:

1. Track the Trigger. Reflect on recent moments that threw you off. What specific action, word, or setting activated you?

2. Explore the Pattern. Ask: "What did I feel? Where did I feel it? What old story might have been playing in the background?"

3. Plan the Pivot. Identify one alternative move you can try next time: a breath, a question, a pause, or a boundary.

The best leaders aren't untroubled. They're just self-aware enough to know what bothers them and prepared enough to lead themselves through it. They don't deny their reactions. They widen their range.

FROM ONE LEADER TO ANOTHER

Steve Carrier

English Teacher, Bloomfield Public Schools
As heard on Othman's Leadership Podcast, Episode 25

Choose Trust Over Control

For Steve Carrier, emotional intelligence isn't a concept, it's a practice. And it starts with how leaders show up in moments of tension, transition, and trust. Early in his career, Carrier worked under a supervisor who rarely offered praise but was quick to criticize. "He didn't yell or belittle," Carrier said. "But the way he asked, 'Where were you?'implied his distrust." That single question, delivered with suspicion instead of curiosity, stuck with him. Carrier responded with professionalism in the moment, but the emotional undercurrent shaped his leadership forever. "I never wanted anyone to feel the way I felt in that hallway," he reflected. That one interaction became a compass for how he'd communicate for the rest of his career.

Carrier believes the heart of leadership is relational, and relationships are built on how people feel in your presence. "I make a conscious decision never to embarrass someone publicly," he shared. Whether working with students or adults, he avoids criticism that stings more than it teaches. "If I humiliate a student in front of the class, I've lost them for the year," he said. That principle holds true for team members too. Carrier chooses private, respectful conversations, and focuses on separating the behavior from the person. His goal isn't to win, it's to build bonds. "Feedback should never cost you a relationship," he added.

Emotional intelligence also means knowing when to let go. Carrier shared how he supported colleagues who outgrew their roles and it was clear they were ready to move on. "I've written recommendations that cost me great team members," he admitted. "But if someone needs to grow, and I stand in the way, I'm not leading. I'm managing my own fear." In those moments, tuning in means doing what's best instead of what's easiest. That shift requires self-awareness and empathy, two qualities Carrier has cultivated intentionally across every level of his leadership.

But his emotional intelligence doesn't end at work. "You lead at home too," he said. "And your family deserves the best of your self-awareness, not just the leftovers." He reflects often on his tone, his presence, and the example he's setting, not just in meetings, but in conversations over dinner, in moments of stress, or during long car rides with his kids. For Carrier, leadership is a daily decision to tune in to who you are, how you're being received, and who's watching. "You can't lead people you don't see," he said. "And you won't see them clearly until you see yourself."

STRATEGY IN A SKETCH

Most leaders know emotional intelligence matters but few know how to teach or practice it. That's where RULER comes in. Developed by the Yale Center for Emotional Intelligence, RULER is a science-backed framework to help individuals and organizations build emotional skills that stick.

The acronym stands for:

- Recognizing emotions in yourself and others

- Understanding the causes and consequences

- Labeling emotions accurately

- Expressing emotions appropriately

- Regulating emotions effectively

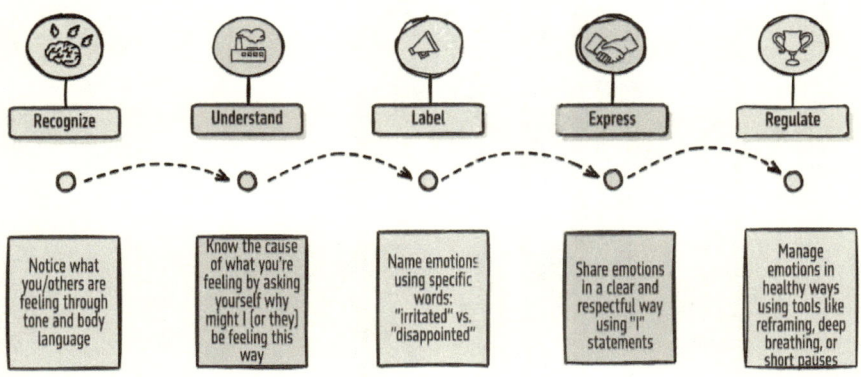

The RULER Approach

Recognize	Understand	Label	Express	Regulate
Notice what you/others are feeling through tone and body language	Know the cause of what you're feeling by asking yourself why might I (or they) be feeling this way	Name emotions using specific words: "irritated" vs. "disappointed"	Share emotions in a clear and respectful way using "I" statements	Manage emotions in healthy ways using tools like reframing, deep breathing, or short pauses

Based on Marc Brackett's framework from Permission to Feel (2019).

MAKE IT YOURS

- What's the ratio of my talking to my listening for spoken and unspoken messages?

- What patterns do I see in how I react under pressure, and how might that affect others around me?

- What feedback, tools, or reflections will help me tune in more deeply?

6

Be Confident

How Can Your Inner Self Match Your Outer Actions?

> Leadership is solving problems. The day soldiers stop bringing you their problems is the day you have stopped leading them. They have either lost confidence that you can help or concluded you do not care. Either case is a failure of leadership.
>
> Colin Powell

Strong and Steady

At Silver Oak Elementary, the beginning of the school year had come with its usual whirlwind of late enrollments, tech issues, and a new reading curriculum that arrived two days before students. But amid the chaos, Principal Nguyen moved with a quiet steadiness that set the tone for the entire building.

She didn't rush through the halls. She didn't bark orders. And she didn't pretend everything was perfect.

Instead, she made her rounds each morning, stopping into class-rooms, asking teachers how the first few days were going, and listening without jumping to fix. When the fourth-grade team men-tioned that the new curriculum pacing felt off, she nodded and said, "Let's pilot it for two weeks, then come back together and adjust as necessary."

She didn't posture. She didn't need to be the smartest voice in the room. She just trusted her people and invited them to join in the process.

At the first staff meeting, the projector glitched, the snacks were forgotten, and her opening remarks were shorter than planned. She smiled and said, "Well, we're off and running, imperfectly and to-gether. Which is exactly how we'll grow." The room relaxed. Teach-ers leaned in. Not because she had all the answers, but because she wasn't afraid of not having them.

When a parent email went school wide, questioning decisions about recess coverage, she didn't get defensive. She called a brief meeting with the staff and said, "We're doing our best. Let's respond with clarity, not reactivity. And if we need to make adjustments, we will. Not because we failed but because we're learning." The culture of Silver Oak began to shift.

People spoke more freely in team meetings. Mistakes were shared openly, not to be judged, but to be understood. New teachers felt comfortable asking questions. Veteran teachers started mentoring more naturally. No one felt the need to pretend.

Ms. Nguyen led with confidence but not the kind that comes from perfection or performance. She wasn't afraid to say, "I don't know yet," or "Let's find out." Her calm didn't mask the truth; it revealed a deep belief in the team's ability to figure things out together. Her job was to show up, tune in, and trust in herself and her team.

PRINCIPLES

Principle 1: Earn Your Confidence in the Doing

Confidence is not a fixed trait reserved for the charismatic or accomplished, it is a capability that grows through experience, practice, and resilience. Contrary to the myth that leaders are born confident, research reveals that confidence is developed over time through the consistent act of showing up, learning from setbacks, and doing the work of leadership even when doubt is present.

Carol Dweck's (2006) research on growth mindset shows that those who believe abilities can be developed through effort are more likely to take risks, persist through setbacks, and embrace feedback. Confidence, in this light, isn't the absence of failure, it's the product of showing up again after it. In contrast, those with a fixed mindset tend to avoid challenges that might expose them, waiting until they feel "ready" before stepping forward. But readiness rarely comes before action. Action builds it.

Consider Howard Schultz, former CEO of Starbucks, who didn't begin his journey with boardroom polish or business degrees. Raised in public housing, Schultz built his confidence by facing rejection, convincing investors, and learning through trial. He didn't wait to feel credible, he became credible by doing the work. He learned that confidence isn't inherited, it's earned.

Ryan Holiday (2014) captures this truth with clarity: "What stands in the way becomes the way." Challenges should be viewed as invitations more than interruptions. When leaders take action in the presence of doubt, they don't eliminate fear, they outgrow it. Confidence expands in the aftermath of effort, especially when the outcome is uncertain.

Hibberd (2019), in *The Imposter Cure*, adds that high achievers often struggle with confidence not because they're unqualified, but because they believe their fears are facts. "Just because you worry you're an imposter doesn't mean you are one," she writes. Leading through doubt requires us to treat thoughts as significant information to process. The goal isn't to erase insecurity, it's to move forward with it in your pocket.

Here's a confidence-building practice to try:

1. Take a Micro-Action. Choose one thing that feels just beyond your comfort zone and do it anyway.

2. Track Evidence. Afterward, list what you handled well, even if it felt awkward.

3. Name the Pattern. Reflect on how many hard things you've survived over time and know that confidence grows in that pattern.

In the end, confidence isn't bravado or false certainty, it's quiet and courageous trust in your ability to be, do, and learn.

Principle 2: Lead from Strength, Not for Show

Confidence loses its power the moment it becomes a performance. Real confidence isn't loud, flawless, or staged; it's grounded. It comes from knowing who you are, what you bring, and leading from that place without apology. When leaders try to lead for show and chase validation, applause, or titles, they burn out fast. But when they lead from their strengths, their impact deepens and their presence becomes undeniable.

Marcus Buckingham (2007), in *Go Put Your Strengths to Work*, makes the case that authentic performance comes when you align your work with your innate talents. He introduces the "SIGN" framework, Success, Instinct, Growth, and Needs, as indicators that you're operating in your zone of strength. The more you design your day around these markers, the more naturally confidence flows. You're not pretending, you're aligned.

Ryan Holiday (2016), in *Ego Is the Enemy,* draws a sharp line between ego-driven leadership and strength-driven leadership. He asks his readers whether it is more important "to be somebody or to do something?" The ego wants to be seen, celebrated, and right. But confident leaders don't need to perform. They lead for impact, not impression. Their confidence is quiet because it's real.

Consider Satya Nadella, CEO of Microsoft. When he took the helm, he didn't try to become the next Steve Jobs or Bill Gates. Instead, he leaned into his own strengths of empathy, curiosity, and collaboration. By doing so, he reshaped Microsoft's culture from one of competition to one of learning. The results were both cultural and financial. Impacting was more important than impressing.

Here's a practice to shift from show to strength:

1. Audit Your Energy. What tasks make you feel alive, not just accomplished?

2. Clarify Your Values. What traits or priorities do you want your leadership to reflect daily?

3. Don't Pretend. Where do you find yourself putting on a performance more than accessing your strengths?

The most trusted leaders aren't the ones trying to impress a room. They're the ones rooted in purpose, clear on their strengths, and steady in their presence.

Principle 3: Check Your Motive Before You Step Forward

There's a quiet power in leading without needing to be seen. One of the most confident things a leader can do is step back from ego and root their decisions in a purpose. Ego demands attention, approval, and control. Purpose asks better questions: "What cause am I here to support? What matters most right now?" Confidence that lasts isn't built on image, it's built on intention.

Holiday (2016) writes that ego pushes us to be seen as great, rather than to do great work. It resists feedback. It fears uncertainty. It clings to the mask of being "right." True confidence, by contrast, doesn't depend on external validation. It lives in the steady decision to keep showing up for something bigger than yourself.

The antidote to ego is purpose. Susan David (2016), in *Emotional Agility*, invites leaders to "walk your why" by aligning daily behaviors with core values and long-term commitments. Leaders who are purpose-driven are more resilient under pressure, less reactive to criticism, and more grounded in their decisions. They don't lead for the applause of others. They lead from an alignment to their goals.

Consider Angela Merkel, former chancellor of Germany. She didn't seek the spotlight. Her leadership was marked by stability, responsibility, and a commitment to service, even when her decisions weren't popular. Her strength came not from showmanship but from substance. She didn't need to be loud to be respected. Her results grounded in a greater purpose spoke volumes.

Practice strength in humility:

1. Ask the Anchor Question: "Am I doing this to be seen or to be of service?"

2. Name the Why: "What value or mission am I aligning with?"

3. Welcome Feedback: "What prideful thought or action might block personal growth?"

Confidence rooted in ego is fragile because it depends on outcomes and opinions. Confidence rooted in purpose is resilient. It's not afraid to fail, because it's not performing, it's contributing.

Principle 4: Lean Into Legitimacy

According to John Gravois, in the Chronicle of Higher Education (2007), seventy percent of people will experience imposter syndrome at least once in their lives, including those in leadership positions. That statistic reveals that far too many leaders feel they're going through the motions, afraid that someone will soon expose their inadequacies. They find their skills and achievements lacking, compared to others, despite evidence to the contrary. Hibberd (2019) explains that those who struggle with imposter syndrome equate their worth with flawless performance. Mistakes feel like exposure, not information. But as she writes, "Overcoming imposter syndrome doesn't mean you'll stop making mistakes; it means accepting that they're part of life."

Dweck's (2006) research demonstrates leaders with a growth mindset don't see setbacks as threats to their identity. They see them as signs of learning. Every time they step into the arena, they reinforce their own capacity and remove the feelings of professional fraudulence.

Don Moore (2020), in *Perfectly Confident*, shows that both overconfidence and underconfidence undermine sound leadership. Overconfidence can lead to reckless decisions and blind spots, while underconfidence causes hesitation and missed opportunities. Moore (2020) argues that the real goal is calibrated confidence, a balance where your belief in your judgment matches the actual evidence and probabilities. Leaders who calibrate in this way project assurance without arrogance, and act decisively without ignoring risk.

David (2016) encourages leaders to untangle their identity from their performance. The ability to lead isn't contingent on having it all figured out; growth and worth can coexist. Self-confident leadership is rooted in values and purpose rather than perfection and performance.

Here's a confidence practice to try:

1. Normalize Imperfection. Remind yourself that humans are not flawless and growth can be messy.

2. Name the Attempt. Celebrate the effort, not just the result.

3. Anchor in Purpose. Strengthen your commitment to the principles that drive your work

When you reaffirm the core values that anchor your leadership and believe that mistakes can foster growth, your confidence will be real and your actions authentic.

FROM ONE LEADER TO ANOTHER

Betty Dannewitz

Truth Teller and Confidence Coach, ifyouaskbetty
As heard on Othman's Leadership Podcast, Episode 33

Confidence Isn't a Trait - It's a Skill

"Confidence is a muscle," Betty Dannewitz shared. "And like any muscle, it needs consistent work." Throughout her leadership journey, Dannewitz has encountered the same doubts many professionals face, especially when doing something new. She recalled times when feedback from a new manager made her question everything she thought she was good at. "We start to think their version of us must be true," she said. But Dannewitz didn't just sit with the self-doubt, she challenged it by turning to her personal "board of directors," a trusted circle of people who know her well enough to give honest, constructive truth. "Sometimes the feedback is spot on, and sometimes it's just a misread," she explained. "But when you're shaken, you need people who will remind you who you are."

Many assume that confidence has to be loud, bold, or charismatic, but Dannewitz pushes back on that narrative. "Some of the most confident people I know are the quietest," she said. What matters most, she emphasized, is an alignment when how you feel inside matches how you show up on the outside. "If you're pretending to be confident, you'll never feel confident," she warned. Her message is simple: stop performing and start owning. In a world that often rewards volume over value, Dannewitz encourages leaders to embrace congruence, not bravado. Quiet doesn't mean weak and loud doesn't mean strong.

Dannewitz also spoke to the inner voice that tells leaders to stay quiet. "We worry we'll sound dumb or ask the wrong thing," she said. But she challenged that fear with a simple truth: "Say it anyway. Because someone else in the room is thinking the same thing and is just waiting for permission to speak." She recounted meetings where leaders held back only to discover that their question would have helped everyone. "The moment you speak up, you give others courage," she explained. Confidence, in this light, isn't about certainty, it's about service.

Another overlooked skill in building confidence? Receiving praise. "Most people deflect it," Dannewitz said. "'Oh, it was nothing. 'It was the team.' We smack the compliment away before we even hear it." But accepting the compliment, believing it, and thanking someone for it is a discipline. "Your voice agreeing with the praise is what allows it to stick," she said. That's when confidence starts to take root. It becomes more than a feeling, and promotes the habit of self-acknowledgement. Own the compliment, speak your truth, and build your own board of directors. Your confidence will be grounded and authentic.

STRATEGY IN A SKETCH

The Confidence–Competence Loop, rooted in Albert Bandura's research on self-efficacy, shows how growth feeds on itself. Every time we take action and succeed, our competence increases. That success, in turn, builds confidence and the belief that we can take on the next challenge. The loop strengthens with each cycle, creating momentum for both learning and leadership. In schools, this is easy to see. A new teacher may hesitate to lead a parent conference, worried they will be caught off guard. But after preparing thoroughly and guiding one difficult meeting successfully, their competence grows. That success fuels the confidence to step into the next conversation with steadiness instead of fear. The loop reminds us that confidence is something you earn by acting.

The Confidence–Competence Loop

Confidence doesn't come before action—it comes from action. Every time you try, you build competence. That builds confidence.

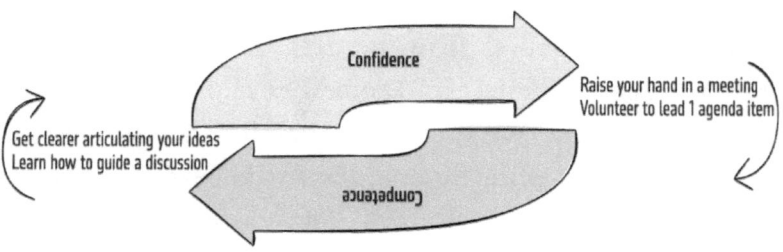

Adapted from Albert Bandura's classic work on self-efficacy (1997).

MAKE IT YOURS

- In what areas has experience and practice increased my confidence?

- What values drive my work?

- What confidence skill-builders can I begin today?

7

Be Relentless

How Can You Shift Setbacks Into Steps Forward?

Enthusiasm is common. Endurance is rare.

Angela Duckworth

Move Forward

For months, Maya was in a relentless stretch. She was searching for a job, but not just any job. She was pursuing work that aligned with her purpose. She was after something that matched her experience, honored her credentials, and gave her the chance to make a real impact.

She applied. She interviewed. Again and again. Many roles looked like perfect fits on paper. She advanced through rounds, only to be met with silence. No offers. No feedback. Just a quiet inbox and the growing weight of doubt.

It would've been easy to stop. But Maya didn't. She stayed rooted in purpose and steady in her practice. Even in the quiet, she kept moving.

When uncertainty pressed in, she poured herself into the work she could control. She also started choosing her circle more deliberately. She stepped away from conversations that drained her and stopped explaining her path to people who didn't get it. She gravitated toward those who saw her clearly and who reminded her of her strength and reflected her resilience when she couldn't see it herself.

She didn't give up. She kept honing her craft. She kept applying. She kept going. Her mantra was simple and unshakable: Move forward with purpose, with persistence, and with people who lift you.

PRINCIPLES

Principle 1: Reconnect to Your "Why" When the Work Gets Hard

Grit is defined as the sustained passion and perseverance for long-term, meaningful goals, even in the face of challenges, boredom, or failure (Duckworth, 2016). Grit is not talent or raw effort alone, it is the disciplined commitment to develop skill, navigate setbacks, and pursue purpose with endurance.

Grit isn't stubbornness, it's commitment with direction. It's not about grinding mindlessly, but persisting with purpose. When your work connects to something bigger than yourself, setbacks feel less like dead ends and more like detours on a meaningful path.

Duckworth (2016) explains that grit is the combination of passion and perseverance over time. She highlights four psychological assets that nourish this kind of commitment: interest, practice, purpose, and hope. Of these, purpose, the belief that your effort serves others, acts as the emotional power source that sustains resilience. When you know your work matters, the hard moments don't stop you. They strengthen you.

In McKinsey's leadership research, Kristensen, Liu, and Sherman (2025) found that purpose-driven leaders were more adaptive and resilient in the face of disruption. Purpose became a compass, not just for personal endurance, but for galvanizing team commitment. Leaders who embed purpose into their goals build organizational grit in addition to personal grit.

Duckworth (2016) is clear: passion and purpose aren't handed to you, they're cultivated by you. Passion matures through repetition and effort. Purpose emerges as you begin to connect your skills with service. Momentum builds at the intersection of what you love, what you're good at, and what helps others. When leaders define that connection with clarity, they fuel their own drive and spark energy in others.

Lee and Duckworth (2018) also showed that when organizational purpose matches individual calling, employees report greater job satisfaction, persistence, and resilience. In education and healthcare, where burnout runs high, this association is especially powerful. Purpose creates identity. It gives meaning to struggle and makes progress visible.

Here's how to bring this into your practice:

1. Ask Your Anchor Question, "Who benefits when I keep going?"

2. Name Your Values in Action. Connect your goal to a bigger 'why.'

3. Share the Story. Make purpose explicit in your team meetings, feedback, and celebrations.

Grit that's rooted in meaning is sustainable and encouraging. Purpose transforms pressure into progress.

Principle 2: Stretch Beyond Comfort - Every Single Day

We often admire grit in moments of glory when the athlete finishes the race, the underdog overcomes odds, or the subordinate delivers the results. But real grit is forged in quieter places like the second draft, the third rehearsal, the meeting no one sees you prepare for. Grit isn't just about pushing harder. It's about practicing smarter. The most relentless leaders don't rise by accident. They train like it matters.

Duckworth (2016) emphasizes that gritty individuals pursue intentional application. Unlike an easy routine, deliberate practice is uncomfortable by design. It targets your weak spots, requires full attention, demands immediate feedback, and depends on repetition with intention. This kind of practice isn't glamorous. It's a grind. But it's also where true growth happens.

Anders Ericsson, the prominent researcher known for his work on expertise and expert performance, explains that excellence doesn't come from experience alone, it comes from how that experience is structured (Ericsson, 2006). "Deliberate practice" sharpens performance through disciplined feedback loops. Sustained effort and focused practice are key to achieving high levels of performance.

Organizations like the Mayo Clinic and Cleveland Clinic build cultures of excellence around these principles. As Lee and Duckworth (2018) describe, they embed deliberate practice into leadership development, team debriefs, and real-time feedback systems. These structures create safe environments for growth through failure and reflection, the hallmarks of sustainable performance.

But there's another layer, and that is emotion. Without a sense of purpose, deliberate practice can be an emotional drain. That's why grit and purpose must work together. The hard work of getting better only becomes meaningful when it's in the service of something you care about. Purpose gives your practice context and staying power.

As Duckworth notes, "Enthusiasm is common. Endurance is rare" (2016). The difference-maker isn't the burst of inspiration, it's the daily decision to stretch beyond comfort, especially when progress is invisible.

To build this habit:

1. Target One Weakness. Choose a skill, not just a task, to improve this week.

2. Design One Practice Loop. Set a micro-goal, get real-time feedback, and refine.

3. Repeat with Intention. Don't just do more. Do better, each time.

The kind of leader people trust when stakes are high are those who train like it matters. Deliberate practice creates a leader whose competence matches their commitment.

Principle 3: Create a Culture that Upholds

Grit is often painted as a solo act where a leader grinds forward alone while others cheer when the work is done. But in real life, the most persistent people are often supported by a culture that runs alongside them in the race.

Perseverance is a team sport. Research by Cross, Dillon, and Greenberg (2021) found that high performers draw significant energy from what they call relational resilience. They depend on the positive emotional energy generated by trust, connection, and shared commitment. When you're surrounded by people who persist, encourage, and model purpose-driven effort, it becomes easier to do the same.

Leaders who embed grit into the culture of their schools or organizations create a climate where perseverance isn't the exception, it's the expectation. As Lee and Duckworth (2018) describe in their research on health care organizations like Cleveland Clinic and Mayo Clinic, environments that prioritize feedback, reflection, and collective goals help normalize struggle as part of growth. These cultures encourage people to keep going, even when it's hard, because support is built into the structure.

McKinsey's model for CEO resilience calls this full-body resilience, a combination of internal drive, operational rhythm, and external support systems that help leaders recover and reengage during difficult seasons (Kristensen, Liu, & Sherman, 2025). Wise leaders design cultures that make resilience visible, habitual, and shared.

Consider the example of Brad Smith, former CEO of Intuit, who modeled vulnerability by sharing his own performance reviews with his team. This act didn't signal weakness, it strengthened the norm of transparency and accountability. As Dewar, Keller, and Malhotra (2022) note, these cultural behaviors made it safer for others to admit struggles and to stay engaged throughout them.

To build this habit:

1. Talk About the Difficult. Normalize moments of struggle as part of excellence.

2. Model the Middle. Share in-progress goals, not just polished wins.

3. Build Support Systems. Create regular touchpoints, peer feedback loops, and micro-celebrations that reinforce effort and connection.

The grit you build isn't only within you. It's around you, and it's contagious. Strong cultures don't eliminate adversity. They absorb it. They remind people they're not alone. And in the moments when people falter, the culture of resilience keeps them moving in a supportive, positive direction. As Rob Cross, Karen Dillon, and Danna Greenberg say in The Secret to Building Resilience (2021) note resilience is not a solo sport, it's built and sustained through our connections.

FROM ONE LEADER TO ANOTHER

Gail Jorden

State-Level Education Leader, Connecticut
  As heard on Othman's Leadership Podcast, Episode TBD

Keep Your Goal in Mind, Give Yourself Grace

For Gail Jorden, grit wasn't just an idea, it was a disciplined pursuit of purpose. When she ran for secretary of the Connecticut Education Association, it wasn't about titles or ambition. It was about impact. She believed deeply in the power of educators to shape the future, and she wanted to help lead that charge.

It was her first real campaign, and she was running against an experienced incumbent with broader name recognition. The learning curve was steep. "I had to run a full campaign, and I had never done anything like that," she said. "It was completely different from anything I'd done before." But Jorden didn't back down. She approached the challenge with intention and drive, treating the experience not as a test, but as a chance to grow.

Her success wasn't accidental. It was the result of focused, consistent effort. Jorden kept her goal in sight and built systems to stay on track. Her method wasn't fancy, but it helped her measure progress. She could look at what she had done and know she was moving forward.

Equally important was the community she built around her, people who were also working toward something meaningful, who brought energy, encouragement, and accountability. "Not just yes people," Jorden explained. "But folks who are striving too. People who challenge you and remind you what you're capable of."

Through every twist in the process, she held her purpose close and gave herself permission to adapt. "Keep your goal in mind," she said, "but give yourself grace. You may need to shift your approach, but stay true to what you're aiming for."

The experience didn't just earn her a leadership position. It reshaped her approach to growth and leadership. Today, Jorden brings that same clarity and passion to the people she supports. She encourages them to lead with purpose, stay disciplined in the practice, and lean into a community that lifts them higher.

STRATEGY IN A SKETCH

Angela Duckworth's Grit Framework explains why some people sustain effort long after initial motivation fades. Grit develops through four key capacities: interest that sparks curiosity, practice that builds skill, purpose that gives meaning, and hope that keeps belief alive. This model helps leaders focus on what truly fuels perseverance instead of just demanding more effort. Used with intention, it becomes a tool for nurturing lasting drive in yourself and others. This model is especially important when long-term goals feel daunting or teams are struggling to stay engaged. It helps leaders shift from simply pushing harder to understanding what's missing. It may not be a question of perseverance, but about where the grit-building process broke down.

Angela Duckworth's Framework

"Grit is not about avoiding failure—it's about refusing to let failure end the story."

"Effort counts twice" — Duckworth explains that talent × effort = skill, and skill × effort = achievement.

Based on Angela Duckworth's research in Grit (2016).

MAKE IT YOURS

- What disciplined commitment have I made to develop a specific skill?

- What goal is more important than the difficulties in achieving it?

- What sustained effort and focused practice do I need to begin?

- What support systems do I need to build?

8

Be a Learner

How Can Growth Become a Daily Habit?

> The capacity to learn is a gift; the ability to learn is a skill; the willingness to learn is a choice.
>
> Brian Herbert

From Task to Turning Point

It started with a simple homework assignment: "Take the Meyers-Briggs Type Indicator (MBTI) assessment." No big deal. I (Reda) was just beginning my doctoral program in leadership at Bay Path University and, like most of my classmates, I clicked through the questions and moved on.

Weeks later, during a virtual session, our professor asked us to revisit our results and focus on one specific page of the seventeen page report. That's when everything shifted. It felt like someone had put words to the patterns I'd lived for years. It illuminated my habits, strengths, and even the internal tensions I rarely voiced.

That night, I didn't just skim the report, I studied it. I followed up by reading everything I could find on MBTI: the framework, the research, the real-world application. I built a system for deepening my understanding and carved out time each morning to read, keep notes, and track questions I wanted to explore. I created a habit of reflection and asked myself what I was learning, but also, how it was shaping me.

I approached it all with a growth mindset. I didn't expect mastery overnight. I focused on daily effort, curiosity, and the belief that ability develops through deliberate practice. Learning became a practice in itself. And then the revelation came to me: this is helping me so much, it could certainly help others, too. So, within weeks, I made the decision to pursue certification as an MBTI Practitioner.

Was it convenient? Not at all. I was managing doctoral course-work, deadlines, and a demanding schedule. Some suggested I wait until life was more manageable. But I'd built momentum that was rooted in daily discipline, structured time, and internal reflection. I knew this was the time.

I enrolled. And that choice reshaped the trajectory of my work. Today, MBTI isn't just another credential, it's a core part of how I help others unlock potential, lead with awareness, and grow with intention.

So here's what I've learned: growth doesn't come from waiting for the perfect time. It comes from building consistent habits, having systems that support your goals, and making time to reflect on what you're learning. Say yes, then move forward day by day, system by system, thought by thought. That's how transformation takes root.

PRINCIPLES

Principle 1: Build One Skill at a Time

Imagine walking into a store where the only accepted currency is knowledge. Not titles. Not tenure. Just the skills you've built and the ones you're actively developing. That's not fiction, it's today's workforce. In a fast-changing world, learning isn't a luxury. It's leverage. The most adaptable leaders are those who treat learning as a habit, not a phase.

James Clear (2018) reminds us in *Atomic Habits* that "success is the product of daily habits, not once-in-a-lifetime transformations." In the same way compound interest builds wealth, consistent learning builds leadership capacity. Whether you're learning how to coach a team, analyze performance data, or communicate across differences, the right skills unlock both confidence and opportunity.

Dweck's (2006) research on growth mindset reinforces this. When you believe abilities can be developed, you're more likely to persist through discomfort and view mistakes as feedback. She writes, "Becoming is better than being," a reminder that your identity is not fixed. It's shaped, stretched, and strengthened by what you choose to learn next.

Andersen (2016) reminds us that a leader's edge is not found in holding onto what we already know, but in the willingness to keep learning. The cycle of learning, unlearning, and relearning becomes a discipline that prepares leaders for uncertainty. What worked yesterday may not serve tomorrow, and those who stay agile are the ones best positioned to navigate change. Robert Greene, in *Mastery* (2012), echoes this: "The future belongs to those who learn more skills and combine them in creative ways."

But today's greatest threat to learning isn't capacity, it's distraction. In *Stolen Focus*, Hari (2022) reveals how modern conveniences can sabotage deep work. Shallow, fragmented activities crowd out the sustained focus needed for meaningful skill building. That's why learning must be intentional and included in your daily rhythm.

To turn this into a habit:

1. Start a Learning Ledger. Track one micro-skill you're developing each week.

2. Create a 20-Minute Practice Block. Protect it like a meeting.

3. Ask "What Did I Learn?" each Friday. End the week with a reflection, not just a task list.

Lifelong learners don't wait for permission and they're not obsessed with being right or doing things perfectly. They're committed to getting better and forging through discomfort. In a world where information is abundant and relevance is earned, skills are the new currency. And the leaders who succeed will be the ones who continue to learn.

Principle 2: Create a System That Works for You

We all want to grow. But wanting isn't enough. What separates consistent learners from occasional dabblers isn't intelligence, it's infrastructure. As Clear (2018) puts it, "You do not rise to the level of your goals. You fall to the level of your systems." If growth is something you hope to achieve eventually, it won't happen. But if learning is built into how your day flows, it becomes inevitable.

Systems are how habits stick. Fogg (2019), in *Tiny Habits*, explains that behaviors rooted in positive emotion and simplicity are far more likely to last. Instead of dreading two hours of study at night, start with a quick plan that's easily implemented. For example: "After I brush my teeth, I'll listen to a podcast of my research topic."

This method of habit stacking makes learning easy to start and hard to skip. The smaller the barrier, the bigger the follow-through.

James Clear's 2-Minute Rule is a slightly different take on the same idea. It states that a new habit should take two minutes or less to start. Once you've begun, it's much easier to continue. It's a small but powerful "gateway habit" that leads to a cascade of more productive behaviors. When learning begins with friction, we resist it. But when it starts small and smooth, it becomes a rhythm. Over time, these micro-habits compound into real transformation.

Systems don't just refer to routines, they include your environment. Do you surround yourself with reminders to learn? Do you keep your favorite books visible, set calendar nudges for practice blocks, or track your micro-skills with a habit app? Erika Andersen (2016) calls this "mental scaffolding," external support that makes internal change easier to maintain.

To build a system that works:

1. Stack It. Attach one micro-learning activity to an existing habit.

2. Track It. Use a visual habit tracker or learning log to mark progress.

3. Share It. Join an accountability group where you share what you're learning.

Your calendar, your environment, and your routines can either hinder your goals or reinforce them. Build systems that make important actions automatic. Consistency beats intensity.

Principle 3: Learn It, Use It, And Grow From It

It's easy to confuse motion with progress. In a world obsessed with doing, the appearance of learning can look like mindlessly watching a video, finishing a chapter, completing a training. But real learning doesn't stick until we stop to think. Reflection is where growth gets processed. Without it, knowledge stays shallow. With it, learning becomes wisdom.

Horsley (2014), in *Unlimited Memory*, explains that "learning is connecting new information to old information." Our brains thrive on connection in addition to consumption. Reflection strengthens these neural links. When we pause to ask, What did I learn? and How does it connect to what I already know?, we move from memorizing facts to reshaping our mental models.

Clear (2018) builds on this in *Atomic Habits*, describing mastery as "the process of narrowing your focus to a tiny element of success, and repeating it until it's internalized." But repetition without reflection becomes mechanical. Growth happens when we step back, extract insight, and adjust course.

Greene (2012) calls this the "emotional pit stop." It's a brief pause that allows high performers to make sense of failure, pattern recognition, and self-correction. These pauses build self-awareness and momentum. Without them, we keep churning, but not learning. Oliver Burkeman, in *Four Thousand Weeks*, (2021) adds to the importance of pausing for reflection. He warns against falling into the trap of hyperproductivity without purpose because learning systems aren't about optimization for its own sake, they're about designing your life around what matters most. When your systems reflect your values, learning isn't another task, it's an expression of who you're becoming.

To build this habit:

1. Use the 3-2-1 Check-In. After a learning activity, write down 3 things you learned, 2 that surprised you, and 1 action you'll take.

2. End Each Week with One Question. What did I learn this week that I can use next week?

3. Create a Monthly Growth Review. Revisit the past 30 days.

Ask: What am I proud of? What felt like friction? What pattern is emerging?

Reflection doesn't slow learning, it secures it. It creates space to align learning with values, revisit assumptions, and pivot when needed.

FROM ONE LEADER TO ANOTHER

Dr. Jono Hey

Creator of Sketchplanations
   As heard on Othman's Leadership Podcast, Episode 39

Start Small with What Makes Sense to you

Dr. Jono Hey didn't start out trying to become a global thought leader. In fact, when he launched Sketchplanations, his only goal was to sketch one idea each week. "I started doing one sketch a week, and that's what I've done ever since." No grand strategy, just a steady habit of making sense of the world. That rhythm, built on repetition, turned into hundreds of visual explanations shared around the world. "It's amazing how powerful one sketch a week becomes over time," he reflected. The magic, he insists, isn't in the polish, it's in the practice.

But consistency, he said, only works when it's tied to curiosity. "A lot of the ideas come from something I've read or just something I've been thinking about," he explained. "Could I explain this visually? Would this help someone understand it?" For Hey, sketching is how he thinks, not just how he teaches. "When I sit down and try to sketch something, it quickly becomes obvious where I don't understand it." That tension between knowing and not knowing is exactly where learning happens.

He also spoke candidly about the challenges of creative discipline. "There are definitely weeks when I think, 'I don't have a sketch in me,'" he admitted. But he shows up anyway. "It's like running. You get better at doing it, and better at being okay with the fact that sometimes it's hard." His advice to others: keep it simple. "Make your learning practice something small and repeatable," he said. "That's what makes it sustainable."

Hey didn't frame himself as an expert on learning, he found what worked for him. "I learn so much from doing them," he said. "I learn about the thing I'm explaining. I learn about myself." That's the heart of his practice. Learning isn't a goal to reach, it's a mindset to live. The people who grow most aren't the ones who master everything. They're the ones who build habits that support their learning, create systems to sustain it, and reflect deeply enough to turn knowledge into lasting growth.

STRATEGY IN A SKETCH

The 3A Learning Cycle is a practical model rooted in well-established educational theory and organized into three clear stages. It reflects how adults develop skills over time by acquiring new knowledge (Bloom, 1956), applying it in authentic contexts (Kolb, 1984), and amplifying it through reflection, integration, or teaching (Bandura, 1977; Schön, 1983). At its core, this cycle turns passive learning into active growth by helping leaders move beyond just knowing to actually doing and deepening.

The mistake many leaders make with this learning cycle is stopping after the first step. They consume ideas without committing to practice or teaching others. The power of this model lies in repetition with intention.

The 3A Learning Cycle

Acquire
Learn new skills through study, experience, or coaching

Apply
Practice and use the skill in real-life contexts

Amplify
Teach it, reflect on it, or combine it with another skill

Put your current skill focus in the center and check: Am I only acquiring? Or also applying and amplifying?

Adapted from classic frameworks by Bandura (1977), Bloom (1956), Kolb (1984), and Schön (1983).

MAKE IT YOURS

- What new skill or topic can I explore this week, this month, this year?

- What routines or systems do I need to establish to make learning time possible?

- How can I build in time to pause, reflect, apply and internalize my learning?

9
Be Mindful
How Present Are You in the Moments That Matter?

The most precious gift we can offer anyone is our attention. When mindfulness embraces those we love, they will bloom like flowers.

Thich Nhat Hanh

The Project That Changed Everything

At Lincoln Middle School, the eighth-grade team had a tradition: the end-of-year science fair. Every spring, it looked the same, with tri-fold boards, vinegar volcanoes, and a panel of judges with red pens and score sheets. It was neat, efficient, and entirely predictable.

But in a team meeting one morning, Mr. Reilly, a relatively new science teacher known for starting class with a few deep breaths, asked a question that made everyone pause.

"Why do we still do it this way?" The room went quiet. Ms. Walker, who had been teaching for over 25 years, shifted in her chair.

"Because it works. The kids know what to expect. It's organized. It checks the boxes."

"But do they care about it?" he asked. "Does it reflect the way real science works, curious, collaborative, and uncertain? Are we choosing this format because it's meaningful, or just because it's familiar?"

That moment was more than a challenge. It was a practice in mindfulness, of noticing a pattern, pausing before reacting, and questioning whether the automatic choice still served a purpose.

Ms. Johnson, who taught math, spoke up. "What if we changed the format? What if the focus wasn't the product, but the process?"

From that seed, the Innovation Challenge grew. Instead of producing perfect final projects, students would choose real-world problems they cared about, experiment over time, and reflect on their progress, including failures. They'd be evaluated not just on what they achieved, but how they observed, adapted, and learned.

At first, students were uneasy. "So... we're allowed to fail?" one asked. Mr. Reilly nodded. "Absolutely. Just be curious. Pay attention. Learn from it. That's real science, and real growth."

Some parents were skeptical. "Will this hurt their grades?" "What if my child doesn't finish?" But as the weeks passed, something deeper started happening. One group studied whether students focused better after mindfulness breaks and presented real data from their classmates. Another tested solutions to reduce lunchroom noise, noticing how stress levels dropped when small changes were made. A student who rebuilt a solar-powered phone charger five different times never got it to work but gave a powerful reflection on patience, problem-solving, and persistence.

Throughout it all, mindfulness was threaded into the process. Students wrote short reflections after each work session. They noted what they did, but also how they felt, what surprised them, what they noticed. They learned to pause before rushing to fix something, to sit with confusion, to see failure as information and not judgment.

The final event wasn't their traditional fair. It was a celebration of the learning process. Students gave presentations with live demos, open-ended questions, and real-time challenges. They didn't pretend to have it all figured out. They were present, honest, and engaged.

Afterward, Ms. Walker stood near the back of the room, watching students animatedly explain their messy, beautiful projects. She turned to Mr. Reilly. "I assumed they needed strict procedures to succeed. I didn't realize how much they could grow when we gave them space." He smiled. "I think we all learned that. It's amazing what happens when we stop doing things on autopilot."

In the months that followed, that one change sparked many more. Teachers across subjects began rethinking routines. Morning pauses became part of the school day. Students talked more openly about their mistakes, and less about getting it "right." The culture shifted and people became more aware, more intentional, and more willing to live with questions instead of rushing to answers.

At Lincoln Middle School, they learned that leadership, learning, and progress don't come from doing things the way they've always been done. They come from noticing the moment, challenging assumptions, and having the courage to move forward, even without knowing exactly how it will all turn out.

PRINCIPLES

Principle 1: Clear the Lens

Leadership often fails not from lack of effort, but from lack of perspective. When leaders operate from old routines, they begin to rely on mental shortcuts like reacting from assumptions, missing nuances, and recycling outdated solutions. The practice of mindfulness interrupts this autopilot by inviting leaders to observe their surroundings, their thinking, and their judgments with curiosity. When practiced intentionally, mindfulness becomes a powerful tool for breaking patterns and noticing what others miss.

Several authors highlight the benefits of mindfulness, noting that it deepens self-awareness, supports emotional regulation, and sharpens decision-making. They emphasize it as an essential skill for leaders facing complexity and high-pressure environments. (Kabat-Zinn, 2003; Langer, 2014; Goleman & Davidson, 2017).

Ellen Langer (2014) defines mindfulness as "actively noticing new things." This definition reframes mindfulness from a quiet, internal process into a dynamic cognitive act of openness. Langer (2010) argues that mindlessness, the belief that we already know, is the real threat to effective leadership. True awareness comes not from certainty but from wonder. Noticing novelty fosters learning, innovation, and adaptability.

In high-stakes environments, leaders are trained to default to what's worked before. But Tan (2015) says even a six-second pause to observe without judgment can create a micro-opportunity to reassess. The most effective leaders habitually question their first impressions. They practice what Achor and Gielan (2016) call "attentional hygiene," a deliberate shaping of focus to widen what they see and who they hear.

This clarity starts with awareness. Instead of labeling someone as lazy, resistant, or difficult, pause and ask, "What else could be true?" You might notice tone, timing, or tension that changes the story. Another practical strategy is to observe your assumptions out loud: "I'm assuming she doesn't agree; let me check that before I act." These simple reflections interrupt bias and open the door for better decisions.

Clearing the lens is about making space for accuracy. Leaders who can see without distortion communicate with more empathy, listen more deeply, and lead with sharper insight.

Principle 2: Rethink the Past to Act Wisely in the Present

When leaders react to situations based on outdated narratives, they risk making decisions that serve the story and not the situation. That's the danger of unexamined frames: they filter reality, often without our awareness. But what if that story you're telling yourself about a colleague's attitude, a failed initiative, or even your own leadership was never fully accurate to begin with?

Ellen Langer's work on mindfulness reveals that our perceptions of the past are often selective, reconstructed, or influenced by the meaning we assign to it now. Leaders often bring rigid labels like "resistant staff," "failed project," "high performer" into new contexts, unaware that those labels may be outdated or incomplete. Unless prompted by crisis or deliberate reflection, most people rarely revise the categories they use to interpret the past.

In one of Langer's examples, a couple's previous arguments are perceived as signs of incompatibility until they reconcile, and the same moments are reframed as growth. This applies directly to leadership. A principal might recall a teacher as "difficult" based on moments of disagreement. But when that teacher secures a financial grant that benefits the school, the principal touts their dedication.

Which story is true? Possibly both. That's the power of reframing. It opens the door to multiple truths, not just the one our bias prefers.

To put this into practice, leaders can use mindfulness as a tool for narrative clarity. Before you act, ask:

- What is the story I'm telling myself about this person or situation?

- What past event might I be overvaluing or misinterpreting?

- How would this moment look if I assumed positive intent?

Sometimes, leadership is about looking back with fresh eyes, and seeing what you missed the first time.

Principle 3: Embrace the Unfinished

We live in a world that praises certainty and closure. Yet leadership is often anything but certain. From shifting goals to unexpected feedback, today's leaders are constantly navigating change. Life is not black and white. Rather than resisting uncertainty, the most resilient leaders learn to stand steady in the gray, treating uncertainty not as a threat, but as a teacher.

In *The Power of Now*, Eckhart Tolle reminds us that "uncertainty is the fertile ground of pure potential." When we fixate on control, our world contracts. But when we accept that not everything needs to be solved or predicted, we expand into presence and possibility. This is echoed in *Buddha's Brain*, where Hanson and Mendius (2009) explain how the brain's threat system lights up under ambiguity. But mindfulness removes the threat by activating the prefrontal cortex, our center for reflection and wisdom, and enables us to respond calmly instead of reacting impulsively.

Uncertainty doesn't mean instability. When leaders embrace the unfinished, they build cultures that value learning over perfection, dialogue over conclusions, and growth over guarantees. Research in

Finding Flow (Csikszentmihalyi) further shows that engagement and creativity often peak not in perfect conditions, but in dynamic ones. Leaders grow not by mastering every variable, but by building the muscle to adapt while staying grounded in values. Meanwhile, McKeown (2021) in, *Effortless*, offers a counterintuitive insight: trying too hard to force outcomes adds friction. Progress is more sustainable when we make peace with progress that's still in motion.

FROM ONE LEADER TO ANOTHER

Dr. Amanda Thayer

Administrator of the Early Childhood Initiatives Program, Holyoke Community College
As heard on Othman's Leadership Podcast, Episode TBD

Modeling Mindfulness Moment by Moment

For Dr. Amanda Thayer, mindfulness as a leader didn't begin with journaling or finding quiet moments to reflect. Those practices came later. What started it all was a moment of honest vulnerability when she chose to speak up.

It happened during a meeting with colleagues she respected and genuinely enjoyed working with. But Thayer has a hearing impairment, and when conversations move too fast or people begin talking over one another, she struggles to keep up. Lip-reading across multiple voices just isn't possible. That day, as the discussion spiraled ahead, she felt herself withdraw. She grew quiet. The voice in her head said, Don't make it a big deal. Just get through it. But something deeper rose up and pushed back: No, this matters.

She spoke plainly and clearly, without irritation in her voice. "I want to be a part of this, but I can't keep up with how fast it's moving."

There was a long pause. Thayer felt exposed. Then someone nodded. Another chimed in, "I felt the same way and didn't know how to say it." And something shifted. The group slowed down. They adjusted. It wasn't perfect, but it was better.

That moment clarified something Thayer had been sensing for a while: mindfulness in leadership isn't about appearance. It's about presence. It's about noticing what's unfolding in real time and responding with care. It's about recognizing that others may not see what you see or feel what you feel, and not assuming they do. It's about staying open, especially when the outcome isn't certain.

In the months that followed, Thayer began to build small, steady habits to support her presence. She created what she calls her "internal pause button." When tensions rose or emotions ran high, she pressed it. Sometimes it meant taking five quiet breaths. Other times it meant saying, "Can we pause? I need a moment to think." It gave her space to return to her values and show up with intention and stay grounded in integrity.

She kept it simple. Every day, Thayer made a cup of tea. No phone. No multitasking. Just the act of making and drinking tea. She started running without headphones, tuning in to the rhythm of her breath, the crunch of gravel, the wind through trees. She called it sensory grounding. Before every meeting, she asked herself, What energy do I want to bring into this space? That one question helped her enter each room, not with certainty and a need to control, but with clarity.

Mindfulness started showing up at home too. One afternoon, Thayer's 16-year-old son mentioned that when he played video games, he was totally focused, but when he was out walking with friends, he barely noticed his surroundings. Thayer smiled. He was beginning to notice attention itself. That evening, they stepped onto the deck, and she invited him to find just one thing to notice. No instructions, no time limits, just, "Pick something, and really look at it."

He did. And to Thayer's surprise, he didn't resist. Later, they talked about how mindfulness teachers sometimes ask people to hold an orange and feel the texture, smell the skin, and observe its details before eating it. It's not about the orange. It's about learning to pause long enough to see what's already there.

Moments like that reminded Thayer that mindfulness doesn't require perfect conditions. It doesn't mean always knowing what to say or do. It means choosing to be present, even in uncertainty. It means letting go of assumptions, recognizing that perception isn't always reality, and staying open to what's unfolding. Whether with a team or a teen, Thayer had learned that even three seconds of shared stillness can shift a moment from reaction to reflection.

And for anyone unsure where to begin, Thayer would say: Don't start with a bold resolution. Start with one breath between tasks. Just one. You'll forget. Then you'll remember. And in that moment of remembering, you'll begin again.

STRATEGY IN A SKETCH

The Langer Mindfulness Framework invites leaders to trade automatic reactions for deliberate noticing. The model sharpens awareness by asking leaders to observe changes, challenge assumptions, and eliminate rash conclusions. Used in moments of tension, decision-making, or group dynamics, it creates space for better insight and fewer blind spots.

Langer draws a sharp distinction between "making the right decision" and "making the decision right." She warns that leaders waste time and energy trying to make the "right" decision, when in truth, there is no way to know for sure. She tells the story of a student agonizing between Harvard and Yale, caught in endless "what ifs" that can never guarantee the perfect choice. That's where regret and stress creep in, fueled by mindlessness: treating uncertainty as if it were certainty. The healthier mindset is to make the decision right. Once you have chosen, direct your focus toward shaping conditions so the choice succeeds. For teachers and school leaders, this shift means less wasted energy and less time spent second-guessing themselves.

The Langer Mindfulness Framework

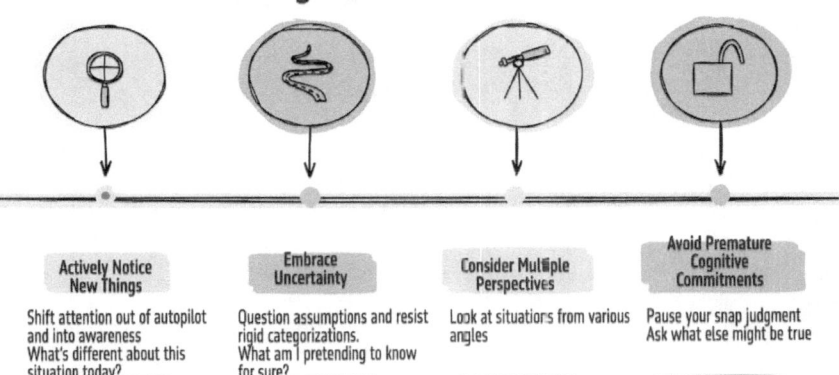

Actively Notice New Things	Embrace Uncertainty	Consider Multiple Perspectives	Avoid Premature Cognitive Commitments
Shift attention out of autopilot and into awareness What's different about this situation today?	Question assumptions and resist rigid categorizations. What am I pretending to know for sure?	Look at situations from various angles	Pause your snap judgment Ask what else might be true

Based on Ellen Langer's classic work Mindfulness (2014)

MAKE IT YOURS

- What assumptions do I carry about certain people or situations, and how might those be distorting my leadership decisions?

- What story am I telling myself about a current challenge and what happens when I look at it from another angle?

- Where might I be trying to control situations instead of embracing uncertainty?

10

Be Grateful

What Happens When You See the Good First?

Gratitude is not only the greatest of virtues, but the parent of all others.

Cicero

The Way We See The World

Reda and I (Suzanne) come from very different worlds. Our backgrounds, cultures, and experiences don't match on paper. Yet we became friends while working at the same high school. I asked him for assistance with a project and when others said they didn't have time or they needed to be compensated for extra work, he didn't hesitate. A few months later, he reached out to me for support, and I was happy to return the favor. Those early exchanges were simple and sincere. We showed up with real concern for each other, and through those moments, we discovered a shared mindset. Even in the face of challenge, we both believed in showing up, pitching in, and finding a way forward.

Not until writing this chapter did I realize that our connection is rooted in how we view the world. We both bring a strong sense of optimism to our work and our lives. It's not that we ignore problems. Our outlook comes from daily habits of practicing gratitude, staying grounded in service, and choosing to see challenges as chances to learn and grow. We also know this mindset is not something we sustain on our own. We are deeply thankful for our families, friends, and coworkers who support us, believe in us, and remind us of what truly matters. Their presence gives us the perspective and strength to keep showing up with purpose.

We believe a leader's mindset can be one of their greatest tools. Gratitude does not ignore difficulty. It allows us to respond with clarity and intention. It helps us see progress in small steps and focus on what is possible even when things are hard.

Christensen, Allworth and Dillon, 2012, the authors of *How Will You Measure Your Life?*, make a compelling case that real professional happiness comes from alignment between values and work, inspiring intrinsic drive, personal growth, meaningful contribution, and an evolving sense of purpose. We agree.

PRINCIPLES

Principle 1: Cultivate The Attitude

Gratitude isn't a feeling you wait for, it's a focus you practice. Just like physical strength comes from consistent reps, emotional strength grows from an intentional perspective and conscious practice. If you want to lead with clarity, connection, and calm, gratitude can't be optional. It must be daily.

Pasricha (2019), author of *You Are Awesome*, highlights that happiness is 90% influenced by internal mindset, not external circumstances. One of his simplest strategies? Write down three things you're grateful for each week. This quick practice rewires your brain to search for what's working instead of what's wrong. Over time, you train your attention to favor possibility over pessimism.

Rohn (1996) calls happiness "a way of interpreting the world." The same is true of gratitude. It isn't about ignoring challenges, it's about choosing what lens you look through. Leaders grounded in gratitude don't react from stress; they respond from perspective. They know how to recognize progress, even when perfection isn't possible.

In education or organizational life, it's easy to focus only on undesirable situations, like poor test scores, employee vacancies, and last minute policy changes. But gratitude helps you zoom out and see the full picture. For example, a principal who opens staff meetings by sharing small wins, like a student breakthrough or a colleague's quiet support, builds a culture of positivity. These micro-moments create macro-impact.

Hay (1984) writes, "Every thought we think is creating our future." When we anchor our thoughts in appreciation, we generate emotional energy that fuels creativity, connection, and resilience. Leaders who express gratitude are strategically boosting morale, reducing burnout, and cultivating loyalty.

To build this habit:

1. Start a Gratitude Log. Write three wins, learnings, or connections each morning or evening.

2. Model It Publicly. Begin meetings or emails with one genuine appreciation.

3. Reframe what's Difficult. Ask, "What did this challenge teach me?"

When practiced consistently, gratitude reshapes how you see, speak, and lead. It helps you build environments people want to return to, even on the hard days.

Principle 2: Choose Purpose Over Praise

Leadership built on external validation is always at risk. When energy hinges on others' perceptions, direction blurs, resolve weakens, and choices start to reflect fear rather than purpose. Decisions become more about approval than impact. Effective leadership begins when your motivation doesn't come from praise, but from purpose.

Pasricha (2016), in *The Happiness Equation*, explains that extrinsic rewards like titles, recognition, and approval often lead to short-lived satisfaction. Intrinsic motivation, on the other hand, sustains joy. It drives leaders to act not because someone's watching, but because they believe in the work itself. Pasricha calls this the happiness formula flipped: doing what energizes you first, and finding that success follows, not the other way around.

This insight is echoed by Rohn (1996) who wrote, "Reasons come first, answers second". When your "why" is personal and rooted in your values, identity, or a vision for who you're becoming, you build staying power. You're no longer chasing approval. You're channeling conviction. This becomes your driving force when momentum dips or criticism rises.

Consider a school leader implementing a new equity framework. If they pursue it to meet compliance, their resolve may fade when resistance shows up. But if they act from a belief that every child deserves access and dignity, their conviction becomes contagious. Their leadership grows from alignment, not applause.

Hay (1984), in *You Can Heal Your Life*, writes that many of our self-sabotaging patterns stem from the belief: "I'm not good enough." Leaders chasing validation are often trying to fill this gap. But confidence is built on a steady sense of self, not on praise. It's only when we shift from performing to contributing that we lead with grounded power.

To build this habit:

1. Reconnect to Your "Why" Weekly. Ask, "What values am I honoring this week?"

2. Audit Your Yes. Before saying yes to a new task or project, ask, "Is this in sync with my purpose or am I trying to prove something?"

3. Replace People-Pleasing. Trade approval-seeking for values-anchored action.

When you look beyond the applause and are rooted in purpose, you lead from a place of contentment and confidence. And that's the kind of leadership that inspires others not just to follow, but to find their own voice too.

Principle 3: Wear The Right Glasses

More than reacting, leaders influence outcomes by how they frame situations. And in that meaning lies the power to shift morale, mindset, and momentum. Seeing the world through a happiness lens isn't about blind optimism. It's about disciplined interpretation. It's about pausing to ask not just what's happening, but how am I choosing to see it?

Rohn (1996) framed happiness not as a mood, but "a way of interpreting the world." That perspective is echoed in Pasricha's research (2016), which shows that only 10% of happiness is determined by external circumstances. The other 90%? It comes from mindset, habits, and intentional interpretation.

Leaders who adopt this lens train themselves to view setbacks as setups, questions as invitations, and feedback as fuel. Take the example of a school principal rolling out a new policy who receives resistance. They could think, "They don't respect my leadership." Or they could reframe it as, "This pushback means people care, and I now have a chance to build trust by listening." The facts don't change. The lens does. And that makes all the difference.

This shift echoes the abundance mindset taught by Zander and Zander (2000) in *The Art of Possibility*. Leaders stuck in a world of measurement, where value is tied to comparison, perfection, or approval, often default to stress and scarcity. But when they interpret events through a lens of growth, creativity, and connection, they stop asking "How do I fix this?" and start asking "What's possible here?"

Christensen, Allworth, and Dillon (2012) adds another layer in *How Will You Measure Your Life?* by reminding us that true success is about coordinating values with actions. Leaders who define progress this way are far less rattled by daily turbulence. They don't need constant wins to stay steady. Their lens is internal, grounded, and resilient

To build this habit:

1. Name the Story. In moments of tension, ask "What story am I telling myself about this?"

2. Choose a Reframe. Ask "What's another way to see this that honors truth but offers growth?"

3. Lead with the New Narrative. Use the reframe to guide your response in personal interactions and emails.

Leadership is meaning-making. The stories you believe become the stories your team lives. When you choose the more empowering, honest, and hopeful lens, everyone sees better.

Principle 4: Interpret Events with Purpose and Possibility

Many leaders walk into rooms carrying an invisible weight of not enough. Not enough money, time, support, credit, or recognition. This scarcity mindset may not be spoken aloud, but it shows up in turf wars, rigid plans, and fear-based decisions. It stifles innovation and corrodes trust. To lead with energy, creativity, and courage, we must shift from guarding what is to imagining what could be.

Zander and Zander (2000) describe this dynamic as the "world of measurement,"a paradigm obsessed with comparison, competition, and control. Leaders stuck here see life as a zero-sum game. But when we shift into what they call the "universe of possibility," we trade fear for vision. We stop asking, "How do I protect my slice?" and start asking, "How can I help expand the whole pie?"

This doesn't mean ignoring constraints. It means reframing them. Imagine a school superintendent whose budget has been reduced. A scarcity lens sees only layoffs and cuts. But an abundance lens looks at partnerships, innovation zones, or community-led solutions that make more from less. The lens doesn't change the facts, it changes the strategy.

Rohn (1996) reminds us that true wealth involves internal fulfillment which comes from applying simple principles with consistency. Gratitude, generosity, and resourcefulness aren't soft skills, they're strategic and essential tools. Leaders with an abundance mindset look at their team's talents, their school's assets, and their own inner resilience and leverage these to the organization's advantage

To build this habit:

1. Reframe Scarcity Statements. When you hear "We don't have enough," counter with, "What do we already have that we're not fully using?"

2. Name and Share Wins Generously. Celebrate others' progress as if it were your own to reinforce a culture of rising together.

3. Model Possibility in Meetings. Be the voice that shifts the tone from "limited options" to "new ideas."

When leaders model abundance, they change mindsets and they change systems. They move from gatekeeping to stewardship. From tension to trust. From scarcity to strategy. And that's the kind of leadership that creates significance and success.

FROM ONE LEADER TO ANOTHER

Michael Merline

Learning Experience Design Consultant, Citizens Bank
   As heard on Othman's Leadership Podcast, Episode TBD

Be the Same Grateful Leader in Every Room

Early in his career, Michael Merline saw how one moment of recognition could lift an entire team. "There are some projects that are highlighted by upper management, and they communicate their interest in that project and how well it was done to a manager." When that praise was shared with the entire team, "it makes all of us feel good about the teammate, and it makes all of us feel good about each other that the work we're doing is being seen, and it's spread throughout the organization." For Michael, moments like these reinforced that gratitude isn't just a feeling, it's something leaders choose to express in ways that ripple outward.

Merline's own foundation for gratitude comes from his parents, who "never preached to us, but we were taught our values by example." He continues that approach with his son, "showing thanks and gratitude throughout our lives, personally and professionally." When results don't match the effort or trust is broken, he draws on that grounding. "I stay calm, keep a level thought process, level emotions, and a level conversation and communication with the other people that are involved." Gratitude, in his view, is steady, not situational; it's how you show up even when things don't go right.

A constant theme in his leadership is authenticity. "If I step out of the office, you're not going to see a different person than is in the office." Gratitude is woven into how he interacts with peers and leaders: "I show how I feel, and gratitude is a big part of what I show and when I feel it." For him, authenticity protects against performative gestures. "Bringing and being your true authentic self with your peers is the best way to be and the best way to be around other people."

Merline also believes gratitude can strengthen improvement-driven cultures. "We are each other's cheerleaders." In practice, that means supporting colleagues through difficulties. "I can help you with this difficulty, or I can show you how to overcome this difficulty," and making recognition a team-wide habit. In meetings, "everybody highlights each other at the same time to make everyone feel a part of a tight-knit community." Those conversations often go beyond work, celebrating "something they've achieved in their personal lives" and "supporting each other as much as possible."

For leaders who want to become more grateful but don't feel it yet, Merline suggests starting small. "Read positive thoughts, hear positive thoughts, repeat positive thoughts, and share positive thoughts on gratitude with other people in their lives." Over time, that practice becomes a habit, one that can spread "from themselves to teammates, managers, coworkers, and even friends and family." In challenging moments, he grounds himself in a simple reminder:

"I'm grateful to be working with many good people. I'm grateful that it's the work that I enjoy doing. I'm grateful that I can not only learn from others, but educate others when anything difficult is going on."

STRATEGY IN A SKETCH

Developed by psychologist Martin Seligman, the founder of positive psychology, the PERMA framework distills what it means to feel well and lead well into five accessible habits. Each domain plays a distinct role: emotion fuels energy, engagement sharpens focus, relationships anchor resilience, meaning provides direction, and accomplishment builds momentum. Leaders can use PERMA to shape team culture, design professional development, and reflect on what keeps them personally engaged and inspired.

PERMA: The Five Habits That Fuel Well-Being

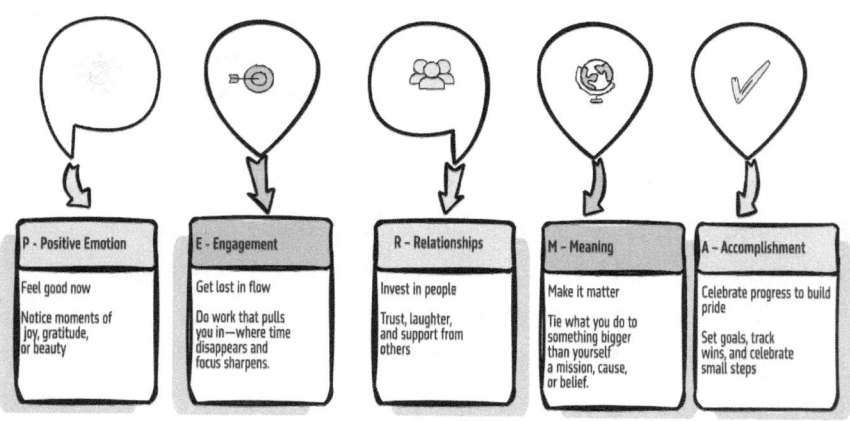

P - Positive Emotion	E - Engagement	R – Relationships	M – Meaning	A – Accomplishment
Feel good now	Get lost in flow	Invest in people	Make it matter	Celebrate progress to build pride
Notice moments of joy, gratitude, or beauty	Do work that pulls you in—where time disappears and focus sharpens.	Trust, laughter, and support from others	Tie what you do to something bigger than yourself: a mission, cause, or belief.	Set goals, track wins, and celebrate small steps

Based on Martin Seligman's well-being framework in Flourish (2011).

MAKE IT YOURS

- How can I make gratitude a visible and consistent part of my daily leadership routine?

- What decisions am I currently making to gain approval from others, and how might I reconnect with my foundational purpose and values?

- When faced with challenges, do I default to scarcity thinking or reframe the situation through a lens of possibility and growth?

11

Be a Public Speaker
How Do You Project and Connect?

The success of your presentation will be judged not by the knowledge you send but by what the listener receives.

Lilly Walters

Lessons from the Front of the Room

Ms. Flores often recalls a striking statistic: nearly 77 percent of people fear public speaking more than death. She understands why. Standing in front of a room full of people can feel deeply vulnerable. But over the years, she has learned something essential. Public speaking is not about being fearless. It's about being prepared and remembering who it is for.

One of her early presentations as a superintendent was to a room of teachers, administrators, and school board members. She was leading a session on instructional vision and professional learning, and the stakes felt high. Yet instead of focusing on impressing anyone, she focused on helping them connect to the work.

She reminded herself that the session wasn't about her, it was about them. She practiced the message out loud, refined the structure, and chose language that felt clear and authentic. She built in moments to pause, to breathe, to adjust her pace, and to check for understanding. She paid close attention to body language: Were people engaged? Were they taking notes? Did they look confused or curious?

That mental shift made all the difference. After the session, a principal approached her and said, "That's just what we needed. People were listening." A teacher shared that she left not only informed, but energized. Those comments stayed with Ms. Flores. It was nice to receive compliments, but she was happier to receive confirmation that physical and mental preparation is the key to a successful presentation. When she prepares with intention, she can be fully present and better able to serve the people in the room.

She also remembers what it feels like to do the opposite. Once, she accepted a speaking invitation out of obligation, not purpose. She rushed through the content, spoke too quickly, and failed to connect. She didn't slow down to listen or observe. The room was polite, but distant. The audience seemed disappointed, and she certainly was.

That experience became a turning point. It taught her that being present is not enough. Speakers must prepare with care, speak with clarity, and make space for genuine engagement. Whether it's a staff meeting, a parent forum, or a professional development session, Ms. Flores returns to three grounding principles before every talk. She remembers the purpose, she practices with focus, and she brings presence by being aware of her breath, her pace, and the people in front of her. To Ms. Flores, public speaking is not a performance, it is an opportunity to serve. When leaders prepare with skill and intention, they create moments that support learning, build trust, and move people forward.

PRINCIPLES

Principle 1: Think First

Dynamic communication begins before you say a single word. Whether you're facilitating a team training or leading a workshop, your mindset is your microphone. While most people focus on words, effective communicators first master what they think and feel before stepping in front of an audience.

Allison Shapira (2022), a former opera singer turned public speaking coach, offers a powerful reframe: nervousness and excitement are two sides of the same coin. Both activate similar physical responses, a racing heart, dry mouth, and shaky hands. The difference? What you call it. Saying out loud, "I'm excited about this opportunity" right before you speak shifts your brain's perception from threat to thrill. It's direction rather than denial.

Nancy Duarte (2012) takes this further by identifying four types of pre-talk rituals:

- Empathy-based - Connect with the audience beforehand

- Exertion-based - Use movement to reset your body

- Spiritual - Offer a short gratitude or grounding practice

- Mantra-based - Repeat an anchoring phrase like "I'm here to help"

These rituals regulate your nervous system. They remind your brain that you're safe, centered, and capable. Choose the ones that match your personality and the tone of your session.

And don't underestimate the physical aspects of a presentation. A quivering voice or rushed speech may stem from shallow breathing. Practice as Shapira (2015) recommends: place one hand on your stomach and one on your chest. Inhale deeply through the nose, exhale slowly, and let your words ride the breath. Think of your breath as the foundation of your message. If it's solid, your message stands strong.

Gershman (2019) teaches that fear often arises from the belief that all eyes are on you. It's primal, and your amygdala interprets attention as danger. But generosity neutralizes fear. Shift the spotlight: instead of "What will they think of me?" and ask, "What do they need from me right now?" You're not performing. You're serving.

And finally, rehearse like a pro. Art Markman (2018) points to stand-up comedians as models of high-stakes communicators who practice out loud. They don't aim for perfection. They aim for resonance. Use visualization, as Duarte suggests, to mentally walk through the full arc of your session, from the moment you stand up to your final line. It tells your brain: You've been here before.

One facilitator's routine before a school leadership training:

1. Five quick jumping jacks backstage.

2. Three deep breaths with hand on heart.

3. Self-talk, "You're here to serve."

4. Visualizing smiles and questions during Q&A.

Remember: mastering your mindset doesn't mean you stop feeling nervous. It means you stop being ruled by it. You walk in with your thoughts aligned, your body grounded, and your focus placed where it belongs, on your purpose of serving your audience.

Principle 2: Sync Your Voice, Message, and Movement

Great communicators share ideas and shape experiences. They coordinate their voice, body, and message in service of connection, not theatrics. Whether you're facilitating a training, leading a workshop, or delivering a school-wide update, your delivery determines how your message feels, and that's what people remember.

Start with clarity. TED curator Chris Anderson (2016) says it simply: "The only thing that truly matters in public speaking is... having something worth saying." But how you say it matters just as much.

Then comes the voice. Your voice is a tool to be used for sculpting, not hammering. Albrecht Enders and Robin de Haas (2025) explain how voice, breath, and posture work together to shape how others receive your message. Use pace to create rhythm, use pauses to emphasize meaning, use tone to convey intention. A steady breath grounds your delivery. Practicing vocal exercises before a session can reduce tension, calm nerves, and unlock energy.

Delivery also lives in your body. Carmine Gallo (2020) reminds us: "Your face is a message." Whether it's Steve Jobs pacing across a stage or a school principal making eye contact during a tough announcement, nonverbal cues shape trust. Open gestures, grounded feet, and expressive hands all communicate confidence and connection before a single word is spoken. Today's audiences need more than words. They need engagement. Matt Abrahams (2023) breaks it into three types:

1. Physical - Ask participants to raise hands, write, or move.

2. Mental - Prompt reflection, prediction, or debate.

3. Linguistic - Use phrases like "Imagine this..." or "Have you ever...?"

Wardle (2024) suggests thinking like a designer: engage all modalities. Use sketches, objects, tone, and interaction to create a learning experience, not a lecture. Facilitation should be a partnership, not a performance. Delivering with presence is like offering a well-wrapped package, but also placing something meaningful inside. When you align your intention, voice, and physicality, your message leaves a lasting impact.

Principle 3: Engage the Audience

Public speaking is never a solo act. While your voice may be the only one heard aloud, the audience is always responding through body language, energy, and attention. The best communicators know that true presence means reading the room, not just reading the slides. Whether you're leading professional development, coaching a team, or delivering training, your success hinges not only on what you say but how your audience feels seen and engaged in the moment.

Deborah Grayson Riegel (2022) focuses on great communicators who "put the audience first." This mindset shifts you from self-consciousness ("How am I doing?") to contribution ("What do they need?"). Start with their world. What do they care about? What are they worried or curious about? This shift from ego to empathy opens trust and increases receptivity.

Once you've centered the audience, the next step is to invite them in. Sabina Nawaz (2018) emphasizes that presentations fail when they become one-sided monologues. Even senior leaders, she notes, respond best to conversations and not content dumps. Create space for connection with simple invitations like "What information is important to you so far?" or "What questions are coming up as you hear this?" Think of the time as an opportunity to co-create understanding.

Trust is the undercurrent that makes interaction meaningful. According to Shapira and Horsager (2022), speakers who build trust through clarity, compassion, and transparency create the conditions for real engagement. Sharing a story, admitting when you're still learning, or simply affirming a tough question with "That's a fair point" makes your audience feel respected.

And when it comes to handling the Question and Answer session, Caroline Webb (2020) offers a mindset shift: Q&A isn't a threat. It's your best chance to deepen the impact. Acknowledge questions with gratitude, echo them for clarity, and use phrases like "Let me think aloud for a moment" to model thoughtful leadership. Even when you don't have a perfect answer, how you respond models presence and poise under pressure.

Imagine you're not at a podium but at a dinner table. Your job isn't to impress, it's to host. Notice who's quiet. Invite perspectives. Adjust the pacing. When people feel they're in the conversation and not just watching it, they're far more likely to remember, reflect, and apply what you shared.

FROM ONE LEADER TO ANOTHER

Jesse White

Principal, Bloomfield High School
  As heard on Othman's Leadership Podcast, Episode TBD

Speak to Their Story, Not Just Your Script

Jesse White knows the power of a message that matters. As both a principal and a preacher, he's learned that what truly transforms audiences isn't polish, it's presence. He shared the story of a woman from South Carolina who stumbled across one of his sermons on YouTube. "She said it was a tough day. Her husband was sick, and she was overwhelmed," Jesse recalled. But something in his message reached her. "She said, 'It was what I needed.'" For White, that moment reminded him that public speaking is less about delivering a perfect performance and more about stewarding a message that speaks to people's lives.

What makes a message resonate? According to Jesse, it starts with this mindset: "There's a radio station everyone listens to: WIFM - What's In It For Me?" Whether you're leading a meeting or addressing a crowd, your job is to make the message matter to them. He explained it with a metaphor: "Even if you're standing in front of the Leaning Tower of Pisa, people will look at a photo and search for themselves first." When you speak with awareness of your audience's needs, values, and context, "you'll land every time."

White's path to confident communication wasn't built overnight, it took practice. He shared the impact of a mentor, Jimmy McMichael, who told him plainly: "Speakers speak." Jesse took that to heart. He began watching master speakers like Dr. Martin Luther King Jr., listening not just to what they said but how they said it, their cadence, tone, and repetition. "Like anything in teaching," he said, "you make adjustments. If something's not landing, you modify."

White also reminded us that confidence doesn't mean showing off. "You're not the most important person in the room," he said. "You're not the sage on the stage; you're the guide on the side." The goal is not to perform for people, but to walk with them. That mindset shift from authority to service frees speakers to connect instead of grandstand.

White's advice is simple, but powerful: "There's nothing I can't do. There's nobody I can't touch." That personal belief resulted in the design of his clothing brand, Anti-Can't, which carries the message that limitation is a lie. His brand is a reminder that the words we speak and wear can shape how we lead. "It might seem insignificant to you," he said, "but it could mean everything to somebody else." That's why White speaks with intention. Because for him, confidence isn't about ego, it's about impact.

STRATEGY IN A SKETCH

Charisma is a measurable blend of Presence, Power, and Warmth. Olivia Fox Cabane's model demystifies personal magnetism by showing how these three traits work together to shape influence. Presence means being fully attentive in the moment. Power signals confidence and competence. Warmth communicates care. The sweet spot? When all three overlap. You command attention and connection.

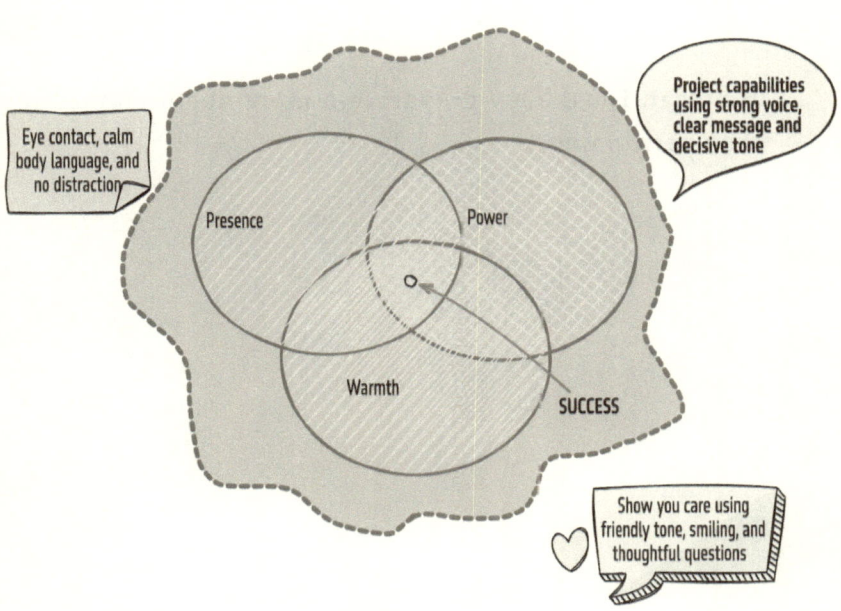

Based on Olivia Fox Cabane's book The Charisma Myth (2012).

MAKE IT YOURS

- What mindset shift and physical ritual could help me re-frame nervousness into energy?

- Using one sentence, can I clearly state the purpose of my message and why it matters to my audience?

- How can I make my preparation more about connecting than performing?

12

Be Steady

How Do You Cope With Dangerous Stress?

Every 40 seconds, someone loses their life to suicide. Workplaces must take mental health as seriously as physical safety.

World Health Organization (WHO)

Leading with Eyes Open

Two weeks ago, Principal Mark Denning sat at his desk when the message arrived. A colleague, someone he had mentored side by side, traded stories with at conferences, and shared quiet laughs with during long district meetings, had taken his own life.

The news landed with a kind of weight Mark couldn't immediately process. This was someone who had always seemed steady. Smart. Respected. Well-liked. He ran a high-performing school. He dressed sharply. He knew his data, spoke with clarity, and had a calm confidence that put others at ease. If you had asked Mark a month earlier who might be struggling, this colleague's name wouldn't have crossed his mind. And maybe that was exactly the point.

Stress doesn't always look the way people expect. It doesn't always erupt or unravel in front of others. Sometimes it hides in the polished ones. The capable ones. The people others look to for strength. It says things like, "I'm good," even when the ground beneath them is giving way.

Mark sat with that reality for days. He replayed old conversations. He thought about moments he may have missed, pauses too long, a tone too flat, a laugh that didn't quite reach the eyes. More than anything, he thought about the assumptions he had been making.

He began to look differently at the people around him. He thought about his assistant principal, who always said yes, the veteran teacher who stayed late but seemed quieter lately, and the custodian who nodded every morning but never really spoke. Who else was hurting in silence? Who was carrying a load that no one else could see?

In schools, the pace is constant. There are schedules to follow, students to support, evaluations to write, and scores to raise. The pressure can be relentless, and in the drive to keep things moving, it's easy to overlook what is most human. We forget to ask real questions. We miss the signs because we're managing our own stress. Or we assume people are "handling it" because they look like they are.

That loss changed Mark. Not in a dramatic, sweeping way, but in small daily choices. He began slowing down long enough to really check in with staff, with students, and with himself. He started asking questions that mattered more than metrics. He listened with fewer answers in mind and he began speaking more honestly about his own challenges, hoping to make space for others to do the same.

Mark's initial response to the terrible situation was to grieve. And then, slowly, a quiet resolve grew. He would not let the title of principal become a shield that made it harder to be human. He would lead with his eyes open and his heart tuned in because no one's salary or resume protects them from the weight of invisible pain. And sometimes the most powerful thing a leader can do is make it safe to say, "I'm not okay," and know that it will be met not with judgment, but with care.

PRINCIPLES

Principle 1: Reframe Stress as a Signal

Stress is not a verdict, it's a voice. A voice that says, "Something you care about is on the line." Most of us have been conditioned to treat stress as a warning sign of failure. But what if it's not a sign of weakness, but a cue to engage? Instead of trying to eliminate stress, emotionally intelligent leaders learn to listen to it.

McGonigal (2015) flipped the stress conversation on its head. In a landmark study of 30,000 adults, she found that those who experienced high stress and believed it was harmful had a 43% increased risk of premature death. But what about those with high stress who viewed it as helpful? They had the lowest risk of all participants. Mindset didn't just shape perception, it shaped outcomes. Stress itself wasn't the issue; the relationship with it was.

Reframing stress begins with awareness. Brené Brown (2021) explains that stress and feelings of being overwhelmed aren't caused solely by external events but by the perception that we lack the ability or control to manage what's coming at us. That's why the first skill of steady leadership is noticing. What's driving the stress? Is it a threat to your sense of control, purpose, impact, or safety?

Here's a simple reframe practice:

    1. Name It. "I'm feeling stressed because..."

2. Locate the Value. "This matters to me because..."

3. Choose the Response. "What would support or action look like right now?"

Think of stress like your car's gas light coming on. You wouldn't interpret it as failure, you'd interpret it as a signal requiring attention and action. It doesn't mean your car is broken. It means your system needs support. A teacher staying late to reach every student isn't falling short, they're deeply dedicated. A leader losing sleep over a high-stakes decision isn't fragile, they're fully engaged and navigating great responsibility.

Resilience begins by translating stress into insight. Stress is the indicator that you care. Your leadership task is to respond to that signal, not with shame, but with strategy. When we shift from resisting stress to reading it, we grow through it.

Principle 2: Use Truth and Structure

Stress becomes toxic when it's carried in silence. For many school leaders, the pressure to appear composed, competent, and in control feels non-negotiable. Projecting strength while carrying burdens in silence isn't sustainable leadership. What looks like composure can be an attempt to hide what's really happening. The antidote isn't perfection; it's connection.

The first step is telling the truth to someone who can hold it with care. Neuroscience confirms what lived experience already tells us: being seen heals. When we speak honestly to someone we trust, oxytocin rises, cortisol drops, and our bodies begin to shift from survival mode into steadiness. In *Buddha's Brain*, Hanson and Mendius (2009) explain how empathy activates the brain's social bonding systems. We are literally wired to regulate through relationships.

This isn't just theory. Another study cited by McGonigal (2012) shows that physicians who participated in daily stress debriefs experienced major drops in burnout. The practice didn't remove the workload but it removed the loneliness. Over time, depression rates dropped by two-thirds.

So if one key to resilience is truth-telling, the other is structure. You need a system. Leadership is too heavy to carry solo. The idea that we must handle everything ourselves is not only false, it can be dangerous. McGonigal (2012) introduces the concept of the tend-and-befriend response to stress. Unlike fight-or-flight, this response is rooted in connection. Oxytocin, the bonding hormone, increases under pressure, prompting us to seek help, offer empathy, and anchor ourselves in community. Reaching out literally makes us stronger.

Handling stress as a leader does not mean pushing through alone. It means knowing when to set something down and turning to those who are willing to carry it with you. And it doesn't take much. Ten minutes of emotional honesty on a regular basis with a few people you trust can build a foundation of resilience and community of support to accomplish goals in good times and bad.

Principle 3: Incorporate Stillness and Light

In a world obsessed with hustle, stillness is an act of leadership. When paired with the practice of noticing small moments of light each day, it becomes a powerful strategy for stress resilience, emotional regulation, and clarity of purpose.

Leaders who build daily rituals of stillness through breathwork, meditation, mindful walking, or even a few quiet moments between meetings become more emotionally regulated and are able to work more effectively. In moments of overload, the pause becomes a power move.

Neuroscience supports this. Hanson and Mendius (2009) explain that stillness activates the parasympathetic nervous system, the body's "rest and digest" mode. When triggered through intentional practices like deep breathing or slowing down, this system helps repair the brain, lowers cortisol, and improves emotional processing. It's a physiological reset.

James Nestor (2020), in *Breath*, reinforces the impact of slowing your breathing to 5.5 breaths per minute, showing how this simple practice calms the nervous system, optimizes oxygen use, and lowers blood pressure. It's a matter of biology.

And McGonigal (2012) reframes rest as a performance strategy. She explains that skipping recovery keeps the brain's default mode network overstimulated, which elevates anxiety and reduces creativity. Stillness, she argues, is not the opposite of action. It is what makes intentional action possible.

Stillness doesn't require a mountain retreat. Consider it a simple reset. It can be stepping away from your screen, sitting quietly with your coffee, or closing your eyes between meetings for three deep breaths. Without the pause, stress can accumulate silently until it erupts.

Here's the metaphor: your brain is a snow globe. Constant motion keeps everything swirling and unclear. Stillness lets the flakes settle. The picture returns. Clarity is restored.

But stillness alone is not enough. When life feels heavy, our brains narrow their focus to what's wrong. Over time, this tunnel vision blocks out even the smallest joys. That's why one of the most powerful resilience habits is also one of the simplest: track one moment of light every day.

It might be the sound of laughter, sunlight through your window, a friendly word, or a quiet nod in a meeting. These moments help rewire the brain to notice what's good, not just what's urgent.

Hanson and Mendius (2009) describes the brain's negativity bias to cling to the bad. But when we pause to absorb a positive moment, even for ten seconds, we literally reshape our neural pathways. Calm and gratitude become more accessible. This isn't toxic positivity. It's neuroplasticity.

Hay (1984) said, "What we focus on grows." Attention is a form of nourishment. When we make space to notice what is working, we nourish a mindset of resilience. A kind gesture. A solved problem. A deep breath. These are not throwaway moments. They are scaffolding for strength.

For leaders, this practice is vital. Too often, attention is focused solely on challenges and deficits. However, recognizing and acknowledging positive moments restore energy and foster resilience. A principal might celebrate a teacher's successful implementation of a new strategy. A teacher might reflect on a moment when a struggling student had a breakthrough in understanding a difficult concept. These moments become more than memories, they serve as mental anchors that bring you back to presence, purpose, and peace.

FROM ONE LEADER TO ANOTHER

Kate Field

Teacher Development Specialist, Connecticut Education Association

As heard on Othman's Leadership Podcast, Episode 19

Put the Phone in the Drawer

Kate Field knows how quietly burnout creeps in. For her, it wasn't a dramatic collapse, it was realizing that her mind was never fully where her feet were. "I was at home, cutting vegetables, but I was mentally drafting a reply to an email," she shared. Like so many educators, she didn't notice the toll until the edges started to fray. She began to have difficulty sleeping, was more irritable, and felt a constant undercurrent of tension. "My email was really messing with my work-life balance," she admitted. That realization led to a small but powerful habit of putting her phone in a drawer with the Saran Wrap. "I check it a few times, and it goes right back in," she said. That one little change helped her reclaim presence.

Her message is clear: being steady doesn't require grand transformations, but it does require intentional micro-practices. Field is certified in mindfulness-based stress reduction. She teaches real-world tools that fit into chaotic days. "Good habits start really small," she explained. "Even ten minutes of quiet in the morning can change your day." One of her most requested sessions across the state is on stress and self-regulation, not standards or assessments. "Teachers are exhausted," she said. "And if they don't take care of themselves, they can't take care of anybody else."

That's why she asks a simple question during her workshops: What brought you joy today? The answers are telling. "No one ever says their email," she laughed. "They say things like, 'My cat' or 'I saw a student laugh.'" For Field, that question is more than an icebreaker, it's a diagnostic tool. It shows how far people have drifted from what fuels them. And often, it uncovers how systems have made joy feel optional, rather than essential. "We're spending a lot of time doing things that actually make us unhappy," she said. "And we wonder why we're burning out."

But Field doesn't stop at naming the problem. She invites educators to reflect on their patterns through a simple practice of tracking where their minutes actually go. She calls it a "time audit." "Once you see it, you can start to reclaim it," she said. And she speaks to leaders directly when she warns them not to expect others to slow down if they're sprinting through everything themselves. "Take care of yourself," she urged. "We need you. The country needs you. Our kids need you." Her tone is tender, steady, and fiercely hopeful.

For Field, steadiness isn't stillness. It's the ability to choose what matters and let go of the rest.

STRATEGY IN A SKETCH

Every leader needs some pressure to lead a balanced life. The Stress Performance Curve, rooted in the Yerkes-Dodson Law (1908), shows that performance increases with stress only up to an optimal point, after which it sharply declines. Leaders operate at their best when demands stretch them just enough to stay alert and engaged, not overwhelmed or disengaged. This model is especially helpful during peak seasons, high-stakes projects, or when you're pushing for innovation, when it's easy to confuse overwork with impact. The key is the self-awareness to regularly ask, "Where am I on the curve?" and "What's one shift that could move me closer to peak performance?" Misreading this curve can lead to personal burnout and team fatigue. A clear interpretation allows you to stay in the comfort zone where challenge sharpens your mind, restores your body, and revitalizes your spirit.

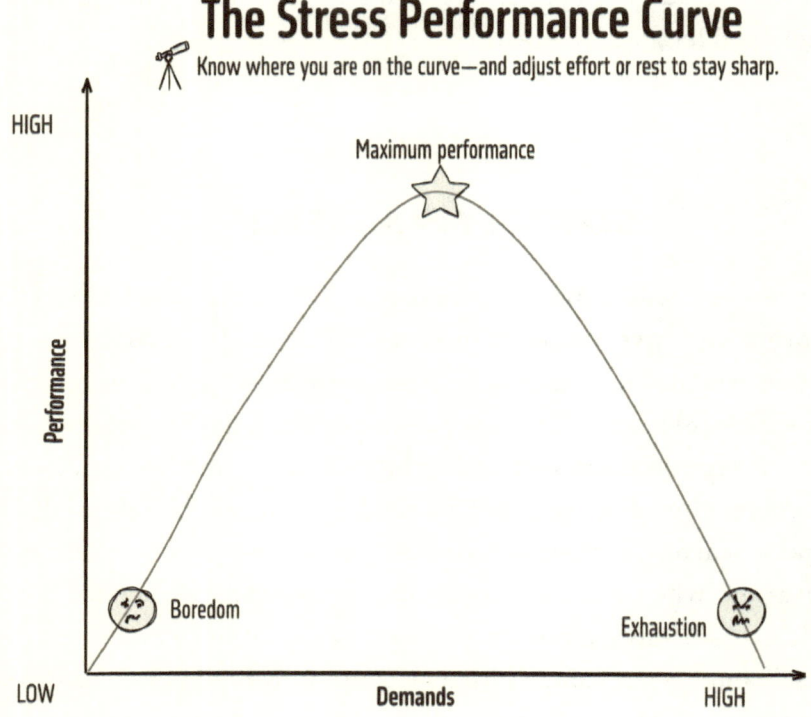

The Stress Performance Curve

Know where you are on the curve—and adjust effort or rest to stay sharp.

Maximum performance

Boredom

Exhaustion

Performance

HIGH

LOW   Demands   HIGH

Adapted from Yerkes and Dodson (1908)

MAKE IT YOURS

- What is this stress trying to tell me about what matters most to me right now?

- Who are the people I trust and can depend on for a regular stress debrief?

- What small daily ritual could help me pause and take note of moments of light?

Part Two

LEAD

Engage in the practices and skills that empower leaders to inspire action, overcome obstacles, and guide teams from strategy to results.

13

Lead with Purpose

How Do You Bring Vision and Mission to Life?

Employees who find their company's vision meaningful have engagement levels 68% higher than those who don't, and they are 52% more likely to stay with their employer long term.

Gallup (2016)

The Best 99 Cents I Never Spent

It was a Friday. I (Reda) had just come home from work around 6:00 p.m., checked the mailbox like I usually do, and then settled into family time. Nothing out of the ordinary except for one small box mixed in with the usual flyers and bills.

I opened it, expecting paperwork. Instead, inside was a small, gold-colored compass. It came from my doctoral program at Bay Path University, with a note that read: "A true leader knows their North Star."

That compass has been in my work bag ever since. I carry it to keep me on course. Whenever I feel uncertain about a professional decision, or a project feels a bit off, I open the top zipper of my bag and look at it. I don't use it to literally navigate, of course, but to pause and ask myself, "Does this activity align with my mission and vision, or is it just busy work?"

There was a time not long after receiving that compass when I was offered a consulting project with a state department. It looked great on paper with a decent budget, government affiliation, and a short-term timeline. But the further I read into the proposal, the more uncomfortable I felt. The way they structured the project, the outcomes they wanted, the approach they insisted I use, it didn't match how I serve or deliver. It was more about checking boxes than making an impact.

I sat with it for a moment, unsure. Then I unzipped my bag. I looked at the compass and remembered the note: "A true leader knows their North Star." And I realized, this wasn't my direction. That tiny, gold compass gave me permission to say the two hardest, clearest words in consulting: "No, thanks."

I've looked up that compass since. It's sold online for 99 cents. And I'll say this with no hesitation: it's the most valuable present anyone could have given me. Because that small symbol reminds me to use my purpose, vision, and mission statement as a filter. It's how I decide what to say yes to. And sometimes, more importantly, what to walk away from.

Your North Star might become more visible with time. Mine has. And its light illuminates my path and guides my steps.

PRINCIPLES

Principle 1: Discover Your Why

Before any strategic plan takes shape, before you draft a vision, write goals, or define metrics, you must answer the question: "Why do we exist?" Purpose is not a slogan that shifts with leadership or a trendy tagline for external audiences. It is the unchanging reason your organization exists. When the purpose is clear, it becomes the filter through which all plans, actions, and adaptations must pass.

Simon Sinek's *Start With Why* (2009) makes the case that inspiration begins at the center. His Golden Circle framework starts with "why," then moves outward to "how" and "what." "People don't buy what you do," he writes, "they buy why you do it." Clearly communicated, that belief builds trust with the outside world and provides direction for the inside. Leaders who articulate and embody a compelling purpose create organizations that outlast trends and weather disruption.

Jim Collins and Jerry Porras, in their 1996 *Harvard Business Review* article titled "Building Your Company's Vision," emphasized that determining an organization's purpose is a foundational task for long-term success. They argued that purpose, what they called "core purpose," is distinct from strategy or specific goals. Instead, it's the organization's enduring reason for being, beyond just making money.

A clearly articulated purpose should be:

- Timeless - It holds true regardless of shifts in leadership, market, or metrics.

- Aspirational - It speaks to your desired contribution to the world, not just your outputs.

- Motivating - It influences decisions, hiring, investments, and communication.

Purpose doesn't eliminate uncertainty but it does guide actions. In moments of ambiguity, it keeps leaders from chasing approval or trends. It brings discipline to decisions and alignment to strategy. Before you ask where you're going or how to get there, start with why you began in the first place. Everything else builds from there.

Principle 2: Envision Your Future

Vision connects the "why" of purpose to the "where to" of strategy. It answers the questions, "What does the organization want to become and what impact does it want to make in the future?" Vision gives leadership its forward motion and when done well, becomes the flowing current that directs the team, unifies actions, and sustains belief. It forges your identity.

The envisioned future, according to Collins and Porras (1996), should be bold and tangible: a vivid picture of what the world will look like when your mission is fulfilled.

Stewart Friedman (2009) emphasizes that vision is most powerful when it is personal and shared. In his research on leadership development, he found that leaders who speak their vision aloud, and turn aspiration into narrative, build deeper trust and engagement. People will commit to a future they can see and feel. That's why vision must be emotional, not just intellectual. It must move people, not just inform them.

The University of Kansas, *Community Toolbox*, documents these common characteristics of meaningful vision statements. They should be:

- Understandable and accepted by the people involved

- Inclusive of various voices and experiences

- Motivational

- Shared and short enough for all to remember

These two frameworks are also useful when designing a vision statement: John Doerr's OKRs (Objectives and Key Results), and Marc Benioff's V2MOM (Vision, Values, Methods, Obstacles, and Measures). The creators believe that a strong leadership vision should be daring and future-oriented, painting a vivid and emotionally compelling picture of what lies ahead. It must be grounded in your core purpose and values, providing a sense of meaning and direction. At the same time, it should align clearly with your strategy and execution plans, ensuring that daily actions are connected to long-term goals. Finally, they conclude that a powerful vision is measurable, with clear outcomes and milestones that allow progress to be tracked and celebrated.

Principle 3: Lead with a Living Mission

The difference between a vision and a mission statement is that the first provides inspiration and direction, while the latter directs daily actions and operations. They work together. The mission statement is like a set of blueprints, detailing the structure and steps needed to build the future envisioned in the vision statement. The power of a mission statement is in its use.

Too often, mission statements sit untouched in handbooks or websites, losing relevance. But when mission is spoken of often, embedded in action, and connected to real choices, it becomes the heartbeat of the organization. It's how purpose becomes practice.

Peter Drucker (2008) was clear: a mission must be something you "know is right," something you're willing to return to again and again as a daily guide. And in dynamic systems like schools or fast-moving organizations, mission matters most when things feel messy. When the path ahead is unclear, a living mission grounds you in the why and sharpens the how.

A living mission brings clarity to three core questions: Who are we serving, what are we committed to doing consistently, and how do we know we're doing it well? These aren't philosophical questions. They drive how you spend time, hire staff, allocate funding, and shape the culture in classrooms or teams.

Jim Collins and Jerry Porras (1996) stress that great organizations preserve their core while adapting their practices. This distinction is essential for mission. The delivery methods may evolve, but the essence must stay rooted in purpose. If vision points to a preferred future, then the mission outlines daily actions to get there.

Richard Rumelt (2011), in *Good Strategy Bad Strategy*, cautions that too many organizations confuse slogans for strategy. A living mission resists that trap. It guides decisions about what to pursue, what to pause, and what to say no to. It gives leaders permission to prioritize not just what's urgent, but what's aligned.

To lead with a living mission, leaders must:

1. Revisit the mission in team meetings, professional development sessions, and decision-making conversations.

2. Connect it to current realities and evolving needs.

3. Ensure alignment with both purpose and long-term vision.

4. Translate it into habits, routines, and visible systems.

When a mission moves from the wall to the workflow, it becomes more than a statement, it becomes culture. And culture, not compliance, is what sustains meaningful change. In fast-changing environments, a living mission will create the future you foresee.

FROM ONE LEADER TO ANOTHER

Dr. Melissa Morriss-Olson

Provost Emerita | Author of IngenioUs Leadership: Creating Solutions to Wicked Problems in Higher Education
   As heard on Othman's Leadership Podcast, Episode 36

The Hardest Work Is Staying Anchored to Who You Are

Throughout her career in higher education leadership, Dr. Melissa Morriss-Olson witnessed a troubling pattern of leaders who began with clarity but lost their way amid competing priorities. "It's very easy to get distracted by shiny things," she warned. "We call it strategic mimicry, doing what others are doing just because it looks successful." This tendency, she observed, often pulls institutions away from their core identity. In her role as provost, she worked closely with presidents who faced declining enrollment and pressure to innovate. But the most successful, she said, were those who asked: Is this aligned with our purpose? One president she admired had the discipline to turn down millions in grant funding because the project didn't reflect the institution's mission. "That takes courage," she reflected. "But it's also leadership at its best."

Morriss-Olson's passion for purpose is deeply personal. Growing up in rural Minnesota, she watched her mother push through hardship with grace, service, and unshakable values. "She didn't talk about purpose," Morriss-Olson said. "She lived it." That early example shaped her view of leadership not as positional power, but as a commitment to something larger than oneself. Later in her career, when she was asked to step into senior leadership, she paused to reflect: What do I stand for? Who do I want to be in the lives of others? That reflection wasn't a one-time exercise, it became a rhythm. "I have a journal I've kept for twenty years," she shared. "When I'm lost or overwhelmed, I go back to my core questions."

That commitment to alignment shaped how she helped leaders lead. In her executive coaching work, Morriss-Olson often asks clients, What does success look like for you, and how do you know when you're off course? She recalled one leader who felt pressure to expand aggressively. Instead of charging ahead, they held small listening sessions with faculty, students, and community members. "They realized the expansion wasn't just off-mission, it would actually erode the very trust they were trying to build," she said. By slowing down and returning to their values, the leader found a different path forward. It was smaller in scale but greater in impact.

Morriss-Olson encourages emerging leaders to engage in what she calls "mission reflection." That includes clarifying your values, naming your non-negotiables, and listening with empathy to the communities you serve. "Purpose doesn't live on a wall," she said. "It lives in how you show up every day, in the questions you ask, the choices you make, and the relationships you build." Her advice isn't abstract. It's alive. It's repeated. And it's rooted in the belief that clarity of vision and mission is the starting point for purposeful action. "If you don't know what you stand for," she said, "someone else will decide it for you."

STRATEGY IN A SKETCH

Simon Sinek's Golden Circle framework (2009) offers a strategic approach to leadership and communication by beginning with Why the organization exists before addressing How it fulfills that purpose and What it delivers. By leading with purpose rather than products or processes, organizations can foster stronger alignment, engagement, and trust among stakeholders. This model encourages leaders to articulate a clear sense of mission that drives decision-making, strategy, and culture from the inside out.

The Golden Circle

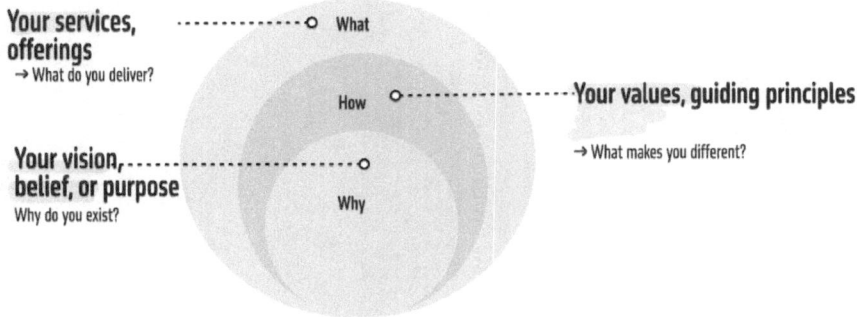

Based on Simon Sinek's leadership framework in Start With Why (2009).

MAKE IT YOURS

- Can I clearly state the purpose of my organization?

- What is the vision for the future of my organization? Can everyone articulate it?

- How does my mission statement direct daily actions and operations?

14

Lead by Example

Are You Cultivating Leadership in Others?

The function of leadership is to produce more leaders, not more followers.

Ralph Nader

Modeling Through the Mess

Part of my role is mentoring new teachers for two years, helping them build their confidence, instructional habits, and voice. That year, I (Reda) had two strong teachers who were committed, coachable, and growing fast. The first half of the year, they were thriving. But midway through, life knocked the wind out of me. My father passed away.

Grief isn't something you schedule. It shows up and takes over. For nearly two months, I was physically present but emotionally drained. My energy was going toward family, routines, and simply staying afloat. Without meaning to, I pulled back. I didn't check in regularly. I didn't offer guidance. I didn't coordinate support.

Later, when I had the clarity to look up, I noticed that my absence had taken a toll. Their classroom performance had slipped. Not because they weren't capable, but because no one was helping them see around the next corner. That was supposed to be my role.

So I sat down with them. I didn't pretend. I didn't make excuses. I told them the truth about what had happened and why I hadn't been as present. And they responded with grace.

But more importantly, that moment gave me a chance to model something they'll need later in their own leadership journey: what to do when life hits hard.

I walked them through the lessons. I shared what I wished I had done differently. I talked about communication, backup plans, and systems that support people when we can't be there ourselves. I showed them that leadership doesn't mean never falling, but it means acknowledging when you do and helping others learn from it.

That conversation wasn't just a reset, it was a real-time lesson in leading through crisis. Because the truth is, if we only lead well when things are easy, we're not really leading. And if we want to develop other leaders, we have to show them what to do when life doesn't go according to plan.

PRINCIPLES

Principle 1: Model Accountability to Cultivate It in Others

Leadership is a great responsibility. Authors and researchers who have studied the field for years cite numerous requirements of the role. A leader is someone who influences others toward achieving a shared vision by modeling desired behaviors, building trust, and empowering people to act through credibility and relational connection. Effective leadership is grounded in influence, not position, and is characterized by behaviors such as clarity of purpose, authenticity, and service to others (Kouzes & Posner, 2016; Maxwell, 2022).

Ultimate accountability starts and stops with the leader. When leaders take full responsibility for their world, they send a message that reverberates through their organization and creates a climate of respect.

Jocko Willink and Leif Babin, in *Extreme Ownership*, argue that true leadership makes no excuses and attempts no deflection (Willink & Babin, 2017). This stance doesn't weaken authority; it strengthens it. When leaders own problems publicly, they create a culture where others feel safe to do the same. One act of visible ownership becomes a permission slip for others to claim and correct mistakes with a supportive environment cheering them on.

Kouzes and Posner (2016) reinforce this mindset in *Learning Leadership*, explaining that exemplary leaders don't wait for permission or perfect conditions before they initiate change or fresh ideas. Accountability isn't just about responding to problems of the past. It is also about looking forward to what's needed and stepping in. When leaders habitually ask, "What part of this do I own and need to take charge of?" they begin to shift the organizational default from blame to responsibility, and from reactivity to proactivity.

Consider a principal who sees student engagement dipping. Instead of blaming curriculum changes or teacher energy, she begins by examining her own tone, her priorities, and her systems for support. She listens, reflects out loud, and adjusts. The result? Others around her begin doing the same in their classrooms, and within their teams. The cultural gravity begins to shift due to a model, not a mandate.

Ownership is contagious and spreads through action. When leaders own the wounds as well as the wins, they unlock a deeper level of trust and build positive relationships. Leaders who prioritize this type of connection create conditions for engagement. This might look like knowing each person's story, showing up consistently, or creating rituals that celebrate effort as much as outcome.

Psychological safety, a term popularized by Amy Edmondson (2019), isn't achieved through grand gestures. It's built in the everyday moments: how you respond to a mistake, whether you listen fully, or whether your feedback includes care as well as candor. That trust becomes the soil where initiative, courage, and shared responsibility can grow. Leaders go first, and when they do, others follow.

Principle 2: Model Continual Learning

Setting the example should be a top priority for leadership. And one of the most important examples is to be a lifelong learner. Organizations maintain relevancy and resilience when all involved are invested in growing. They don't see learning as an extracurricular activity, but treat it as essential to staying effective. Kouzes and Posner (2016) put it plainly: "The best leaders are the best learners." They argue that leadership is not an innate gift but a set of skills that can be developed through deliberate practice and reflection. Similarly, Willink and Babin (2017) emphasize that in high-stakes environments like the military, the best-performing leaders are those who adapt quickly, absorb feedback, and refine their approach after setbacks. Learning isn't a side project, it's part of the job.

One of the clearest modern examples is Satya Nadella's transformation of Microsoft. By replacing a rigid "know-it-all" mindset with a "learn-it-all" culture, he catalyzed a shift in everything from product innovation to employee engagement. Nadella modeled what he expected: curiosity, humility, and openness to being wrong. His leadership grew the company's bottom line and its people (Kouzes & Posner, 2016; Willink & Babin, 2017).

Leaders committed to learning do more than read books or attend workshops. They ask tough questions, sit with criticism they'd rather ignore, and seek perspectives that challenge their worldview. In meetings, they admit what they don't know and turn decisions into learning moments for the whole team. Instead of signaling weakness, these behaviors create psychological safety, drive performance, and normalize growth.

Principle 3: Build Leaders by Empowering Others

Leadership isn't proven by holding onto power, it's revealed in how willingly you share it. When leaders lift others into leadership, they don't lose influence, they multiply it. Empowerment, at its core, is not delegation of tasks but development of people. It is a strategic move to build capacity.

Empowerment begins with trust in oneself and others. As Kouzes and Posner (2016) assert, "Exemplary leaders enable others to act" by fostering competence and confidence. Leaders who hold back authority often do so out of fear, fear of losing control or being outshone. As Maxwell (2022) notes, "Only secure leaders give power to others." Empowerment demands a shift from command to coaching, from supervision to sponsorship.

This shift isn't abstract. Consider a district manager at a national retail chain who gave store managers the authority to design local promotional strategies. The central brand standards remained in place, but autonomy was granted on the methods they each used to accomplish the goal. The result? Within a year, sales rose by 15%, and employee retention surged. Empowerment created ownership, and ownership fueled innovation.

Empowered leadership also strengthens accountability. Willink and Babin (2017) describe how junior leaders of Navy SEAL teams were expected to make frontline decisions. This decentralized command made missions more agile and leaders more invested in outcomes. Empowerment is strategic trust. When people are trusted with important responsibilities, they prepare more, engage more, and accomplish more.

FROM ONE LEADER TO ANOTHER

Nikki Vassallo

President, ATD Central Massachusetts
  As heard on Othman's Leadership Podcast, Episode 41

Stretch Them So They're Ready

For Nikki Vassallo, leadership is never about holding onto power. Some of her most memorable lessons came from leaders who didn't stay in their office or judge from a distance, but walked alongside her. She remembered a supervisor who didn't just say, "Go network," he showed her how. "He came with us," she said, "and modeled how to connect with others, how to tell your story, how to build real relationships." That example stuck with her, not because it was polished, but because it was shared. "That's what helped me become the kind of leader who's involved in the work, and not just assigning it." Now, she carries that mindset as she engages with her own team.

But being in the work also means knowing when to step back. One of the barriers Vassallo sees most often in leaders is ego, especially when individual performance used to be their measure of success. "Sometimes the people who get promoted are the ones who were great at the job," she said. "But now they hold on too tightly." She recalled managers in banking who wouldn't let team members take on mortgage applications, the highest-earning transactions, because they feared losing control. "You'll never develop your team if you keep the good stuff for yourself." Her own mantra is clear: "If I'm not here tomorrow, my team should still know what to do."

To get there, Vassallo's first leadership lesson came with an equally practical challenge: learning to ask better questions. "Most people think coaching is about giving advice," she said. "But real coaching is about curiosity." Rather than just tracking outcomes or giving feedback, Vassallo aims to understand what fuels her team. "What fills your cup? What would you like to try next?" These questions are door openers. In one case, a team member worried a project was going off track. Vassallo invited the person to take the lead in addressing it. "You're the learning expert," she reminded them. "That's why you're on this project. Advocate for learning." That experience didn't just resolve the issue, it also built the team member's confidence and respect from others.

Her next lesson? Visibility. "I've seen leaders unintentionally take credit for their team's work," she noted. Vassallo flips that habit on its head by lifting people when they're not in the room. "Give them the credit. Say their name," she advised. When people know their work will be seen and appreciated, they take more risks, contribute more ideas, and stay more engaged. "People want to shine, and when you elevate them, they shine even brighter," she said.

But Vassallo's most powerful strategy may be how she uses stretch assignments as a leadership tool. "Someone came to me and said they wanted more project experience," she recalled. Rather than sending them to a course or waiting for the perfect opportunity, Vassallo threw them into the deep end - strategically. "I put them on a project that matched their strengths in some areas so they could focus on learning others." The outcome? New skills that elevated competency and new ideas that improved organizational direction. "That wouldn't have happened without them in the room," Vassallo reflected.

Trust, empowerment, and the next step, delegation, all go togeth-er. "Early in my career, I used to do everything myself. It was easier," she admitted. But that approach blocked her team from growing. So she began pulling people into live client situations, standing beside them while they opened accounts or handled complex tasks. "Sometimes they were nervous, but I'd say, 'You're going to do this, and I'll be right next to you.'" Over time, those team members felt comfortable enough to take over the entire task. And that freed Vassallo to step into strategic projects she previously didn't have time for. It's a win-win situation.

STRATEGY IN A SKETCH

Kouzes and Posner's *Five Practices of Exemplary Leadership* outline essential behaviors that help leaders earn trust and inspire meaningful results. At its core, this framework reminds us that leadership is not about authority, it's about behavior. The five practices include: model the way, inspire a shared vision, challenge the process, enable others to act, and encourage the heart. They work together to form a blueprint for leading by example. People watch how you act more than they listen to what you say. In schools, that might look like a principal who stays calm during a crisis, a department chair who takes risks first before asking others to innovate, or a teacher who admits mistakes openly so students see that growth is a lifelong process.

The Five Practices of Exemplary Leadership

Leadership Starts With You

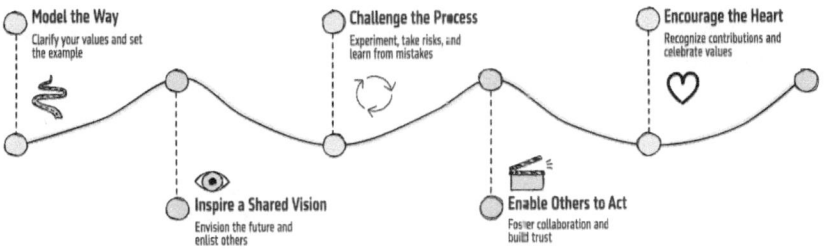

Model the Way
Clarify your values and set the example

Challenge the Process
Experiment, take risks, and learn from mistakes

Encourage the Heart
Recognize contributions and celebrate values

Inspire a Shared Vision
Envision the future and enlist others

Enable Others to Act
Foster collaboration and build trust

Based on Kouzes and Posner's leadership framework in The Leadership Challenge (2017).

MAKE IT YOURS

- Am I in the habit of owning my mistakes or shifting the blame to others?

- What am I learning through deliberate practice and reflection?

- What have I let go of and trusted others to handle in their own way?

15

Lead Through Change

How Do You Bring Structure to the Challenges of Change?

It's not the strongest or the most intelligent who survive, but those most adaptive to change.

Ken Chenault

This Time, It Was Different

When Dr. Maya Thompson was hired as the new principal of Lincoln Elementary, most teachers didn't react. They had been through several new faces over the years.

In fact, some joked quietly in the staff lounge that they'd start a bingo card for "new leader catchphrases." Words like innovation, transformation, and reimagine had all been used before and nothing ever stuck.

So when Dr. Thompson began the year with a clear vision and a calm confidence, no one rushed to buy in. They listened politely, and guardedly. But this time, it was different.

She didn't open with a new initiative or flashy slogan. She opened with listening. For the first month, she held small group conversations with every grade-level team and every department. She included paraprofessionals, specialists, and bus drivers. She asked about what was working, what wasn't, and what had been promised in the past that never came to life.

Instead of rolling out an entirely new program, she introduced a research-based framework for change. It was clear, structured, and grounded in professional learning. She invited teacher leaders to co-design the rollout, and decisions were made transparently, with timelines, goals, and support.

As one teacher put it, "She didn't just say, 'Here's the new vision.' She said, 'Here's how we'll build it together and here's what you'll have to make it possible.'"

Planning time was protected. Coaching support was expanded. And when early adopters took risks in their classrooms, Dr. Thompson was the first to show up to celebrate.

By spring, the tone in the building had changed. Skeptics weren't magically converted, but they were curious. And those who'd been burned before were invited into the process. Because Dr. Thompson understood something essential. Change doesn't happen because someone at the front of the room says it's time. It happens when a change management system is developed and those implementing the change are part of the process.

PRINCIPLES

Principle 1: Treat Change as a Continuous Capability, Not a One-Time Event

Change management is a core leadership capability. It is the structured process by which individuals, teams, and organizations transition from a current state to a desired future state in order to achieve strategic outcomes and sustain performance improvements. It involves preparing, equipping, and supporting people through change by aligning leadership, communication, learning, and feedback systems to reduce resistance and accelerate adoption (Association for Talent Development, 2014; Hiatt, 2006; Kotter & Rathgeber, 2016).

In a world where most organizations navigate three or more major transformations a year, treating change as a one-time project is a leadership blind spot (Association for Talent Development, 2014). Leaders must build systems, cultures, and mindsets that are adaptive by design because change is no longer the exception, it's an expectation.

DevOps, which combines software development (Dev) and IT operations (Ops), is a movement that illustrates this well. High-performing organizations use iterative cycles and fast feedback loops to reduce deployment time from months to hours (Kim et al., 2016). But this mindset doesn't belong only to the technology industry. Any organization can build in small tests, tighten learning loops, and replace rigidity with responsiveness. Change becomes a norm because it's embedded in the operation.

Still, the capability to change without the buy-in of those who need to do it, is just meaningless motion. As Kotter and Rathgeber (2016) reminds us, "Change sticks when people see it as beneficial." Without a compelling reason to move, teams don't. Heath and Heath (2010) go further. People resist not because they're lazy, but because the destination is vague. Change leaders give more than just directions, they give people something to care about and a clear path to follow.

That's why effective leaders connect change to strategic purpose. They name what's at stake, why it matters now, and how it ties to the organization's future. In doing so, they unlock commitment where there might otherwise be reluctance.

To lead change well, leaders need to normalize uncertainty through repetition and make learning visible. They tell the story of progress in motion. Change management is not a moment, it's a muscle. And leaders who train that muscle daily are the ones whose teams outlearn, outlast, and outbuild the rest.

Principle 2: Build Multi-Level Change Competency

Change can't be the sole responsibility of executives and administrators. For transformation to take root, organizations must build change competency at every level, from senior leadership to the front lines. This principle moves beyond top-down directives and centers on equipping everyone with the tools, mindset, and capacity to lead change within their own sphere of influence.

The ATD report *Change Agents* highlights a telling gap: only 17% of organizations rate themselves as highly effective at managing change (ATD & i4cp, 2014). What separates high-performing organizations is in the preparation. They develop role-specific tools, embed feedback loops, and prioritize resilience-building habits across the entire system. Change-readiness isn't isolated to leadership retreats or professional development workshops. It is woven into the fabric of everyone's work, every day.

When the logic of change and the ensuing emotions are aligned, individuals are far more likely to commit to and sustain meaningful transformation. Heath and Heath (2010), in *Switch: How to Change Things When Change is Hard*, illustrate this point with a metaphor of "The Rider and the Elephant." The Rider represents the rational, logical, and analytical side of a person, while the Elephant embodies the emotional, intuitive, and instinctual side. The Heath brothers argue that to achieve lasting change, you must engage both the Rider (directing it with clear instructions) and the Elephant (motivating it with feelings and appealing to its desires). People need to understand the "what," while feeling connected to the "why," and being shown "how" to act.

Michael Watkins (2013) reinforces the need for tailored support. In *The First 90 Days*, he argues that leaders at different levels face distinct challenges and thus need different change strategies. A new supervisor, for example, may require tools for navigating peer relationships, while an executive might need frameworks for aligning strategy and culture. One-size-fits-all won't work; change competency must be contextual.

When everyone is change-capable, organizations become agile and resilient. Multi-level change competency distributes ownership, strengthens alignment, and reduces friction. And in times of adjustment, it's not just strategy that saves you, it's who's ready and able to carry it out.

Principle 3: Communicate Transparently and Frequently

During change, silence sends a loud message. When leaders don't fill the space with clear, honest, and timely communication, people fill it with fear, doubt, and speculation. In moments of uncertainty, clarity is critical.

One of the top reasons change efforts fail is poor communication (ATD & i4cp, 2014). When frequency is inconsistent or the message is vague, teams are left to interpret the silence. That ambiguity breeds resistance. Transparent, repeated communication builds trust and psychological safety. Both of these elements are essential for sustaining engagement through times of transformation.

Kotter and Rathgeber (2016) places communication at the heart of his 8-step model for leading change. In *Our Iceberg Is Melting*, effective leaders repeat and reinforce the case for change using stories, images, and actions that make people grasp what's at stake. That emotional resonance is what moves people.

Heath and Heath (2010) offer a similar insight: resistance is often just confusion in disguise. "We're making changes" is not a strategy. People need to know: What's changing? Why now? What does this mean for me? Leaders must script the critical moves and paint the destination vividly enough that teams can walk toward it with confidence.

Transparency also means vulnerability. Senge et al. (1994) remind us that surfacing mental models for the leader and the team, is key to system-wide learning. In the face of the unknown, it's powerful to say: "Here's what we know. Here's what we're still figuring out. Here's how we'll keep you updated." Uncertainty becomes more tolerable when leaders show up with honesty.

The best change communicators don't talk at people, they talk with them. They repeat the message without sounding robotic. They customize it without losing consistency. They create two-way channels for questions and feedback. In change, trust travels through communication.

Principle 4: Design for Early Wins and Momentum

Momentum fuels belief. In any change effort, early wins are proof points because they show that progress is happening and the effort is worth it. Without clear early successes, skepticism creeps in. That's why great change leaders engineer small, visible victories that build confidence and energy from the start.

Kotter and Rathgeber (2016) names "generate short-term wins" as one of the most critical steps in his 8-step model. These wins should be concrete, clearly linked to the larger effort, and easy to spot. In *Our Iceberg Is Melting*, the penguin colony gains traction through symbolic and practical moves by appointing scouts, and celebrating milestones. The positive momentum encourages continued movement forward.

Chip and Dan Heath (2010) deepen this idea with "shrink the change." When people see progress, they're more likely to keep going. Their famous example of a loyalty card with two bonus stamps already filled illustrates that a head start, real or perceived, makes all the difference. Change feels more manageable when we can see we're already partway there.

This principle powers DevOps teams. They don't wait for a perfect launch. Instead, they release small updates regularly, celebrating every stable deployment. Those wins reinforce shared ownership, learning, and cultural momentum (Kim et al., 2016).

The key is in making progress visible so your team and stakeholders see change working in real time. It's about finding early success that's credible, relevant, and tied to your broader vision. When you design for early wins, you shift the story from "Will this work?" to "This is working." And that belief serves as a critical driver for meaningful and practical advancement.

Principle 5: Institutionalize Learning and Feedback

Sustained change doesn't come from a single initiative. It comes from turning every change effort into a feedback loop. When learning is embedded into the culture, change shifts from a one-time push to a repeatable process of reflection, adjustment, and shared growth.

Peter Senge (1994) describes learning organizations as those that "continually expand their capacity to create their future." At the heart of this is team learning, the discipline of reflecting together, questioning assumptions, and making meaning out of experience. In this context, feedback is not just about evaluation, it's about alignment, clarity, and course correction.

The DevOps movement offers a model of how learning can become operationalized. Practices like blameless post-mortems and continuous integration ensure that every error or success becomes a data point, not an endpoint (Kim et al., 2016). These habits make improvement part of the workflow, not an afterthought. The question isn't "Who messed up?" but "What can we learn, and how do we share it?"

Watkins (2013) reinforces this at the leadership level. In times of transition, he notes, leaders who build feedback loops early accelerate alignment and reduce missteps. But this mindset must extend beyond individuals. Teams and departments need shared practices like retrospectives, learning reviews, and dashboards that keep feedback flowing and learning public.

Consider Toyota's Andon Cord, which lets any worker on the factory floor stop the line when a problem arises, triggering investigation and collaborative learning. It's a signal that growth is everyone's job. Outside of manufacturing, leaders can recreate this spirit by designing psychologically safe spaces where people are encouraged to surface issues, test solutions, and reflect openly on outcomes.

To institutionalize learning, leaders must model curiosity, celebrate reflection, and build rituals that make feedback routine. When learning becomes the norm, growth becomes inevitable.

FROM ONE LEADER TO ANOTHER

NLS

Director of Pricing Strategy in a Fortune 500 Retail Organization
As heard on Othman's Leadership Podcast, Episode TBD

If You Waste the Crisis, You Miss the Opportunity

When the inflation crisis hit, Ned and his team didn't just adjust pricing, they reimagined how the organization responded to change. "We had to move fast," he said. "There wasn't time for perfection. We needed progress." That urgency became fuel. Drawing on Kotter's 8-Step Change Model, Ned created what he called a "heartbeat of wins," small, visible successes that built momentum and trust. "If you only communicate the finish line, people burn out," he explained. "You have to show that something's working now." One early move, changing how inflation was framed, transformed employee engagement. "Instead of saying, 'We're behind,' we said, 'Here's where we're headed.' That shift changed everything."

But saying it wasn't enough. Ned had to build belief. "We had all the usual challenges," he shared, "skepticism, legacy systems, data chaos." To create alignment, he built a guiding coalition. "I found a few people who had influence but weren't always the loudest voices," he said. "They helped drive the change from within." One key moment came when a cross-functional partner who was initially hesitant became an advocate after a collaborative pilot. "She saw that we weren't asking her to change everything, just one thing. And it worked." That single shift cascaded across the business.

Ned also emphasized that change isn't just about what you fix, it's about what you protect. "I told the team, 'Some things will feel uncertain, but our values don't change.'" He believes one of the biggest leadership mistakes during transformation is trying to control everything. "You don't need to write the whole playbook," he said. "Just write the first few pages well, and make sure people know how to write the rest together." That flexibility allowed his team to respond to new data, shift direction, and still stay anchored in purpose.

What made this change effort successful was both the process and the posture. Ned led with honesty, humility, and momentum. "We didn't pretend to have all the answers. We just promised to listen, adapt, and keep moving forward." That promise became a practice. And in doing so, he showed that leading through change doesn't mean eliminating discomfort, it means creating the confidence that growth will occur through it.

STRATEGY IN A SKETCH

The ADKAR Model, developed by Jeff Hiatt (2006) at Prosci, is a change management framework designed to guide individuals and teams through successful transformation. Its strength lies in sequencing five psychological and behavioral conditions. Each element must be addressed in order: clarity first, buy-in second, then skills, practice, and finally sustainability. Rather than rushing into implementation, effective leaders use this model to diagnose resistance and guide support.

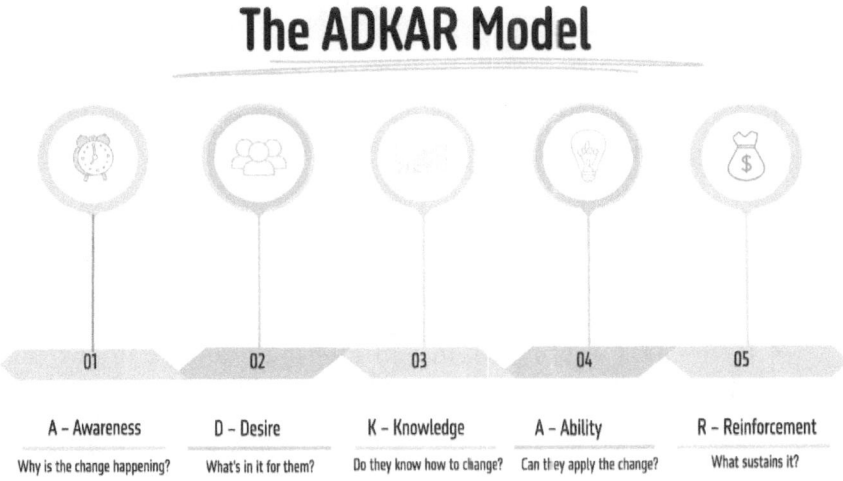

The ADKAR Model

01	02	03	04	05
A – Awareness	D – Desire	K – Knowledge	A – Ability	R – Reinforcement
Why is the change happening?	What's in it for them?	Do they know how to change?	Can they apply the change?	What sustains it?

Based on Jeff Hiatt's ADKAR change model (2006).

Make it YOURS:

- Is organizational change treated as a one-time event or a continuous capability?

- How have I involved my team in the change management process?

- Have I clearly and consistently communicated the purpose and effect of the changes?

- How can I equip people and create an environment that supports change?

- What early wins could I design to demonstrate successful transformation in process?

16

Lead Through Project Management

How do you Maximize Teamwork and Tools?

Talent wins games, but teamwork and intelligence win championships.

Michael Jordan

You Can't Measure What You Didn't Define

At Ridgeview High, nestled in a quiet suburban town, the staff took pride in being known as "a school that cared." From food drives to multicultural nights to the newly launched "Respect Matters" initiative, Principal McClain was always encouraging staff to lead projects that built school culture and community.

One spring, Ms. Daniels, the ESL coordinator, partnered with Mr. Chen, the family liaison, to plan a welcome night for

Ridgeview's multilingual families. The planning was enthusiastic and fast-paced. Flyers were translated, tables were reserved, and student volunteers lined up to serve food and greet families. By all accounts, the event went well. Over 100 people attended. There were smiles, laughter, and even a spontaneous dance performance by a group of 9th graders.

At the debrief meeting the next day, someone said what everyone was thinking: "That was a success." But then Ms. Daniels paused. "Can I ask something?" she said, flipping through her notebook. "What did we actually set out to achieve?" There was silence. Mr. Chen finally said, "We wanted families to feel welcomed and included." "Yes," Ms. Daniels nodded, "but how would we know if that happened?"

During the next week, the group met to talk more. They asked important questions like, "What's the purpose of the project? Who's doing what? What are the actual deliverables? How will we measure success?

Inspired, they brought the idea to Ridgeview's leadership team. At first, there was some skepticism. "We already know what we're doing," someone muttered. But when they used a project outline to plan the next event, a student-led cultural showcase, the difference was evident. They defined clear goals:

- 10 student performances from diverse backgrounds

- A parent feedback form in three languages

- At least 5 teachers committing to a follow-up activity in their classroom

When the event was over, the team didn't have to guess whether it was a success. They had evidence. More than that, they had a blueprint for continued success.

PRINCIPLES

Principle 1: The Picture of Success

According to the Association for Talent Development (2024), project management is defined as the intentional practice of planning, executing, monitoring, and closing a temporary endeavor to achieve a specific outcome. All of this must be accomplished while aligning people, timelines, and resources in a way that maintains both performance and trust. The truth is, most project managers don't follow this practice. Initiatives don't fall apart for lack of effort but because no one slowed down long enough to define what success actually looks like. As Flyvbjerg and Gardner argue in *How Big Things Get Done*, the most successful projects follow the pattern: "Think slow, act fast" (Flyvbjerg & Gardner, 2023). They resist the rush. Before assigning a single task, they start by asking sharper questions, specifying outcomes, and anticipating constraints.

This principle blends the discipline of "Start slow to move fast" with the clarity of "Define what done looks like." The huge task of building the Empire State Building was completed ahead of schedule and under budget. It was a product of deep pre-planning that made execution fast, focused, and precise (Flyvbjerg & Gardner, 2023).

In education and nonprofit spaces, the temptation is to act quickly and prove progress. But real momentum comes from sharing the plan at the beginning. Dan Sullivan's *Impact Filter* (2018) emphasizes the importance of articulating the project's purpose, defining the ideal outcome, and agreeing on success criteria before setting timelines or assigning tasks. If you don't know what you're aiming for, you won't know when you've arrived.

Association for Talent Development (2024) underscores this through its "Initiating" and "Planning" phases. Charters, scope, and stakeholder alignment are not optional, they're foundational. In schools, this might look like starting with a Project Outcome Profile, a single page that clarifies what the initiative will achieve, why it matters, and how progress will be tracked.

Projects succeed when they start with clarity and purpose. Meaningful progress comes from intention and focus. Align before you take action. Clarify before you delegate. Define the outcome before you begin.

Principle 2: Design Together, Deliver Better

Project success includes managing logistics and engaging people. The most impactful leaders co-create, turning shared vision into shared ownership. Association for Talent Development (2024) reinforces this by emphasizing that stakeholder engagement must be embedded throughout the project, not treated as a one-time consultation. When planning happens in silos, whether by central office teams or executive committees, it overlooks the practical realities of those responsible for implementation. The result can be misalignment, unforeseen obstacles, and weak follow-through.

Flyvbjerg and Gardner (2023) warn against what they call "uniqueness bias," the belief that your project is so different, it can ignore past patterns or external input. In *How Big Things Get Done*, they show that failed projects often reflect narrow, insular thinking. Their call is simply to bring in more perspectives earlier and often to design smarter, more resilient systems.

Tony Buzan's *Mind Map Mastery* offers a way to visualize this: map the project as a living system. Instead of a flat task list, you create a web of people, timelines, challenges, and interactions, noting relationships along with responsibilities (Buzan, 2018). This system view invites ownership and surfaces interdependencies.

When the people who carry the work help shape the work, buy-in comes naturally. In schools, this means including teachers in professional development planning, students in engagement design, or community partners in strategic initiatives. Engaging stakeholders throughout the entire process turns good ideas into grounded, sustainable solutions.

Principle 3: The Checklist: A Simple Tool with Serious Impact

In complex projects, even experienced teams forget critical steps. That's why checklists matter. "Use the Checklist, Avoid the Chaos" is a call to embed reliability and accountability into management systems.

Atul Gawande's *The Checklist Manifesto* (2009), makes the case plainly: checklists reinforce professional judgment. Across fields like surgery, aviation, and construction, high-stakes teams habitually use checklists to ensure compliance with intricate procedures. Without serious attention, complexity breeds errors. The same applies in schools, nonprofits, and any organization navigating ambitious initiatives. Projects often stall not from incompetence but from missed conversations, skipped steps, or invisible gaps.

Checklists deliver the essential functions of consistency and coordination. For example, launching a new curriculum might require teacher feedback loops, material audits, professional development scheduling, parent communication, and technology integration. Without a checklist, steps are missed. With one, teams stay on track. In project management terms, checklists reduce variance and support quality control which is vital for hitting timelines and coordinating tasks (Association for Talent Development, 2024).

The Scrum methodology applies this logic. It is a flexible way to manage projects by breaking work into short, focused cycles called sprints. The methodology helps teams work together, adapt quickly, and improve as they go (Sutherland & Sutherland, 2014). Teams can respond to feedback quickly, stay aligned, and continuously improve the quality and impact of their work (Sutherland & Sutherland, 2014).

The checklist tool works best when developed with those performing the tasks. As a living document, it represents on-the-ground realities and increases ownership. When used conscientiously, it has the ability to eliminate preventable mistakes, reduce ambiguity, and give teams the confidence to move expediently with a shared focus on the end goal.

FROM ONE LEADER TO ANOTHER

Dr. Stan Skrabut

Director of Instructional Technology and Design, Dean College | Author of Mastery Through Quizzing
  As heard on Othman's Leadership Podcast, Episode 28

Structure Frees People to Perform

When Dr. Stan Skrabut stepped into a new leadership role, he didn't start with change, he started with structure. "The first thing I asked was, 'What are our objectives? What are our key results?'" he said. That question became the heartbeat of how he managed his team's focus. Drawing from his Air Force background, Stan implemented Objectives and Key Results (OKRs) not to micromanage, but to clarify what mattered most. "Without shared goals," he explained, "people drift. Structure gives direction, but it also gives freedom."

His approach responded to the needs at hand. Leaders, he believes, need to build frameworks that guide without suffocating.

Structure needs to be combined with collaboration to drive performance. Skrabut described how he embedded OKRs into every team meeting. "We kept asking, 'what are we doing this week that supports our objectives?'" That rhythm created accountability without blame. And when things didn't go as planned, he didn't hide it. "I'd say, 'This is where we fell short. What do we learn from it?'" That posture turned failure into feedback. "You're not punishing mistakes," he said. "You're building a team that reflects and improves together."

Skrabut also brought structure to how decisions were made. Rather than hoarding authority, he aimed to remove barriers for his staff. "I see myself as the guy who clears the runway," he said. If someone needed tools, approvals, or cross-departmental support, he stepped in. That philosophy changed how people viewed their work. "They weren't just doing tasks," he shared. "They were owning the outcomes." His job, as he saw it, was to make the work smoother and the purpose visible.

Even his approach to growth was structured. Skrabut described how short, focused conversations after projects were completed, helped his team internalize what worked and what didn't. "If you don't stop and think," he said, "you'll keep repeating the same mistakes." One tool he leaned on consistently was a simple four-question check when things went wrong: Did the person know the standard? Were they trained for it? Did they have the tools? Was the environment right? If any answer was no, he took responsibility. "Then I'm the problem," he explained. That mindset built trust, not fear. His team began to expect reflection, value it, and bake it into their weekly rhythm. That's how structure became more than a system, it became a shared standard of care. Skrabut's story shows that effective project management is about designing systems that unlock ownership, learning, and leadership at every level.

STRATEGY IN A SKETCH

The Association for Talent Development's Project Management Process is a four-phase framework designed to help leaders guide projects from concept to completion with clarity and accountability. The process begins by clarifying outcomes, constraints, and stakeholder roles. From there, it shifts into mapping actionable plans with assigned owners, realistic timelines, and contingency strategies. The real challenge is in the third phase which requires balancing relationships, adapting to change, and making timely decisions under pressure. Closing with reflection ensures learning is captured, success is acknowledged, and momentum is built for what comes next.

ATD Project Management Process

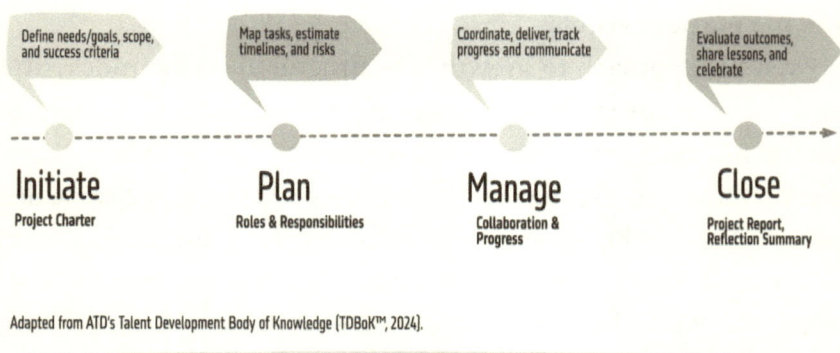

Define needs/goals, scope, and success criteria

Map tasks, estimate timelines, and risks

Coordinate, deliver, track progress and communicate

Evaluate outcomes, share lessons, and celebrate

Initiate
Project Charter

Plan
Roles & Responsibilities

Manage
Collaboration & Progress

Close
Project Report, Reflection Summary

Adapted from ATD's Talent Development Body of Knowledge (TDBoK™, 2024).

MAKE IT YOURS

- How have I defined and communicated what the success of this project will look like?

- Who has been left out of the planning but will be expected to deliver or support the project?

- Have I incorporated checklists or feedback loops?

17

Lead Through Collaboration

Can You Share Power?

Leaders who fail to prune their pride will meet demise. That's not a guess; it's a guarantee.

John Maxwell

Your Idea Might Be Great—But Incomplete

For years, Melissa Carter, a high school instructional coach at Brookside Unified, believed that good teamwork was simply about showing up, sharing ideas, and making compromises. She prided herself on being collaborative, but when strong personalities filled the room, she often struggled to lead the group effectively. That changed when her principal introduced her to the Myers-Briggs Type Indicator (MBTI) during a districtwide leadership training.

Through MBTI, Melissa began to see what she had been missing. People weren't intentionally difficult, they simply had different, natural ways of processing information and making decisions. Her colleague Mr. Sullivan, for instance, always gravitated toward big-picture visioning, while Ms. Carroll was known for her precision and attention to detail. Mr. Ortiz often led with logic and strategy, whereas Mrs. Kim centered discussions around how decisions would impact morale. Instead of growing frustrated, Melissa started asking a new question: "What might they be seeing that I'm not?" That one mental shift transformed how she participated, not just as a teammate, but as a leader.

The real test came when Melissa was selected to serve on Brookside's Teacher Contract Negotiation Team, a seven-member group tasked with shaping the district's most consequential agreement in over three decades. With livelihoods on the line and emotions running high, the potential for division was real. But something different happened.

From the start, the team, which was made up of educators like Mr. Ortiz, Ms. Carroll, and union lead Denise Marshall, took time to learn one another's MBTI profiles. They used that insight to assign roles and balance contributions. Melissa and Mr. Sullivan focused on future-oriented strategy, Ms. Carroll led document review with a sharp eye for technical accuracy, and Mrs. Kim kept relationships strong even through tension-filled meetings. They didn't agree on everything, but they respected what each person brought.

The result was the most favorable contract the district had seen in over 30 years.

Reflecting on the process later, Melissa realized the success wasn't just in the terms they negotiated, it was in the trust they built. By setting ego aside and leaning into one another's strengths, the team created something far stronger than any one person could have achieved alone.

True collaboration, she now says, isn't just about working together. It's about designing a process where every voice matters and every strength finds its place.

PRINCIPLES

Principle 1: Start With Psychological Safety

In today's collaborative workplaces, the foundation of meaningful teamwork goes beyond raw talent and technical skill. Employees must feel psychologically secure. As Amy Edmondson (2019) defines it, psychological safety is a shared belief that a team is safe for interpersonal risk-taking. When people feel safe, they are more likely to speak up, admit mistakes, ask for help, and share bold ideas. Without that protection, even the smartest voices will hold back.

Daniel Coyle (2018) reinforces this in *The Culture Code*, highlighting that great teams are built on "belonging cues," those subtle, repeated signals that say: You matter here. These cues don't just boost morale, they flip the neurological switch from self-protection to openness. That's the moment people stop managing impressions and start contributing with courage.

The data backs this up. Google's Project Aristotle found that psychological safety, more than expertise or tenure, was the single greatest predictor of team performance. Edmondson's own research showed that in hospitals adopting complex new procedures, it wasn't the most experienced teams who rapidly succeeded, it was the ones where nurses felt free to challenge doctors, and junior members could question routines without fear.

But safety doesn't happen on its own. It's built, conversation by conversation, signal by signal. Leaders must model what they want to see: vulnerability, curiosity, and openness. Coyle (2018) points to the power of small, intentional phrases like "What am I missing?" or "I might be wrong, but..." to reshape the emotional climate of a room. These micro-moves tell people: You can speak. You'll be heard. You're safe.

Psychological safety fuels the kind of trust that turns groups into high-performing teams. When people feel secure enough to speak honestly and take risks, collaboration becomes deeper, innovation becomes stronger, and every voice has the power to shape success.

Principle 2: Shift from Inward to Outward Mindset

Collaboration breaks down when people focus only on their own performance, image, or agenda. It thrives when they perceive others' goals, pressures, and stories as equally valuable. The difference begins with a change of the mind and results in a change of behavior.

The Arbinger Institute (2016) describes an inward mindset as one where others are viewed as objects who either help, hinder, or are irrelevant to our own goals. In that mode, we justify blame, avoid responsibility, and treat people as problems to solve rather than partners to support. But when we shift to an outward mindset, we begin to see others as worthy as ourselves. Their needs count. Their perspectives matter. Their success becomes part of our success.

One moment at Ford Motor Company made this real. In a high-stakes leadership meeting, a senior executive reported a major delay by marking his project in red, something unheard of in a culture addicted to "green" status updates. But instead of punishing him, CEO Alan Mulally thanked him. "What can we do to help?" he asked. That single sentence flipped the culture from fear to collaboration, from silence to trust (Arbinger Institute, 2016).

Amy Edmondson (2012) adds that effective teams are built on interdependence. The more people recognize that their actions affect others, the more they contribute with awareness and care.

To lead with an outward mindset, start with better questions: "How might I be getting in the way?" "What do others need from me?" These strategic questions dissolve defensiveness and invite partnership.

Mindset is invisible, but its impact isn't. When we shift from self-protection to shared purpose, we unlock the trust and energy teams need to move forward together.

Principle 3: Redistribute Power and Influence

Collaboration falters when power is hoarded and hierarchy rules the room. But when leaders share power, rooting influence in trust, respect, and shared purpose, teams move from mandated compliance to commitment. In fast-paced, complex environments, control isn't the goal. Contribution is. And contribution grows where power is shared.

Ferrazzi and Gohar (2020) describes this shift as co-elevation, where leadership isn't tied to title, but to mutual responsibility for results. When team members feel empowered to lead from any seat, support their peers, and challenge ideas with care, collaboration stops being a structure and becomes a culture. Ferrazzi's research shows that co-elevating teams break down silos, move faster, and initiate better solutions.

Patrick Lencioni (2022) reinforces this in *The 6 Types of Working Genius*, where influence flows from contribution, not control. A team member may not have a formal title, but their energy can ignite a room. Recognizing and honoring informal leadership based on action, not authority, encourages all members to excel.

A helpful metaphor is that of a rowing crew. If each rower pulls at a different rhythm or direction, the boat stalls or veers off course. But when all rowers are fixed on the same destination and move in sync, the team glides with power and grace. Sharing power creates that synchronization. It reduces friction and amplifies momentum.

Redistributing power unlocks capacity. It invites participation, models humility, and creates space for others to lead. When power is shared, people bring more of their insight, energy, and ownership to the work.

FROM ONE LEADER TO ANOTHER

Maryellen Manning

Chief of Staff, New Britain Public Schools
   As heard on Othman's Leadership Podcast, Episode TBD

Chase Collaborative Outcomes

Collaboration is a lifeline, especially when the stakes are high. Maryellen Manning recalled one of the most intense leadership moments in her district. "We had a traumatic event where it was a swatting event. Luckily, it didn't yield school violence, but it had all the aspects of it and impacted those who lived it for that day." In the aftermath, the entire community mobilized. "We had to work with law enforcement... our leadership team in the Central Office, our building principal, and then all of the building principals... talk to the people that experienced it that day and get their feedback." That level of coordination and empathy didn't happen by accident, it happened by design. "There was no way that could have happened without so many different hands around the table and so many different perspectives."

Collaboration depends on open, consistent, and clear communication across every level. "Communication is really the cornerstone to a collaboration that's impactful, or at the very least, effective," Manning explained. "Unless there is clear communication within that collaboration, you're dead before you even begin." Whether implementing a new curriculum or responding to a crisis, she emphasized the importance of listening and questioning. "You need people around the table that can question whether we're moving in the right way." When something doesn't go as planned, she says the most important move is to "create the condition to talk about the misstep... and elicit everyone's perspective on why it didn't work."

Strong teams collaborate best when they are consistently checking in and offering each other tangible support. "We start meetings with, 'What's keeping you up at night?' or 'What do you need to be successful?" Manning shared. "That allows us to say, 'Hey, I can help you with that." Her team is deeply cross-functional, not in title but in practice. "Even though we have different areas of expertise, we also have this consistent thread of support for one another." That means showing up, unasked. "Sometimes that means I've got to show up at your meeting and be the support, or you've got to show up at mine." Trust is what holds it all together. "It's not just about getting it done, it's about doing it together."

A collaborative culture is only real when people are learning together, out loud, and without fear. "When something doesn't work out, you have to create the condition to talk about the misstep... and elicit everyone's perspective on why it didn't work." She brings that mindset into large-scale change initiatives, like when her district implemented a new digital timecard system for over 2,000 staff. "It was a really big shift... we started simply with the why, and from there had virtual town halls, department one-pagers, and videos." The secret, she says, was constant feedback and iteration. "If you're able to constantly get feedback from people, then you constantly are refining that initiative. And it doesn't just become the cabinet's initiative, it becomes the district's initiative."

Leaders who want stronger collaboration must make space for others to be heard. "Take a moment to really listen to the collaboration and feedback of others... because sometimes that can make all the difference." For Manning, it's about noticing what the room needs. "You have to create a culture where everyone's coming to the table and everyone is accepted for what they have around the table."

STRATEGY IN A SKETCH

Tuckman's Stages of Group Development helps leaders understand that collaboration isn't immediate, it's earned through progression. Teams move through forming, storming, norming, performing, and adjourning. The power of the model isn't in labeling a stage, but in leading with awareness of what each stage demands. Early tension or awkward silence in meetings doesn't always mean something's wrong, it could simply mean the team is storming. A skilled leader recognizes this as part of the process and responds with structure, not alarm. Teams need time to grow into collaboration, and even high-performing ones cycle back when circumstances change. Leadership means discovering the stage beneath the surface and adjusting your support to match.

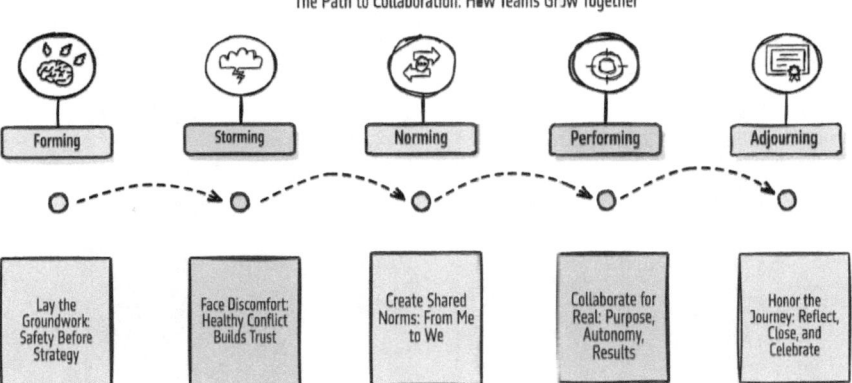

Tuckman's Stages of Group Development
The Path to Collaboration: How Teams Grow Together

Forming	Storming	Norming	Performing	Adjourning
Lay the Groundwork: Safety Before Strategy	Face Discomfort: Healthy Conflict Builds Trust	Create Shared Norms: From Me to We	Collaborate for Real: Purpose, Autonomy, Results	Honor the Journey: Reflect, Close, and Celebrate

Based on Tuckman and Jensen's stages of group development (1977).

MAKE IT YOURS

- What steps do I take to create a psychologically safe space for others?

- In moments of tension or disagreement, do I instinctively lean inward or outward? How does that shape my impact?

- How can team members discover each others' strengths and amplify involvement?

18

Lead Through Tension

Can you Disagree without Disconnection?

In moments of tension, leadership is not about avoiding conflict, it's about creating alignment and shared purpose.

Satya Nadella

Tension as a Turning Point

At Alder Grove High School, two faculty meetings left a lasting impression on Assistant Principal Morrell. It wasn't the agendas that stood out, or even the participants. It was how the facilitators handled moments of tension, and how their responses either strengthened or fractured the room.

The first meeting took place in the library with a cross-campus committee working on restorative discipline practices. As the group neared the end of a heated discussion on accountability, it was clear that not everyone had agreed on the proposed next steps. The energy in the room was tight, and a few teachers had started packing up.

Before closing, Mr. DeLaney, the facilitator, looked around and asked, "Is there anyone we haven't heard from yet?" Ms. Suri, a soft-spoken history teacher who'd stayed quiet during the back-and-forth, raised her hand. Her voice was tentative. "I have a different take I'd like to share." Without hesitation, DeLaney nodded and said, "Please, explain to me what you're seeing."

She spoke deliberately, offering a perspective that challenged the group's direction but grounded it in a student perspective. Her words slowed the room down. People leaned in.

In just a few minutes, tension turned into insight. Mr. DeLaney hadn't avoided discomfort, he'd made space for it. And in doing so, he modeled what restoration looks like: curiosity, humility, and respect. Ms. Morrell left that meeting feeling hopeful and collaborative. So did others.

Three days later, Morrell observed a different team. It was a new professional learning cohort gathered to set collaboration norms. About 20 minutes in, just as they began to reach a fragile consensus on their top three values, Ms. Franklin, a recent transfer, offered a suggestion from her previous school, "We used a quick inclusion check-in at the start of meetings. It helped quieter folks feel like their thoughts mattered."

Mr. Redmond, the facilitator, glanced at the clock and said curtly, "I don't think that would add much. Let's stay focused on the main points." An awkward silence followed. Someone tried to jump in with support by saying, "Actually, I think it could be helpful," but the mood had already shifted.

Ms. Franklin didn't speak again. Her body language changed, arms crossed, and gaze down. She was physically present but emotionally gone. Others mirrored her resistance to speak again. The tension remained palpable and the meeting ended early without final resolution.

Later that week, the assistant principal found herself thinking about both meetings. They both included divergent ideas, subtle conflict, and an opportunity to improve the status quo by sharing ideas. But only one leader made room for it with three little words, "Explain to me." That simple expression transformed tension into trust.

PRINCIPLES

Principle 1: Normalize Constructive Conflict

Disagreements are part of life. Yet for many seasoned leaders, disagreements still feel dangerous, like a threat to unity, momentum, or authority. This discomfort often stems from an outdated belief that harmony equals health. In reality, the absence of conflict may signal repressed voices, surface-level agreement, or a culture of fear.

Patterson et al. (2004) warn that suppressing conflict can result in two negative effects, silence or violence. Silence is demonstrated by disengagement and withdrawal, while violence is quickly obvious through eruptions of emotional outbursts. Both are symptoms of a team that doesn't feel safe. But when leaders model and expect candid dissent, they create groups that can work out tangible solutions using dissenting thoughts in a climate of trust.

Research by Weiss and Hughes (2005) drives this home. Many team failures are the result of unresolved or avoided conflict. When managed well, tension becomes a crucible for clarity, alignment, and innovation. Productive conflict is what keeps decisions honest and solutions creative.

Cultural clarity matters, too. Brett et al. (2006), in the Managing Multicultural Teams article, show how norms around confrontation vary globally. In one international school, leaders introduced a shared norm: "In this space, disagreement means engagement. Please challenge ideas, not people." They backed it with tools to model curiosity, using sentence stems like "Can you walk me through your thinking?" and explained when attendees should expect divergent viewpoints in upcoming meetings. These simple moves bridged cultural gaps and gave people permission to speak up.

As noted by Amy Edmondson and Michaela Kerrissey, "Psychological safety allows good debates to happen when they're needed." Safety doesn't mean avoiding dissent, it means having the freedom to speak up in a culture that sees tension as a path to stronger performance.

Normalizing constructive conflict starts with a leader's posture and is sustained through process. When a team sees conflict as a productive way to include valuable insights, it is welcome as an operational necessity.

Principle 2: View from the Balcony

Leadership under pressure requires composure. In moments of tension, leaders can easily become emotionally hijacked, rushing to defend, dismiss, or dominate. But transformative leadership pauses to evaluate the entire situation. Buchdahl (2024) interviewed William Ury, negotiation expert and co-author of *Getting to Yes*. Ury calls this pause "going to the balcony," a mental and emotional position that lets leaders observe without becoming entangled. From this elevated view, they shift from reacting to responding. It's a foundational move for navigating conflict without losing connection.

Ury reminds us that the greatest barrier to resolving conflict often isn't the other person, it's our reflex to react. Rising above that reflex allows leaders to focus on the deeper goal rather than the immediate trigger. McKinsey research on failed negotiations supports this insight. Over 70% of breakdowns stem from emotional and process mismanagement (Prilepok, 2018). Anticipating flashpoints and practicing grounded delivery, they argue, is what distinguishes effective negotiators.

Stone and Heen (2014), in *Thanks for the Feedback*, show how identity triggers, those moments when feedback threatens how we see ourselves, can cloud perception and spark defensiveness. Their recommendation: build awareness of your internal reactions. Emotional reactivity, whether anger, detachment, or judgment, narrows a leader's field of view. Mindfulness in these moments becomes a strategic asset.

According to Edmondson and Kerrissey (2025), leaders must model a humble receptivity to disagreement if they want teams to learn and grow through times of tension. The choice to listen rather than lash out, and pause instead of pounce, sets a tone of safety. It invites others into the work rather than silencing dissent.

To lead from the balcony is not to float above the fray, it's to bring deliberate restraint to the heart of it. A leader who absorbs tension without spreading it, cools the room by raising the view. This habit doesn't come naturally. But when practiced, it becomes a defining act of wisdom and a signal that calm is part of your leadership contribution.

Principle 3: Tools to Guide Hard Conversations

Candor without structure can feel like an attack. Structure without candor becomes avoidance. Leaders who want to navigate hard conversations with integrity and impact must bring both. Structured candor means delivering truth with clarity, care, and consistency, using tested tools that lower defensiveness and increase understanding. It's a leadership habit that turns tension into progress, not disconnection.

One of the most practical frameworks comes from Rosenberg's *Nonviolent Communication* (2015), which encourages leaders to separate observation from judgment, express needs without blame, and make specific, actionable requests. The goal isn't to be "nice," it's to be clear in a way that preserves dignity. Kim and Mauborgne (2003) reinforce the power of clarity in their concept of Fair Process. When people understand how decisions are made, even those they disagree with, they are more likely to support the outcome. Transparency in communication builds commitment, not just compliance.

Stone, Patton, and Heen's work in *Difficult Conversations* reminds us that every disagreement contains three threads: the facts of what happened, the emotional undercurrent, and the impact on personal identity. Leaders who ignore the emotional and identity layers risk inflaming conflict. But when all dimensions are surfaced and respected, truth-telling becomes less threatening and more collaborative.

And Patterson et al. (2004), in *Crucial Confrontations*, offer another essential tool: the CPR model. It helps leaders deliver feedback by identifying whether the issue is about Content (a single event), a Pattern (a repeated behavior), or the Relationship (when the repeated behavior begins to erode trust or credibility).

This framework keeps conversations focused on impact rather than character. For instance:

"I've noticed you've missed three key meetings this month. I'm concerned because our team counts on your presence to make timely decisions. It's starting to affect how much others rely on your input. Can we talk about what's happening?"

Rather than rush to blame, this message names behavior, names impact, and invites ownership. So how do you know if you've prepared your team for constructive conflict? Ask yourself these questions:

- Have I made the norms of dialogue explicit, not just assumed?

- Have I shown how opposing views will be welcomed and handled?

- Have I modeled disagreement that is firm but respectful?

- Have I framed the conversation with transparency and purpose?

- Have I made clear that disagreement isn't disrespect, but a form of commitment?

Clarity isn't about controlling the conversation, it's about creating enough structure that people can speak freely without fear. And when leaders consistently show that respectful dissent is not just allowed but valued, psychological safety shifts from theory to practice.

Principle 4: Recover Connection After Conflict

What happens after times of conflict and tension? Relational damage must be repaired, trust rebuilt, and purpose restored. Ury (2024) calls this moment the opportunity to build a "golden bridge," a path forward that allows everyone to preserve dignity and walk back into connection. Recovery begins when leaders help others craft their own "victory speech." This narrative promotes acceptance and empathy, moving the team to resolution without residue.

The Arbinger Institute (2015) adds depth to this idea in *The Anatomy of Peace*, warning that conflict festers when we see others as obstacles. Repair starts with mindset. It requires leaders to pause the impulse to fix people and instead focus on reconnecting with them. Being humble, inquisitive, and honest, moves the needle in that direction.

Whether it is interpersonal disagreements of supervisory input, Stone and Heen (2014) point out that even well-intended feedback can cause unintended harm. What matters is not just the message, but the aftermath. Leaders who acknowledge emotional impact before and after sharing difficult information often find that misunderstandings are avoided and safety remains intact.

Fair Process plays a critical role here, too. Kim and Mauborgne (2003) emphasize that people don't need to get their way to move forward but they do need to feel heard. After a rupture, explaining what happened, why it matters, and what comes next reestablishes fairness, even if full agreement isn't possible.

But repair is not complete until leaders guide the team into recommitment. Too often, we move on while leaving questions unanswered and climate unsettled. Recommitment means affirming what was learned, realigning around purpose, and inviting forward motion with clarity.

In high-trust teams, the scars of conflict don't signal damage, they signal growth. Just like muscle strengthens through tension and repair, relationships deepen when teams work through disagreement with honesty and care. Restoration is a catalyst for stronger collaboration, sustained performance, and shared success.

FROM ONE LEADER TO ANOTHER

Aaron Geddis

Educator | Faith Leader
  As heard on Othman's Leadership Podcast, Episodes 7 & 34

Calming the Storm

The pain of judgment changes behavior. "Some people have been abused by leaders in the past," Aaron Geddis said. "And now you're tasked with leading that individual." That kind of pain doesn't just disappear, it changes how people show up. And if leaders don't understand that, they risk doing more harm than good. For Geddis, tension is not a signal to assert authority, it's an invitation to rebuild trust. "They've heard enough talk," he explained. "Now they're watching what you do." He believes trust is earned through lived consistency, when care shows up again and again, even after people stop expecting it.

He offers a simple but powerful metaphor: "People are like plants." You don't yell at a plant to grow. You check the soil. You give it light. You water it daily. And then, you wait. The question becomes, "do you treat that person like something worth nurturing?" In one of his earliest leadership roles, Geddis worked with a younger team who lacked structure, vision, and confidence. Instead of forcing expectations, he started with life conversations, where they saw themselves in five years, how they defined growth. Over time, that relational investment turned into professional transformation. "Sometimes people don't need direction," he said. "They need someone who believes in them before they believe in them-selves."

But belief alone doesn't replace accountability. Geddis recalled giving critical feedback to a new teacher, a moment that could have triggered defensiveness. Instead, the teacher thanked him. Why? Because the message wasn't about judgment, it was about helping him win. "Correction is a form of care," Geddis explained. "But it has to come from the right heart." He teaches his team to receive feedback with discernment: "Take the meat, spit out the bones." Not every note will be perfect, but almost every one holds something useful if we're willing to stay open.

That openness doesn't always come easy. Disagreements can es-calate when egos enter the room. Geddis uses a sports analogy to explain what mature leadership looks like: "Kobe and Shaq didn't get along. But they still won three championships together." For Geddis, the takeaway is simple: you don't have to be best friends to do great work, you just have to align on the goal. The leader's job is to ask, "What do you need from me so you can contribute at your highest level?" Conflict isn't a wall. It's a door waiting to be walked through. Someone needs the courage to take the first step.

Geddis often returns to the role of the leader as the "watchman on the wall." From that higher vantage point, leaders see what others don't. "Your job," he said, "is to keep reminding them why they're building what they're building." Even when morale dips or storms set in, it's the leader's voice that can ground a team. He shared a story from childhood. A violent lightning storm struck while his church group was crossing a bridge. People began to panic until his father calmly explained the storm was temporary and clear skies were ahead. That one voice of steadiness made the journey bearable. "That's leadership," Geddis said. "You don't always stop the storm but you help people move through it without falling apart."

STRATEGY IN A SKETCH

Amy Edmondson's Psychological Safety Model helps leaders assess the culture they're cultivating. The model below maps four zones based on levels of psychological safety and accountability. The goal is to be in the "Learning Zone," where team members feel safe to take interpersonal risks like asking questions, admitting mistakes, or offering new ideas, without fear of embarrassment or punishment. This sense of safety opens communication, promotes collaboration, and makes conflict constructive.

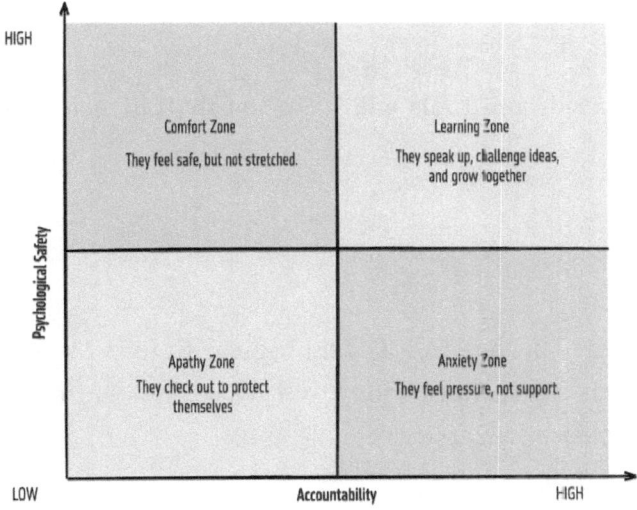

Based on Amy Edmondson's framework of psychological safety in The Fearless Organization (2019).

MAKE IT YOURS

- When conflict arises in my team, do I tend to avoid it, control it, or explore it?

- What norms or structures have I put in place to make disagreement safe, constructive, and expected in my work culture?

- Which principles and tools will I use to rebuild trust after conflict?

- Look at Amy Edmonson's Psychological Safety Model. Which zone is my team in today, and what small shift can move them closer to learning?

19

Lead High-Performing Teams

How Do You Build Norms That Drive Results?

Execution is the ability to focus on the wildly important, act on lead measures, keep a compelling scoreboard, and create a cadence of accountability.

Jim Huling

The Power of Shared Growth

When I (Reda) started a coaching circle for early childhood leaders, I wasn't sure what kind of space it would become. The group brought together a mix of professionals, including teachers, supervisors, directors, and business owners. Each carried their own challenges, frustrations, and hopes. Some were facing low enrollment. Others felt isolated or unsupported. Many were doing their best, but lacked access to research-based leadership strategies.

I launched the circle with a short message: this is a space to build a supportive network, collaborate for growth, and share evidence-based strategies. That was our "why." I shared it in writing before we ever met. But during the first two sessions, I did most of the talking. It felt like people were still testing the waters and wondering if this was any different from every other workshop they'd attended and forgotten.

Then, something shifted. The third session opened with a participant saying, "I'm so exhausted today, but I didn't want to miss this." That comment stayed with me. It wasn't just about showing up, it was about choosing growth, even when tired. Slowly, the group dynamic changed. People started contributing more, asking sharp questions, and building on each other's strategies.

That's when I realized the quiet force behind it all. We had set a norm of shared commitment to growth. The belief inspired the behavior and the behavior modeled the belief. During our time together, one business owner who had been struggling with low enrollment quickly reached capacity and began a waiting list. A director who had shared her communication struggles was later thanked by a partner organization for her clarity and professionalism. These were proof that collective norms lead to individual breakthroughs.

What made the difference was that we chose to show up, to stretch, and to support each other. We turned shared commitment into professional growth. We lived out our sentiment that high-performing teams grow together by choice, not by chance.

PRINCIPLES

Principle 1: Align Vision, Purpose, and Norms

A high-performing team is a cohesive group of individuals who demonstrate a strong commitment to shared goals, trust, accountability, and continuous improvement. They consistently achieve exceptional results through collaboration and mutual support. Such teams operate with clear roles, open communication, and aligned values, enabling them to adapt, learn, and innovate effectively in dynamic environments (Katzenbach & Smith, 1993; Lencioni, 2000; Senge, 1990).

High-performing teams don't happen by chance. They are intentionally developed through a shared vision of where the team is going, a clear purpose that explains why it matters, and behavioral norms that guide how people work together day to day. When these three elements are in sync, teams are unleashed to excel.

Peter Senge (1990) describes shared vision not as a slogan but as a unifying force that builds commitment rather than mandated compliance. It's the difference between showing up to do your job and showing up because you believe in what the team is trying to accomplish. But vision alone isn't enough. As Clifton and Harter (2019) argue, culture is created when that vision is backed by purpose and lived through decisions, conversations, and actions repeated over time.

Too often, organizations write bold statements but fail to define the behaviors that bring them to life. Norms, those unspoken rules of engagement, are where culture becomes real. Are meetings spaces of psychological safety? Do people hold each other accountable with care? Is feedback a welcome routine or a surprise? These daily habits either reinforce or erode alignment.

Consider the U.S. Navy's Blue Angels. Their mission to demonstrate the precision and excellence of naval aviation is expressed not only in performance, but in process. Every day, they conduct open debriefs, regardless of rank, to name what went well and what could improve. Their norms of trust, rigor, and mutual accountability turn a high-risk mission into synchronized success.

Senge (1990) notes, these norms are best when co-created, not handed down. Teams that build shared mental models through dialogue are more likely to take ownership. Tools like OKRs - Objectives and Key Results - are a goal setting framework that pairs bold objectives with specific, measurable results which help translate big goals into concrete steps, so everyone knows how their role supports the mission (Doerr, 2018)

When leaders align vision, purpose, and norms, they create conditions for trust, for contribution, and for results that last. That's what it means to lead for impact.

Principle 2: Build Cohesion Through Psychological Safety and Trust

While high-performing teams are composed of exceptional talent, maximizing their full potential involves ensuring their psychological safety. We've talked about psychological safety several times in this book, but it's well worth repeating. When members have been shown that it's safe to take interpersonal risks, speak up, challenge ideas, or admit mistakes without fear of embarrassment or retribution, the commitment and ability to achieve thrives. Group cohesion naturally follows.

Patrick Lencioni (2016) identifies what happens when the opposite is true. The absence of safety causes the foundational dysfunction of a team. But trust doesn't happen when everything runs smoothly. He argues that trust grows from vulnerability. It's the willingness to say, "I was wrong," or "I need help." In teams where this kind of candor is modeled and protected, collaboration becomes deeper and more durable. Senge (1990) echoes this in *The Fifth Discipline*, noting that team learning requires members to suspend judgment and explore different perspectives with curiosity. Trust, then, is not just emotional, it's also cognitive. It's how people open their minds, not just their hearts.

Google's Project Aristotle reinforced these findings. In their study of effective teams, psychological safety emerged as the top differentiator (Rozovsky, 2015). Teams that felt safe took more risks, offered more ideas, and learned faster from failure. They were more productive because they were more connected.

Lencioni's *Ideal Team Player* model adds another layer. Teams thrive when members are humble (own their mistakes), hungry (take initiative), and people smart (read others well). These traits create behavioral norms that reinforce psychological safety as a daily climate.

Leaders carry the responsibility to model these norms. Practices like weekly check-ins, open feedback loops, or simple acknowledgment of effort and honesty (Blanchard & Johnson, 2015), create the conditions for trust to grow. When safety and trust are strong, teams feel empowered to bring their full selves to the work. Cohesion emerges from the confidence to contribute authentically. That's when collaboration deepens, and performance rises.

Principle 3: Institutionalize Learning and Feedback Loops

In an environment where the sole focus is learning, it's alarming to read the study by Academic Impressions which revealed that the success rate for implementing strategic plans in educational institutions is notably low, with failure rates ranging from 63% to 90%. (Academic Impressions, 2014, March 6)

With high-performing teams, learning is a habit. They don't wait for annual reviews to ask what is and isn't working. They build feedback loops into the rhythm of their work. Reflection is part of their routine. And because of that, they adapt faster and improve more consistently.

Senge (1990) describes this kind of culture as a "learning organization" where people continually expand their capacity to create the results they care about. At the heart of it is feedback that is timely, specific, and safe to give and receive. He reminds us that operational performance is shaped by feedback loops. Teams that wait to act until something breaks remain reactive. But those that reflect and adapt as they go become generative, building capacity, not just fixing problems.

Doerr (2018) echoes this in his work on Objectives and Key Results (OKRs), when he says weekly and quarterly check-ins aren't just for tracking progress, they're built-in moments for reflection, adjustment, and alignment. This regular cadence creates a continuous feedback loop, turning learning into momentum. Instead of relying on hindsight, teams stay engaged, adapt quickly, and move forward with clarity.

Matthew Syed's *Black Box Thinking* (2015) drives the point home with a powerful comparison: the reason air travel is so safe is the discipline of learning from every mistake. Every misstep is documented, analyzed, and shared. The mindset? Mistakes are data. Feedback is an advantage. The same logic can transform teams if they treat evaluation as a feature, not a flaw.

On the ground, this might look like a five-minute WIG session - a weekly check-in on a team's Wildly Important Goal. It's an effective practice highlighted in *The 4 Disciplines of Execution* by McChesney, Covey, and Huling (2022). These sessions keep the most critical priority visible, surface progress blockers, and prompt small next steps. Another productive routine is the One Minute Redirect from

Blanchard and Johnson (2015), where leaders offer quick, specific feedback to guide improvement in the moment.

Leaders create the foundation by showing that feedback is valued and growth is encouraged. In this kind of environment, the focus shifts from getting everything right to getting better every week. When feedback becomes part of the culture, teams deliver, develop, and improve together.

Principle 4: Embed A System and Culture of Accountability

Accountability is the link between intention and execution. It is a shared norm in high-performing teams and is incorporated into daily work habits. Accountability includes a set of routines, metrics, and expectations that make tenacity expected and visible. McChesney, Covey, and Huling (2022) argue that successful execution of a plan comes from effectively managing the 'whirlwind' of urgent daily tasks. Their 4 Disciplines of Execution (4DX) framework provides a system for staying focused. It includes: identifying Wildly Important Goals (WIGs), tracking progress through lead measures, making results visible via public scoreboards, and holding weekly accountability check-ins. These structures transform accountability from a vague idea into a visible, lived habit.

Doerr (2018) makes a similar case in his advocacy for OKRs because it is a goal-setting method that aligns people and priorities through transparency. In companies like Google, OKRs are publicly posted, time-bound, and reviewed regularly. This visibility turns accountability into a team dynamic. When progress is seen by all, ownership increases and performance improves. Unfortunately, an analysis by Gardner (2021) reported that out of 108 strategic plans, 73% lacked clear metrics.

Lencioni (2016) adds that peer accountability is often more powerful than managerial oversight. In cohesive teams, members hold one another to high standards because they care about the mission and about each other. Feedback becomes a shared responsibility, not just a supervisor's job.

Think of a championship sports team. Players aren't just evaluated on their personal statistics, they're measured by how they contribute to the team's system. There are daily rituals like film reviews, debriefs, and metrics dashboards that keep everyone aligned and accountable to a common goal. Performance is tracked for improvement.

Leaders who want lasting accountability do more than set expectations. They create systems that reinforce priorities, highlight progress, and make reflection a regular practice. With a clear operating structure in place, accountability becomes part of a consistent, shared, and sustainable culture.

Principle 5: Leverage Strengths with Role Clarity

When people understand what they're good at and how their role contributes to the bigger picture, they take more initiative and solve problems without being asked. They own outcomes. That's the power of pairing strengths with role clarity; it unlocks intrinsic motivation and shared responsibility.

Gallup research, as summarized by Clifton and Harter (2019), shows that employees who use their strengths daily are six times more likely to be engaged. That's a definite organizational productivity boost! A strengths-based approach means leaders assign tasks that complement talents. They get to know their people well enough to shape roles that elevate natural ability and energy, not just fill gaps.

But talented, engaged people still need direction. *The New One Minute Manager* (Blanchard & Johnson, 2015) emphasizes the importance of short and clear goals that are created with the input of those involved in the work. When team members help define what success looks like, they own it more fully. Role clarity minimizes second-guessing, miscommunication, and turf wars. It replaces ambiguity with focus.

A Formula One pit crew makes this clear. While the driver gets the spotlight, the outcome often hinges on the crew's speed and precision. Each crew member has a defined task, either jacking the car, changing tires, refueling, cleaning the windshield, or making mechanical adjustments. All must be synchronized and completed within seconds. There's no overlap, no hesitation, and no wasted motion. Every action is meticulously planned and executed, with minimal room for error. The pit crew operates as a single unit, with each member relying on the others to perform their tasks efficiently. That's the power of role clarity matched with strengths.

To lead this way, start by knowing your people well. Identify growing strengths and clarify roles often, especially as organizational needs shift. Acknowledge outcomes and celebrate the talents that made them happen. When every person functions as designed, the whole team moves like a well-oiled machine.

FROM ONE LEADER TO ANOTHER

Dr. Kristy Zaleta

Principal, Rogers Park Middle School
As heard on Othman's Leadership Podcast, Episode 18

You Lead by Showing People Who You Are

When Dr. Kristy Zaleta became principal of Rogers Park Middle School, the school carried an undesirable reputation. "It was the school that nobody wanted to go to," she said. Teachers worked in silos, families were disengaged, and students were struggling to meet expectations. But Zaleta didn't start with a strategic plan. She started with presence. "You lead by showing people who you are," she said. "I started by being visible, by listening, by showing I cared."

The real challenge wasn't just the data, it was rebuilding belief. "You have to be able to take a hard look at yourself as a school," she said. "Where are we failing? What's in our locus of control?" The turning point came when she and her team stopped working around each other and began working with each other. "We started talking about flexible grouping, about student needs, not just teaching content," she explained. "We stopped talking about kids as my students and started referring to them as our students."

Zaleta rebuilt team norms with intention and honesty. "If you're not collaborating and you're not communicating your thoughts, and then asking people who are going to poke holes in it, it doesn't help me." She empowered teachers to lead committees, mentor one another, and help shape school-wide decisions. When resistance showed up, she didn't ignore it. "I look for the saltiest person that's going to be looking for every reason this is not going to work... because they want to be perfect. Then it makes me think even harder."

One of the most powerful moments came when students themselves became co-authors of the school culture. "They said, 'Hey, we need to be better at talking about race.' We brought in the ACLU, No Place for Hate. Through a grant I wrote, kids worked on it. They had some amazing, courageous conversations with teachers." In another example, student ambassadors helped revise the school's tardy policy, dress code, and cell phone rules, reinforcing a culture of accountability and ownership.

Zaleta's leadership relied on consistency. "Every decision we make in schools, implicitly or explicitly, communicates a set of values," Zaleta said. And those values showed up in routines, recognition, and results. "We had over a ten percentage point growth... our chronic absenteeism dropped 12.2 percentage points for our high needs students."

The results were unmistakable. Rogers Park moved from one of the lowest-performing schools in the district to one of the most improved. Student engagement rose. Teacher retention stabilized. Family involvement increased. "People felt proud to be part of the school again," she said. And that pride wasn't accidental. It was engineered through intentional culture work, aligned leadership, and deeply embedded team norms. "You can't fake that kind of growth," Zaleta reflected. "It happens when everyone is moving in the same direction and they believe in where they're going."

Zaleta's story reminds us that a positive school culture doesn't come after the work, it is the work. If you want high-performance, start by paying attention to the climate you're encouraging and the norms you're reinforcing through your daily actions and attitude.

STRATEGY IN A SKETCH

The Five Behaviors framework by Patrick Lencioni is designed to help teams function more effectively by addressing the foundational drivers of group performance. It works as a sequential model where each behavior reinforces the next, creating a culture of trust, productive conflict, commitment, accountability, and collective results. The model begins with building psychological safety, then progresses toward performance. Rather than simply improving communication, this framework transforms how a team functions at its core. Leaders can use this model to diagnose team dysfunction and design intentional team norms.

The Five Behaviors of a Cohesive Team
Each behavior enables the next.

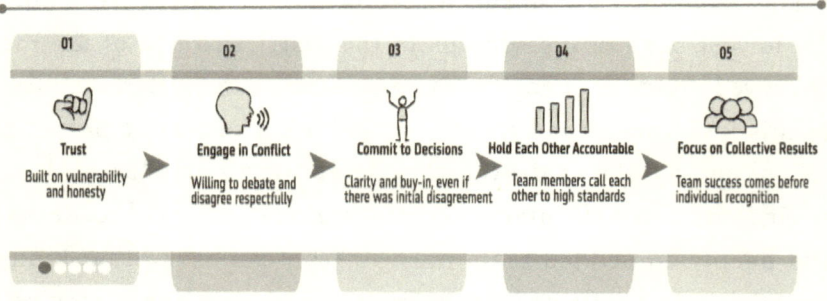

01	02	03	04	05
Trust	Engage in Conflict	Commit to Decisions	Hold Each Other Accountable	Focus on Collective Results
Built on vulnerability and honesty	Willing to debate and disagree respectfully	Clarity and buy-in, even if there was initial disagreement	Team members call each other to high standards	Team success comes before individual recognition

Adapted from Patrick Lencioni's team development framework, The Five Behaviors of a Cohesive Team™ (2014).

MAKE IT YOURS

- How well are my team's vision, purpose, and behavioral norms aligned, communicated, and practiced?

- Where could feedback loops be strengthened to regularly reflect, learn, and adapt from successes and setbacks?

- Are team members' unique strengths and roles identified and maximized?

20
Lead as Coach
How Do You Help Others See Themselves Clearly?

If your actions inspire others to dream more, learn more, do more and become more, you are a leader.

John Quincy Adams

The Power of "You're Ready"

After one of my leadership training sessions, participants were invited to sign up for a follow-up coaching session. Ileana was one of them. A veteran educator with over 25 years in the field, she joined our 1:1 meeting quietly, but it didn't take long before her voice carried something deeper, a mix of hope and hesitation.

She told me she had two goals that had been sitting in her heart for years: to become a director and to go back to school. But she didn't know where to begin. She was feeling stuck, unsure what the first step was, or even if it was still possible. What she needed wasn't a checklist. She didn't need someone to tell her what to do, she needed a sounding board. Someone to listen closely, reflect honestly, and help her hear her own voice more clearly. That's what I tried to be.

As she spoke, I gathered what she shared and painted a picture of what her life could look like after she reached those goals. I described her future self walking into work as a center director, leading with confidence, having earned her next degree, not as a fantasy, but as a real possibility.

She smiled. Then she said something I'll never forget. "That's exactly what I want. And I can do it. Just like the people I've always looked up to." That moment changed everything.

A few months later, I got an email from her. She told me she had applied for a director role and been hired. She also had been accepted into a graduate program. And she wrote, "I finished three classes already and just started the fourth. I didn't give up. I'm so proud of myself."

It reminded me of something I've seen over and over again: People are capable of more than they realize, but they often need someone to see it first, and say, "You can do it."

PRINCIPLES

Principle 1: Question for Introspection

Coaching isn't about solving other people's problems or fixing their personality flaws. It's a process that facilitates self-discovery, unlocks potential, and supports meaningful progress toward personal or professional goals. Rather than telling someone what to do, an effective coach uses reflective inquiry, active listening, and goal oriented dialogue (International Coaching Federation, 2020; Stanier, 2016).

The coach's job is to hold up a mirror so others can see themselves clearly and choose their next move with intention. Michael Bungay Stanier (2016), in *The Coaching Habit*, says the biggest trap coaches fall into is rushing to solve the wrong problem. Instead, he suggests slowing down with a question like, "What's the real challenge here for you?" This invites reflection, helps to uncover obstacles, and reveals a valid picture of the situation.

Kate Murphy (2020), in *You're Not Listening*, adds that a question followed by undistracted listening creates space for people to think aloud, organize their thoughts, and surface insights they didn't know they had. When we listen without interrupting, redirecting, or solving, we offer the rare opportunity for people to hear themselves more clearly.

Imagine a coach working with a new leader hesitant to delegate. Rather than offering tips or advice, the coach asks, "What happens when you hand off work?" or "What feels risky about someone else taking the lead?" These questions don't prescribe a path, they uncover one. The result is deeper self-awareness and longer-lasting change.

Stanier (2016) makes this shift clear. He encourages coaches to ask more and say less, using simple, powerful questions like, "And what else?" The 'AWE' question, as he calls it, pushes the conversation deeper. It opens up reflection, slows the pace, and invites the other person to keep thinking rather than rushing to closure. This kind of inquiry creates space for insight to surface organically.

The same philosophy shaped the coaching of Bill Campbell, the legendary mentor behind leaders at Google and Apple. In *Trillion Dollar Coach*, Schmidt et al. (2019) describe how Campbell rarely gave direct answers. Instead, he asked pointed questions that made people pause, reflect, and arrive at clarity on their own. His wisdom was found in inquiry, not advice.

Imagine a leader supporting a burned-out team member. Rather than offering tips on balance, they might ask, "What's one small change that would give you more breathing room this week?" or "What do you need less of right now?" These kinds of questions empower ownership. They respect the person's context and honor their capacity.

An effective coach creates the space for individuals to uncover their own insights and determine the actions that matter most.

Principle 2: Honor the Person

Transformational coaching begins with a mindset that people are more than the issues they bring into the room. The principle, "Honor the Person, Not Just the Problem" challenges us to see each coaching session not as a puzzle to fix but as a relationship to hold. True coaching affirms the person's worth, capacity, and complexity, even when the path forward is unclear.

In *Daring Greatly*, Brené Brown (2012) reminds us that change doesn't happen through strategy alone. Real growth begins when people feel seen, heard, and valued, and that only happens in a climate of emotional safety. Her research shows that what appears to be laziness or ignorance, can actually be a result of shame, fear, or vulnerability. Coaches who meet individuals with empathy and measured deliberation create the conditions to unearth the truth. By going slow, we create the conditions for real transformation. Not the quick wins of surface-level advice, but the lasting clarity that only emerges when we allow people the time to go inward.

When coaches honor the introspection of the individual, trust deepens. Defensiveness fades. Insight sharpens. Clifton and Harter (2019) reinforce that modern professionals don't want micromanagement, they want development. And development begins by acknowledging the whole person, their values, goals, and life context. When a coach links external challenges to internal drivers, they help the person reconnect with meaning, not just metrics.

Imagine an employee who consistently misses deadlines. Rather than diving into scheduling tactics, a coach might ask, "What does it mean to you when things fall behind?" or "Where did you learn to tie your worth to performance?" These questions uncover the emotional script behind the habit and invite more lasting change.

When individuals feel respected, genuinely heard, and free from pressure, they're more likely to engage in meaningful reflection and take ownership of their growth and progress toward goals.

Principle 3: Challenge with Care

At its best, coaching is a powerful motivating force where candid conversations and emotional support must walk side by side. Effective coaching requires the courage to name what's difficult and the compassion to do so in a way that invites positive transformation and discourages alienation. This balance is built on trust, accountability, and the desire for growth.

Schmidt and his coauthors (2019) describe how Bill Campbell earned the right to be blunt. He was a legendary business executive, coach, and mentor in Silicon Valley who gave direct, often tough feedback but always from a place of deep care. His honesty was never weaponized. It was cultivated by the belief in the person's potential and ability. That's why people listened.

Brené Brown (2012) adds an exclamation mark. *In Daring Greatly*, she writes that "Clear is kind," she says, reminding us that protecting someone from discomfort might feel compassionate in the moment, but it ultimately denies them the opportunity to grow. Kindness and clarity are partners. It's all in the way you say it.

Imagine a coach working with a rising administrator who tends to dominate meetings. Rather than say, "You're not a good listener," the coach might offer, "I've noticed people hesitate to speak after you've shared. What might be causing that?" It's a gentle but obvious nudge for the purpose of introspection.

Challenging with care means speaking truthfully and respectfully, with the other person's growth in mind. When done well, it fosters appreciation, sparks insight, and becomes a powerful catalyst for meaningful progress.

FROM ONE LEADER TO ANOTHER

Kimm Quinlan

Director, Early Childhood Initiatives, Holyoke Community College
    As heard on Othman's Leadership Podcast, Episode 21

Understand with Questions

Kimm Quinlan doesn't believe in fixing people, she believes in unlocking them. Early in her leadership role, she faced a moment that shaped her entire coaching philosophy. "I remember sitting with a staff member who was struggling with confidence," she recalled. "She wasn't sure if she belonged in the role." Instead of stepping in to direct or correct, Quinlan asked a simple question: "What's going well for you right now?" That conversation opened the door to a shift. "She started seeing herself as someone who had something to offer... someone who belonged." It wasn't the feedback that changed the outcome, it was the belief behind it.

Quinlan's first coaching move is simple but powerful: slow down and observe. "So often, we go in with the assumption of what people need but we haven't actually taken the time to ask or watch." She describes coaching as an act of curiosity. "I might sit with someone and say, 'Tell me about your day. What are you enjoying? What's feeling hard?'" These questions aren't accidental. They're designed to build trust. "When people feel seen, they're more open to support. Coaching becomes a partnership instead of a correction." For leaders in fast-paced environments, this reminds us that insight requires presence.

Another strategy Quinlan uses is tailored reflection. "If someone is struggling, I don't start with what they're doing wrong, I start with what they care about." She shared an example of a teacher who was overwhelmed by a classroom management issue. "I asked her, 'When do you feel most confident with the kids?'" That small question opened space for real growth. "She realized she was strong during transitions, but uncertain during group time... that awareness gave us something concrete to build on." For Quinlan, effective coaching isn't about generic advice, it's about uncovering patterns people don't yet see in themselves.

To sustain this kind of culture, Quinlan builds coaching into the daily rhythm of the organization. "We don't wait for formal evaluations. Coaching happens in hallway conversations, quick check-ins, even text messages." She believes leaders have to model the vulnerability they hope to inspire. "I tell my team when I'm nervous. I name when something didn't land the way I hoped." That openness creates safety for others to reflect without fear. "When people know they won't be judged, they're more likely to ask for support before things escalate." In her team, development isn't a program, it's a habit.

Quinlan's advice to leaders is simple: "Don't assume you know the answer. Get curious." She believes the best coaching moments come from genuine listening. "It's not about solving, it's about witnessing. Sometimes people just need to hear their own thinking out loud." For those looking to help others develop, she offers this challenge: "What if your role isn't to direct, but to reveal? What if the growth isn't yours to give, but yours to hold space for?" In a world full of fast answers, Quinlan's coaching offers something rare: reflection that leads to transformation.

STRATEGY IN A SKETCH

The Co-Active Coaching Model is a powerful framework for cultivating transformational conversations built on trust, presence, and partnership. It centers on the belief that people are naturally creative, resourceful, and whole. This shifts the leader's role from problem-solver to possibility-partner. Rather than offering advice, leaders trained in this model listen on multiple levels, ask questions that stretch thinking, and create space for reflection.

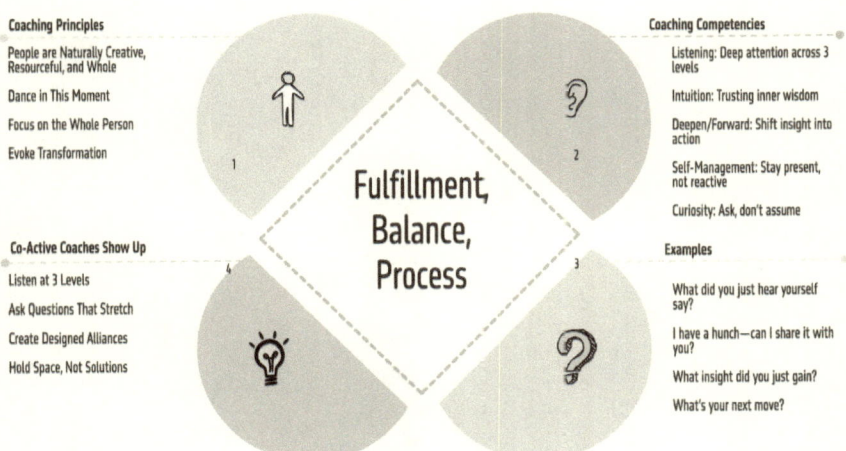

Co-Active Model

Coaching Principles

People are Naturally Creative, Resourceful, and Whole

Dance in This Moment

Focus on the Whole Person

Evoke Transformation

Co-Active Coaches Show Up

Listen at 3 Levels

Ask Questions That Stretch

Create Designed Alliances

Hold Space, Not Solutions

Fulfillment, Balance, Process

Coaching Competencies

Listening: Deep attention across 3 levels

Intuition: Trusting inner wisdom

Deepen/Forward: Shift insight into action

Self-Management: Stay present, not reactive

Curiosity: Ask, don't assume

Examples

What did you just hear yourself say?

I have a hunch—can I share it with you?

What insight did you just gain?

What's your next move?

Based on the Co-Active Coaching framework by Kimsey-House, Kimsey-House, Sandahl, and Whitworth (2018).

MAKE IT YOURS

- Where might I be offering advice too quickly instead of holding space for insight?

- What powerful questions could I ask that would help this person uncover their own truth?

- Am I truly seeing beyond the problem and honoring the person?

21
Lead to Inspire
How Do You Bring Out the Best in People?

The growth and development of people is the highest calling of leadership.

Harvey Firestone

Unlocking Potential

I (Suzanne) met Tina when she was a teacher's aide. It was immediately obvious that she loved the students and poured her heart into the job. But I could also tell she carried a quiet belief that this was as far as she could go. She often said things like, "I'm just an aide" or "I'm not cut out to be a teacher." She didn't think she had the skills, experience, or credentials to do more.

One afternoon, during a casual conversation, I asked her what she would do if nothing stood in her way. She hesitated, then whispered, "I'd be a teacher." That was the beginning of our plan. We started by shaping her resume to reflect the real strengths she had developed over years in the classroom. I asked questions about her experiences to help her see that her patience, classroom management techniques, and ability to connect with students were the very skills great teachers need.

Next, we walked through the process of applying to a teacher certification program. It felt daunting to her at first, but we tackled it step by step by breaking down deadlines, gathering transcripts, and writing her personal statement. I reminded her often, "You've already been doing the work. Now you're just getting the title that matches it."

When she got her acceptance letter, we celebrated like she'd just been handed the keys to her future, because in a way, she had. Over the next two years, she worked full-time and studied at night. Every milestone, whether it was a passed exam, a completed practicum, or a glowing observation report, was a victory we acknowledged together.

The day she received her teaching certificate, she sent me a photo of herself in cap and gown, grinning from ear to ear. In her message she wrote, "I can't believe I'm here. Thank you for believing in me before I believed in myself."

Today, Tina has her own classroom, her own students, and a career she once thought was beyond her reach. She's thriving and it wasn't because I changed her, but because she finally saw what I and others had seen all along. Once she believed in herself, there was no stopping her.

PRINCIPLES

Principle 1: Reinforce Strengths

Each person has a unique set of qualities and abilities that enable them to flourish in various scenarios. These strengths can be both personal attributes and professional skills. Buckingham (2007) defines a strength as something someone does well, and also makes them feel energized, focused, and fulfilled. Strengths, then, are motivators that play a crucial role in navigating challenges, achieving goals, and building positive relationships.

Leaders who help others operate in their "zone of genius" unlock higher motivation, better performance, and deeper engagement. Gallup research shows that teams that focus on strengths daily are 12.5% more productive (as cited in Buckingham, 2017). This is not just feel-good leadership, it's strategic. When people spend more time doing what they're great at and love, their creativity and resilience naturally rise.

Organizations like Google and Facebook have designed systems to support this. Rather than pushing top-performing engineers into management roles they may not want, Google created the "Distinguished Engineer" track, an alternative path that keeps people in their strength zones while still growing their influence.

It's the difference between being a mechanic and a gardener. A mechanic fixes what's broken. A gardener nurtures what's already growing. Strengths-based leadership is gardening that requires patience, discernment, and a deep understanding of each individual's unique potential.

Buckingham's framework to spot strengths in ourselves can also be used to identify them in others. He uses the acronym SIGN: S is for the strengths where you feel successful; I is where you're pulled, your instinct; G is for the growth you experience when you use your strengths; and N represents the needs you feel upon later reflection. The author recommends turning this theory into practice by implementing a "strong week plan." It involves a weekly commitment to two specific actions that amplify strengths and two actions that mitigate weaknesses. The idea is to focus on activities that energize and lead to increased productivity and job satisfaction.

To bring out the best in others, leaders must flip the script from "What's wrong and how do I fix it?" to "What's strong and how can I grow it?" This mindset boosts morale and builds cultures where people thrive at the intersection of energy and impact.

Principle 2: See and Speak Appreciation

People work best when their talents are applicable, exercised, and acknowledged. The most inspiring leaders understand that appreciation is a strategic act that fuels performance, deepens trust, and builds loyalty. As Chapman and White (2019) found, 88% of employees leave jobs for reasons unrelated to pay, most often because they don't feel valued.

Aubrey Daniels, a prominent figure in the field of behavioral science, wrote about the power of acknowledging strengths in her book titled, "Bringing Out the Best in People: How to Apply the Astonishing Power of Positive Reinforcement"(2016). The central idea of Daniels' work is that "What we positively reinforce, grows". This concept underscores the importance of carefully selecting and timing rewards to foster motivation, learning, and lasting behavioral change.

But appreciation only works if it's specific to the individual. Chapman and White (2019) outline five workplace "languages of appreciation": Words of Affirmation, Acts of Service, Quality Time, Tangible Gifts, and Physical Touch (appropriately contextualized). Too often, leaders default to generic praise or bonuses. But the real impact comes from knowing what resonates. For one team member, a thoughtful note lands deeply. For another, five minutes of undistracted time with their manager means more than any award.

Major organizations are picking up on the tangible worth of positive acknowledgement. Southwest Airlines embedded this principle into their culture, using small, intentional gestures to express appreciation in ways that fit the individual. At Google, peer-nominated recognition has created a system where gratitude is expressed throughout the team. These practices aren't perks; they're cultural glue.

Think of appreciation like fresh air that rejuvenates and sustains engagement, confidence, and forward momentum. It must be replenished consistently, not reserved for performance reviews or milestone moments. When leaders make appreciation part of the rhythm of how they lead, they breathe life into everyday moments that shape impact. Ultimately, to bring out the best in people, you have to show them that they matter. And when appreciation is timely, personal, and sincere, it becomes one of the most powerful tools a leader can use.

Principle 3: Listen to Lift and Empower

Listening is one of the most underused, yet most powerful, tools a leader has to empower others. As Murphy (2023) reminds us, real listening isn't passive, it's an intentional act that validates, connects, and invites people to step into their full voice. When leaders listen beyond words to emotion and meaning, they demonstrate sincere consideration.

This kind of listening demands more than open ears. It requires curiosity, patience, and the discipline to slow down. In a world of endless pings and continual distractions, full attention has become a radical act of respect. Murphy (2023) notes that many people today feel lonelier than ever before, despite constant connection. Leaders who offer their attention acknowledge the worth of the speaker.

Kouzes and Posner (2017) found that leaders who build trust and spark collaboration do so by first seeking to understand. When people feel heard, they contribute more boldly, think more clearly, and stay engaged longer. Listening becomes a developmental tool to expand thinking and ownership.

Think of great listeners like trampolines. They don't just absorb, they reflect, elevate, and return energy. Active listening is like that: it bounces people higher. It asks open-ended questions, resists the urge to fix, and creates psychological safety where people feel free to explore their thoughts out loud.

Listening is a leadership skill. When leaders listen to lift, not steer or solve, they unlock potential others didn't know they had. That's when connection deepens, confidence builds, and contribution takes flight.

Principle 4: You Get What You Expect

One of the most transformative acts a leader can take is to believe in someone's potential. This kind of belief isn't silent or internal. It's visible. It's spoken. And it's felt. When people know their leader sees an ability in them that they may not even notice themselves, they often rise to meet that vision.

Kouzes and Posner (2017) argue that great leaders cast a vision for the organization and for each person in it. This idea is echoed in the Pygmalion Effect, where higher expectations lead to better performance, regardless of past abilities. In a landmark study, low-ranking students randomly selected as "high potential" outperformed peers with higher scores, simply because their teachers expected more (Rosenthal & Jacobson, 1968). The belief communicated to them shaped the reality they lived into.

This principle lives in leaders like Coach John Wooden, who emphasized effort and growth over outcomes. His consistent affirmation built a culture of psychological safety and improvement. Or in the work of Marva Collins, the educator who turned "unteachable" into unstoppable students by relentlessly reminding and affirming her belief in them.

Carol Dweck (2006) affirms that people flourish when surrounded by others who expect progress, not perfection. Similarly, Daniels (2016) found that clear, positive expectations can dramatically improve performance. Belief in the potential of your team members, when consistently expressed, becomes an impetus for growth. Ultimately, you get what you expect. If you expect the best from others and show them why you believe they can achieve their best, they rise to the occasion.

FROM ONE LEADER TO ANOTHER

Lisa Garcia

Manager at Thomson Reuters
As heard on Othman's Leadership Podcast, Episode TBD

Let Someone Else Shine First

When Lisa Garcia thinks about what it means to bring out the best in people, her earliest memory isn't from a boardroom, it's from a playground. When she was a child, trying to learn how to flip over the bar on a swingset, she noticed a quiet classmate nearby. "He didn't have much confidence. I was like, 'Can you flip over it?' And he said, 'Yeah, sure.'" And then he showed her.

It wasn't just about play. It was about helping someone feel seen. "A lot of the other cliques would not include him," she said. But in that moment, Garcia instinctively stepped back, made space, and let Andy be the expert. "I think it's the basic element of servant leadership, right? You're not the expert, you let somebody else do their thing."

That instinct to notice people's potential and name it before they see it themselves, has shaped Garcia's entire leadership style. Whether she's managing a team at Thomson Reuters or leading study groups through the Association of Talent Development, Lisa makes a habit of watching quietly, asking questions, and creating moments for others to step into their strengths.

"A lot of people have trouble identifying their strengths... but they also have trouble stepping forward and saying, 'I'm really good at this.'"

One of her go-to strategies? Reverse the spotlight. In one team retreat, she used the StrengthsFinder list - a tool that identifies individuals' top talents - not as a personal reflection tool, but as a peer recognition exercise. Before team members named their own top strengths, they were asked to identify a colleague's. "It was a bit of a love fest," she laughed. But it was also disarming. People heard things about themselves they didn't realize were unique, like their organizational abilities, thoroughness, and insight. Others had quietly noticed all along.

"Every person heard something they didn't think they were... but maybe they thought they could be. Somebody else saw it in them."

Garcia believes these small moves of public affirmation, gentle redirection, and showing trust before proof, are often more powerful than grand gestures. That belief was tested when a highly respected team member made a serious mistake in a legal-facing role. The slip-up could have shattered his credibility. But instead of shielding him from the fallout, Garcia encouraged him to own it.

"He was feeling embarrassed for sure," she said. "But I told him, share what you learned. Help the whole team." He did. And in doing so, modeled vulnerability, accountability, and real-time learning in front of the entire squad. Garcia backed him publicly and framed the experience as a teaching moment. "I just jumped in to say, 'This is why I have high expectations... this is why diligence matters.'" The moment didn't damage the team, it strengthened it.

Garcia's influence isn't always loud. One of her most impactful decisions started as a quiet offer to support someone else's dream. When a board member in her local ATD chapter launched a certification study group, Garcia signed on as her backup. She was the only certified professional in the chapter at the time. "I figured there's no better opportunity than to represent," she said casually.

But when the original lead stepped away, Garcia kept the group alive. Five years later, it has helped over 100 people earn their certification, sparked new chapters to form their own groups, and led to recognition from ATD. "I can't really articulate the ripple effect," she admitted. "But it ties back to Andy on the playground... seeing someone's face light up, seeing them reach a goal."

Her leadership is anchored in one principle she learned from her father early in her career. It was during a season when she almost lost her job over a company incident she didn't cause. She still remembers her dad's words. "He said, 'Lisa, whatever you do, don't let them break your spirit. That's what I love most about you.'" And so she didn't. And she makes sure others don't either.

"Usually mistakes that don't get caught... don't get caught because someone's hesitant to comment, to be vulnerable, to say, 'I messed up.' If you're genuine, human, and fallible, there's no blocking communication."

Her strategy? Speak belief into people out loud. Let them borrow your confidence until they find their own. Then step back and let them shine. Her question? Who's on your team that's waiting for permission to be more than their job description?

STRATEGY IN A SKETCH

The Self-Determination Theory (SDT) helps leaders unlock deeper motivation by supporting three innate human needs. When autonomy, competence, and relatedness are all present, people do more than comply, they commit. The model works by reminding us that long-term engagement grows from internal drivers, not promised rewards. But here's the trap: leaders often focus too much on incentives and overlook what actually sustains performance like voice, growth, and connection. Instead of asking "What reward can I offer?" try "What need isn't being met here?" The strength of this approach lies in meeting the need and igniting the drive.

Self-Determination Theory (SDT)

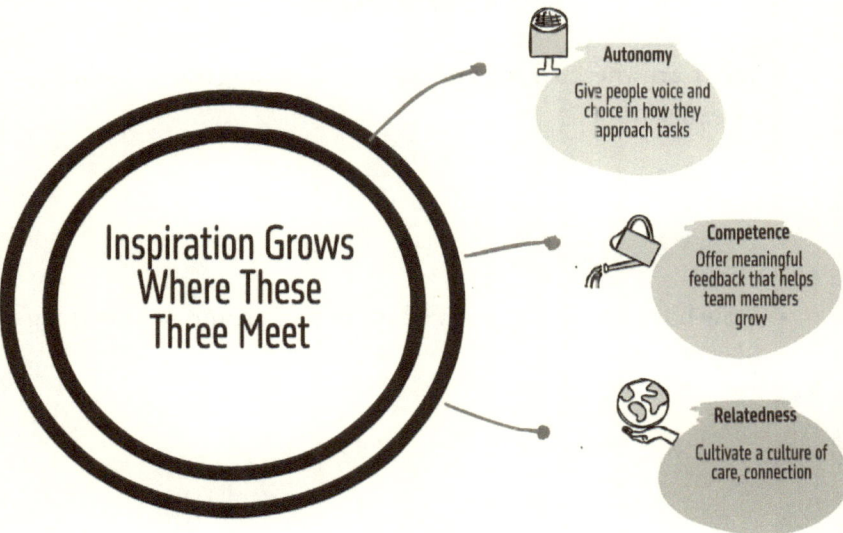

Inspiration Grows Where These Three Meet

Autonomy
Give people voice and choice in how they approach tasks

Competence
Offer meaningful feedback that helps team members grow

Relatedness
Cultivate a culture of care, connection

Watch for the Trap: Over-reliance on External Rewards and Ignoring Individual Differences

Based on Deci, Olafsen, and Ryan's self-determination theory (2017).

MAKE IT YOURS

- What are the current and potential strengths of each team member?

- How have I built a system of appreciation and acknowledgement?

- What are each team member's preferred language of appreciation?

22

Lead as an Instructional Designer

How Do You Train to Transform?

Training is not about the transmission of knowledge, it is about the transformation of the individual.

Tony Robbins

From Words on the Wall to Habits in the Hallway

During a school visit to a middle school in Rhode Island, the principal met with me after dismissal and said, "We have our mission statement everywhere, the front hallway, our website, even posted in classrooms, but if I walk into random lessons, I don't see it lived out." He was in his second year and had inherited a school where the mission sounded compelling on paper: a challenging learning environment that embraces individual differences and inspires high expectations for achievement. But in practice, the instructional culture felt uneven. He noticed teachers teaching to the middle, struggling to differentiate, and falling back on routines that didn't reflect the values they were expected to uphold.

Initially, the principal imagined creating a simple PowerPoint and sharing a few articles, just enough to onboard new staff each year. But when I interviewed twelve teachers, seven couldn't recall a single line from the mission. A few admitted, "I've seen it, but I've never really thought about how it connects to what I do." That disconnect gave us a design opportunity.

Instead of a static presentation, I proposed a self-paced onboarding course built in Articulate 360. I said, "If we want this mission to live in their teaching, we need to go beyond telling. We need to show them what it looks like and invite them to try it." We organized the course around key themes in the mission, using short videos of teachers modeling differentiated strategies, flashcards to reinforce instructional moves, and branching scenarios that asked teachers, What would you do here? Each section ended with a personal reflection prompt or a classroom action they could test the next day.

To deepen ownership, I collected classroom stories from veteran staff - small, honest wins. One teacher shared how shifting her groupings helped one student finally speak up in class. Another shared how using flexible assessments helped uncover strengths that the pacing guide missed. Embedding these real examples made the application of learning practical.

While the course was built with new hires in mind, veteran staff were invited to revisit it and reflect. Several teachers used it as a launchpad for conversations in their Personal Learning Communities. Two months later, the principal forwarded me an email he'd received from a first-year teacher. She wrote, "This was the first professional development that actually made the mission feel connected to my day-to-day. I used the reflection prompt about learning styles, and it made me realize I've been defaulting to one mode of instruction without meaning to." That kind of feedback mattered more than any certificate of completion.

What I learned was simple: don't design for information, design for application. If the goal is culture change, the course must help people see the gap, make meaning, and try something new. That's what turns training into transformation.

PRINCIPLES

Principle 1: Diagnose The Issue

Every year, billions of dollars are spent on professional development programs that yield little to no measurable change. Even though, as Beth McGoldrick noted, "Training isn't a magic bullet" (ATD, 2018), leaders often rush to prescribe training without pausing to diagnose the actual deficiency. When the problem persists, the blame falls on the instruction provided when very often it is the quality of the diagnosis that was faulty.

To lead through learning design, leaders must attend to three areas:

1. Needs Assessment: This is a process to determine the gap between current and desired results. It looks at performance, not preferences (Kaufman & Guerra-López, 2013).

2. Needs Analysis: This involves an exploration of root causes behind the identified gaps. It seeks to explain 'why' the gap exists.

3. Training Needs Assessment: This step is used only when training is verified as the solution (ATD, 2018).

Roger Kaufman (2015) reminds us that needs aren't just preferences or requests, they're measurable gaps in performance. Effective needs assessment clarifies what's missing, why it matters, and what will close the gap. He continues with the importance of digging into what's currently happening and what should be happening instead. The measurable gap in results must be documented with data and specificity.

When leaders skip this step, they risk solving the wrong problem or applying training to an issue that training alone can't fix. As Kaufman and Guerra-López (2013) put it bluntly, "If you skip the assessment, you risk solving the wrong problem."

According to the ATD Needs assessment whitepaper (2018), the most effective assessments begin with business goals and work backward. They ask: What outcomes matter? What capabilities enable them? And what's missing today? Tools like the Skills Gap Action Plan reinforce this backward-mapping process and connect strategic priorities with the knowledge, conditions, and behaviors required to execute them.

When determining needs, effective leaders begin with questions to analyze operations. Like a doctor, the prescription comes after a thorough evaluation and diagnosis. Only then will the remedy be successful.

Principle 2: Define the Need

The most effective leaders take the time to design well-developed questions that surface true deficiencies or inadequacies. In determining how to meet needs, the difference between a surface fix and a transformational solution often comes down to the quality of the inquiry. When leaders ask vague, rushed, or assumption-driven questions, they build solutions on shaky ground.

Asking better questions means going beyond simple checklists. The ATD (2018) encourages leaders to use structured categories:

What is the expected performance? What's actually happening? What are the barriers? What evidence supports this gap? These kinds of targeted questions not only sharpen diagnosis, they also build credibility and alignment across stakeholders.

From a learning design perspective, Shank (2015) adds that many learners in a workshop struggle to prioritize what must be learned deeply and what can simply be accessed later. Asking the right questions beforehand helps clarify what must be trained, what can be supported through tools, and what can be removed altogether.

To ensure precision in defining needs, consider these four levels (ATD, 2015):

1. Business Needs – What strategic goals are at risk? What metrics matter?

2. Performance Needs – What do people need to do better or differently?

3. Learning Needs – What knowledge, skills, or attitudes are missing?

4. Learner Needs – Who are the learners? What supports their growth?

Clarifying the gap is about precision. It's about explicitly defining what behavior, result, or system must change. It's not always individual or team performance. Sometimes the problem isn't a lack of skill but it's a lack of clarity in the process, or the lack of support to accomplish the task. Shank (2015) warns that many training initiatives fail because they ignore environmental or motivational contributors to performance. Leaders who skip this analysis often reach for training when the real fix is a tool, a resource, or a re-structured workflow. Shank reinforces this point by reiterating that training only works when the root cause of the problem is a skill gap. Many so-called training failures happen not because the session was poorly run, but because training wasn't the right solution to begin with. Sometimes the real issue is motivation, unclear roles, flawed systems, or inconsistent leadership. You can't train your way out of a structural problem.

Principle 3: Develop The Program

Once the real need is clear, the work of the instructional designer begins. Goals are translated into a learning experience that leads to growth. Training is built for outcomes and follow-up is embedded for retention and implementation of learning. But equally as important as the information to be presented is the method used to relay it.

Cognitive Load Theory (CLT), developed by John Sweller, explains how the brain processes and retains information during learning. It focuses on how to design instruction that matches how our brains naturally learn, especially when dealing with complex material. From Sweller, J., Ayres, P., & Kalyuga, S. (2011). Cognitive Load Theory. Sequencing for learning, a concept used effectively since the 17th century, is one of these important design strategies. It involves organizing content in a way that supports attention, retention, and real-world transfer. It guides learners from simple to complex, concrete to abstract, and known to unknown. It follows the way we naturally think and uses examples of cause and effect, whole to part, and step by step procedures. Poorly sequenced instruction overwhelms learners and increases confusion. Well-structured learning reduces cognitive load and supports deeper understanding (Allen, 2024).

Yet while 90% of instructional designers report prioritizing learner needs and context, far fewer apply consistent sequencing strategies (ATD, 2015). One proven model to follow is Gagné's Nine Events of Instruction. It provides a structured approach to effective teaching and learning and prompts the presenter to Gain attention, Inform learners of objectives, Stimulate recall of prior learning,

Present the content, Provide learning guidance, Elicit performance, Provide feedback, Assess performance, and Enhance retention and transfer.

The tradition of story telling has been a sequential learning approach to impart knowledge and wisdom for centuries in all cultures on earth. That's why Heath & Heath (2007) incorporate it into their SUCCESs model which outlines six principles to make ideas memorable, understandable, and impactful. The acronym stands for Simple – Strip the idea down to its core message; Unexpected – Capture attention by breaking patterns or surprising people; Concrete – Use clear, sensory details that people can easily grasp; Credible – Include trustworthy sources; Emotional – Help people care by tapping into feelings or values; Stories – Wrap ideas in narratives to inspire action and make them relatable.

Storytelling, simulations, and role play immerse learners in context-rich scenarios where they can safely engage for improvement (Khatib, 2025).

Merrill's First Principles of Instruction add more research-backed scaffolds for designing experiences that stick (Merrill, 2002). Merrill's First Principles of Instruction outline five core strategies that promote effective learning across disciplines: Problem-centered – Learning is most effective when centered around real-world problems or tasks; Activation – Learners build on prior knowledge and experiences; Demonstration – New content is shown through examples, models, or visuals; Application – Learners actively practice and apply what they've learned; and Integration – Learners reflect, discuss, or use new knowledge in meaningful ways.

Principle 4: Follow Through and Follow Up

Training proves its value when the learning endures through action. In addition to pertinent content and delivery, instruction with lasting impact demands active engagement, deliberate practice, and continuous evaluation. The Ebbinghaus Forgetting Curve shows that learners forget up to 75% of what they learn within six days unless reinforced (Glaveski, 2019). Consider an onboarding program that replaces traditional assessments with weekly challenges, journaling prompts, and peer coaching calls. Instead of tests, learners record short videos demonstrating the new skill in action. This makes learning visible, personal, and practical.

As Cole Nussbaumer Knaflic (2015) explains in *Storytelling with Data*, information only becomes useful when it can be retrieved under real-world pressure. That means learning out of context is not as valuable as practicing it where it will be used. Workday routines like team huddles, application challenges, and coaching check-ins create bridges between content and performance.

Consider a leadership development program that runs three live sessions over a month. Between sessions, participants complete weekly prompts, submit video reflections, engage in peer feedback, and apply tools in their teams. This structure builds momentum through consistent, incremental improvements that accumulate over time, leading to significant and self-sustaining growth.

Glaveski (2019) expounds further on the fact that timing of the training matters just as much as the format of it. Too often, we teach the right things at the wrong time. Instead of cramming everything into a single session, he recommends learning that is broken into digestible chunks, layered with micro-assessments, peer coaching, and active experimentation. "Lean learning" delivers micro-sequenced content in the flow of work, when learners need it most. Tipton (2023), also believes in reviewing and delivering key information in small, manageable chunks at increasing intervals over time to help build durable mental frameworks without overload. And both she and the Association for Talent Development (2024) reiterate the need to allow time for application of new knowledge between and after sessions. All of these plans for reminders, micro-challenges, peer reflections, and gradual integration of information into practice, must be built into the instructional design process from the beginning. Learning is less apt to fade when it is applied in context and reinforced over time.

Frameworks like the Kirkpatrick Model and Brinkerhoff's Success Case Method advocate continued engagement by evaluating the effectiveness of training programs according to the subsequent changes. The Kirkpatrick Model evaluates training according to participants responses, knowledge gained, applications demonstrated, and measurable impact on performance (Kirkpatrick & Kirkpatrick, 2006). Brinkerhoff's Success Case Method (SCM) focuses on interviewing to determine most and least successful instances of application after training. It provides a narrative of the real-world impact and how to improve future programs (Brinkerhoff, 2003).

Learning doesn't end when the workshop does. In fact, what happens after the session often determines whether learning is retained and applied, or forgotten.. Building for sustained impact means designing follow-through systems that embed learning into the flow of work.

FROM ONE LEADER TO ANOTHER

Shelly Reed

Senior Training Specialist
As heard on Othman's Leadership Podcast, Episode 24

Training Is Only One Piece of Real Change

Before Shelly Reed designs a single slide, she starts with questions, not content. "What specific behavior or performance gap are you seeing?" she asks stakeholders. "When did you first notice this issue? Have there been any recent changes in tools or processes or expectations?" Her goal is to get underneath the request to understand whether training is even the right solution. "They risk implementing a bandaid solution that addresses the symptoms rather than the root cause," she said. "Without really understanding the true problem, their efforts may fail to create a lasting impact." She's seen leaders misidentify training as the fix when "the real issue lies elsewhere... in process, in communication, or even in leadership."

To ensure her learning design drives clarity, Reed anchors everything in two evidence-based models: Mager's A-B-C-D approach for learning objectives and Gagné's Nine Events of Instruction. "Mager helps ensure clarity and alignment by specifying the audience, the behavior, the condition, and the degree," she explained. "It keeps objectives both measurable and meaningful." Once learning goals are defined, she applies Gagné's structure to guide learners from attention to retention. "It helps support cognitive processing... from gaining attention to providing feedback and overall retention strategies." Whether she's designing for live or virtual sessions, these two frameworks keep her focused on outcomes, not just activities.

One of Reed's most consistent strategies is to embed interaction into the learning itself. "One of my favorite ways to make learning stick is making it fun and interactive—especially through games." She frequently uses "game-based reviews like Jeopardy, poll questions, or scenario-based challenges" to reinforce key ideas and keep energy high. But it's not just competition, she designs for connection. "I collected each learner's favorite songs and made a Spotify playlist I'd play before sessions or during breaks... it was a unique way of building connections on a global level." Whether through music or movement, her sessions are crafted to invite participation. "Participants were more involved, asked better questions, and reported higher confidence using the system afterwards."

Another tool she integrates into her virtual sessions is screen-share walkthroughs paired with reflection. "I might have someone screen share and ask them, 'Show me how you'd create a meeting note,'" she explained. While learners demonstrate live, she tracks their actions against a checklist. Then she shifts to dialogue: "What are your pain points? How might you solve that or how might my team help?" The combination of practice and reflection creates space for both skill building and systems-level problem solving. "Presenting creative ways that engage learners in applying both knowledge and skill is absolutely necessary in my role."

At the heart of Reed's approach is a belief that training is just one piece of real change. "Real change doesn't come from a single training event. It comes from aligning learning with behavior, with culture, and also with accountability." Leaders, she believes, must reinforce learning actively: "Revisit the key takeaways in meetings, emails, one-on-ones... model the behaviors you want to see." She measures success through Kirkpatrick's Four Levels and tracks outcomes with rigor. But her core advice? Stay open. "If you continually are always working on improving the training you've got... you can't really go wrong."

STRATEGY IN A SKETCH

The ADDIE Model is a time-tested instructional design framework that helps leaders create effective learning experiences from start to finish. It guides you through five sequential stages and ensures that each step aligns with learners' real needs and measurable outcomes. A common mistake is skipping the analysis stage; don't do it! Rather than jumping straight to slide decks or training events, first ask: What is the performance gap? ADDIE will help you find it then improve it.

The ADDIE model

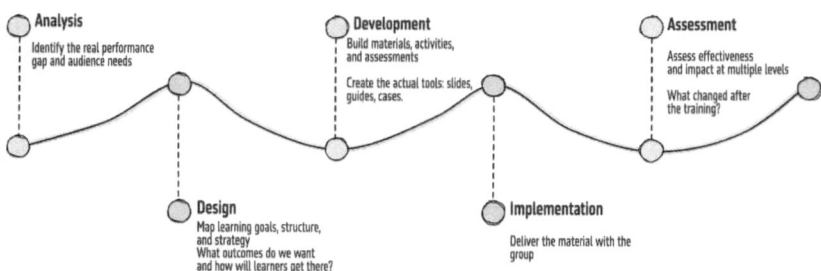

Analysis
Identify the real performance gap and audience needs

Development
Build materials, activities, and assessments
Create the actual tools: slides, guides, cases.

Assessment
Assess effectiveness and impact at multiple levels
What changed after the training?

Design
Map learning goals, structure, and strategy
What outcomes do we want and how will learners get there?

Implementation
Deliver the material with the group

Based on Branch's ADDIE instructional design model (2009).

MAKE IT YOURS

- What problem am I trying to solve?

- What would success look like?

- Are there non-training factors involved (processes, systems, leadership)?

- Is the performance issue due to lack of skill or something else?

- What instructional design models will I follow?

23

Lead by Hiring for Impact

How Do You Hire the Right Talent ?

> The secret of my success is that we have gone to exceptional lengths to hire the best people in the world.
>
> Steve Jobs

The Energy You Can't Miss

Rehab, a seasoned early childhood educator, saw something remarkable during her final days at her first center in Claremont, California. As she prepared to leave, her replacement, Alexandra, arrived. The plan was for Alexandra to shadow her for two weeks. That plan didn't last long, but for a good reason. By the second day, Alexandra was ready. Her energy filled the room. She connected with the kids right away, managed the classroom with care and confidence, and brought a spark that lifted everyone around her. Students were engaged, her teammates felt supported, and even the center's leadership took notice. It was clear that they hired the right candidate. She would continue Rehab's legacy of excellence and build on that momentum to drive further progress.

A few weeks later, Rehab moved to a different child care center. On paper, it had more to offer. They provided better pay, more time off, and attractive staff perks. But the energy? It was nowhere to be found. Each morning began with the same staff chorus: "I'm tired." "I can't wait to go home." One teacher, facing repeated conflicts, said out loud, "Why don't they just fire me?"

All of them had the right credentials. What they lacked was the mindset.

Rehab's takeaway was simple but powerful. A person's mindset and attitude eclipse their impressive resume. Alexandra had experience but more importantly, she had the drive, joy, and initiative that no credentials can promise. If you're leading a hiring process, those are the criteria you should prioritize.

PRINCIPLES

Principle 1: Hire for Mindset, Not Just Metrics

A résumé can tell you where someone has been, but it doesn't reveal their energy and initiative to lead, learn, or respond to change. Technical qualifications and experience may open the door, but they don't guarantee long-term impact. That's why great hiring decisions look beyond credentials. They focus on attitude and outlook. Who stretches under pressure? Who seeks feedback? Who takes initiative when the path isn't clear? These are the traits that do more than just fill the open position.

Laszlo Bock, former SVP of People Operations at Google, found that "role-related knowledge" was the least predictive factor of success in their hiring process. The more powerful predictors? Learning ability, leadership, and "Googleyness," a mix of curiosity, conscientiousness, and comfort with ambiguity (Bock, 2015). Similarly, Patrick Lencioni (2016) argues that ideal team players bring three traits: humility, hunger, and people smarts. These aren't skills you list, they're characteristics you live.

Mindset is how people interpret challenge, feedback, and opportunity. Carol Dweck's research reminds us that those with a growth mindset don't stop at what they know. They stretch, adapt, and take ownership. In contrast, resume-driven hires often wait to be told what to do and stay within the confines of a limited job description. Sullivan and Hardy (2020), in *Who Not How*, warns not to just hire people who know the "how," but it's critical to hire people who take responsibility for the "what." That shift from qualification in word to ownership in deed, is what future-ready hiring demands.

Here's the moment to watch for: You're interviewing two finalists. One has years of experience in the exact role. The other has transferable skills, asks thoughtful questions, and lights up when you describe the vision and mission. Instead of defaulting to the person who has "done it before," pause and ask: Who will grow with us? Who will challenge our team in a positive and productive way? Then go deeper. Ask, "Tell me about a time you failed and what you learned," or "What's a risk you took to support a colleague?" You're not fishing for perfect answers. You're listening for someone who can think critically, take ownership, and demonstrate excitement to be part of a winning team.

Hiring for mindset doesn't mean ignoring skills. It means seeing skills as the foundation and attitude as the multiplier. You're not just filling a position. You're shaping the culture. And that starts with who you invite in.

Principle 2: Your Culture Is Your Filter

Organizational culture isn't just a list of values on a poster. Good, bad, or indifferent, culture is created by what is tolerated, expected, and rewarded every day. When hiring, culture shouldn't be about matching personalities or preferences. It should be about aligning with the behaviors that make your team thrive. Culture becomes a filter that doesn't screen out differences, but funnels in people who can both uphold and enhance your shared commitments.

Patrick Lencioni (2016) shares how one construction company transformed performance by hiring strictly for modesty, initiative, and collaboration. The result? Lower turnover, stronger teamwork, and a culture that reinforced itself through every new hire. Laszlo Bock (2015) explains how Google does the same by anchoring hiring decisions in core values like inquisitiveness, mission orientation, and partnerships. Candidates are, of course, evaluated for competence, but equally important is their potential for contribution to the culture. One of Google's hiring mantras is simple: bring in only those who raise the bar.

Think of culture like a coral reef. It thrives when supported by a diverse mix of organisms that coexist through shared conditions. But it collapses when even a few toxic elements disrupt the balance. Hiring someone who undermines your values can erode the trust, safety, and momentum you've built. That's why strong cultures don't just attract the right people, they also protect against the wrong ones. It's not about a personality "fit." It's about value alignment and behavior integrity.

Define your non-negotiables. What do you absolutely need from every team member regardless of their role? For example: "We speak directly and respectfully." "We own our impact, not just our intention." "We learn in public." When your culture is clearly defined and consistently upheld, it becomes your most powerful hiring filter.

Principle 3: Delegate Outcomes, Not Tasks

The difference between a contributor and a leader often comes down to ownership. Great teams need people who take responsibility to accomplish tasks, but they also need people who take responsibility for results. Sullivan and Hardy (2020) emphasizes that effective leaders understand the value of those who are willing to take full ownership of outcomes and projects (Sullivan & Hardy, 2020). That mindset should start in the hiring process. Look for candidates who ask, "What's the goal?" not "What's next?"

Bock (2015) reinforces this idea of sharing accountability for results in *Work Rules!*. He encourages managers to give "slightly more trust, freedom, and authority than you're comfortable with." That discomfort is where growth happens. Micromanagement suffocates ownership. When you delegate outcomes, not just tasks, you give high performers space to think, adapt, and lead. You hire people not just to execute, but to elevate.

Imagine hiring a coordinator for a school-based tutoring program. A task-oriented candidate might want to know which tutors they should assign where? An outcome-oriented candidate would be more likely to inquire about what success would look like for students in the program and how it will be measured. To discover this mindset, the interviewer could ask: "Tell me about a time when you accomplished something without step by step directions. The way the candidate describes their role as a problem-solver or one who was upset by lack of instructions, reveals whether they'll be a driver or a dependent.

Your hiring lens changes when you're not just asking, "Can they do this job?" You're asking, "Will they own what comes out of it?" Outcome-oriented hires multiply your time and your impact.

FROM ONE LEADER TO ANOTHER

Adam Thomas

Principle at Approaching One
  As heard on Othman's Leadership Podcast, Episode TBD

Finds the One Who Surprises You

When Adam Thomas had only two weeks to replace a failed product manager and turn around a disastrous project, he knew his usual hiring instincts wouldn't be enough. "Everything had been a disaster when I first landed there... there was no product," he said. "The CEO was promising that we would release this product that fall." With no margin for error, Thomas made an unexpected move: "I looked at the world of gaming... people who work in gaming have to deal with delays, explain something new, and launch something unfamiliar." He found someone fast, and the result stunned the organization. "The product he launched was phenomenal... it blew everyone's socks off."

Thomas emphasizes the need to precede a job posting with a thoughtful hiring strategy. "Before you even start to formulate a job description... ask yourself, "In six months, if this person is killing it at the job, what have they accomplished?"" That single question, he believes, changes everything. "It crystallizes what makes your job special... it kicks off your entire process." Too many job descriptions, he warned, are "copypasta," copied from other templates and stripped of context. The result? "You get a lot of bad incoming." To avoid this, he helps teams specify outcomes as well as responsibilities. "No one ever hires because they just want to hire. Hiring represents a problem to be solved."

Once that clarity is in place, Adam uses story as a design tool. "When you have that super clear, you start telling yourself a story about that candidate." He encourages leaders to imagine the new hire's journey: "This is the story they should have in their heads... this is what they're going to accomplish... Here are some of the pitfalls they may or may not find themselves in." The story doesn't just coordinate the thoughts of the hiring team, it shapes the interview. "It makes it easy for them to see not just what type of person they want, but how to frame their own questions to get what they need from that candidate."

To uncover candidates who truly raise the bar, Thomas looks for two core traits: curiosity and accountability through failure. "If they can tell me a story about their failure, it signals they're open to learning." But it's not just about surviving mistakes, it's about integrating them. "Failure doesn't stop them. That failure enhances or pushes forward their curiosity." These behaviors, he says, are contagious. "They're raising the bar not just for themselves but also for those around them." His ideal interviews are designed to bring these qualities to the surface. "I like to limit it to three questions," Thomas said. "That allows for follow-up questions... and creates an opportunity for a two-way conversation." He usually designs a 3 to 4 stage process: a short phone screen, peer interviews both inside and outside the candidate's function, and finally a "workshop" or "wargame" exercise. "I sit you down with the whiteboard... we work out through a wargaming exercise how you would behave." Why? "It doesn't take a lot of time, allows us to see how someone thinks, and we can score it quickly." What he watches for is surprise. "Great hires take you for a loop. They make you see something you didn't see. They can cause people to go, 'Oh, they didn't make me comfortable.'" He remembers one candidate with a PhD in astrophysics. "She was brilliant but scared people," he said. But those candidates, "to a person, turned out to be amazing hires."

For Thomas, hiring impact players is also about designing conditions where those hires thrive. "Great onboarding processes... put the right amount of people around this person so they feel confident... to bring their full selves." Leaders who want to keep top talent, he said, must move out of their comfort zones, also. "This is not your last job. How do you want to grow?" It's a conversation he has with every team member. "As a leader... it is critical that you do this. You need to understand your team and your organization enough to create opportunities that fit their roles and responsibilities." Hiring for the right mindset, cultural fit, and outcome are a two-way street.

STRATEGY IN A SKETCH

The "Culture Add vs. Culture Fit" framework challenges leaders to shift their hiring lens from sameness to stretch. Rather than asking, "Will this person blend in?" it pushes us to consider, "Will this person expand who we are becoming?" Culture Add focuses on the strategic inclusion of hiring people who bring different experiences, identities, or approaches that challenge our thinking in constructive ways. The risk of over-prioritizing fit is that you protect comfort but sacrifice growth. The power of this model lies in its ability to future-proof your team by hiring for who you want to become, not just who you've been.

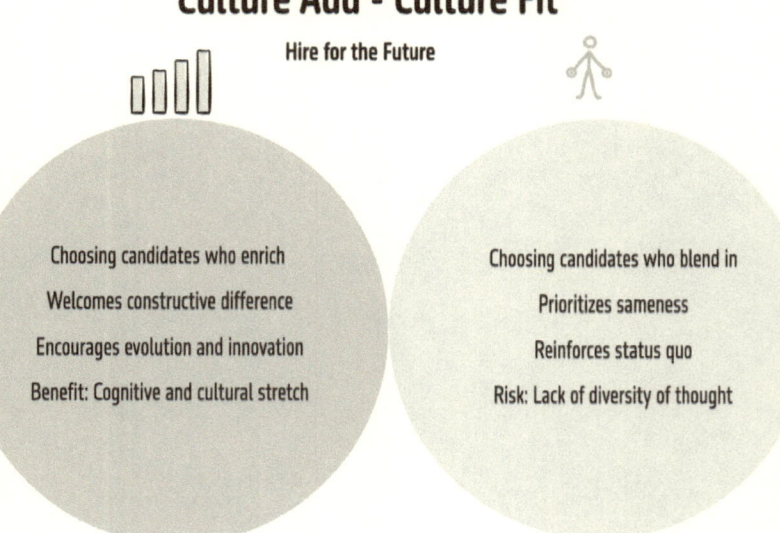

Culture Add - Culture Fit

Hire for the Future

Choosing candidates who enrich

Welcomes constructive difference

Encourages evolution and innovation

Benefit: Cognitive and cultural stretch

Choosing candidates who blend in

Prioritizes sameness

Reinforces status quo

Risk: Lack of diversity of thought

Based on Travis and Nielsen's argument for "culture add" over "culture fit" in Harvard Business Review (2016).

MAKE IT YOURS

- Do I need staff who maintain the status quo, or those who challenge it constructively?

- What mindset will position our future team to drive the organization's long-term success?

- Am I willing to prioritize potential and attitude over credentials when considering who will best advance our organization's mission?

Part Three

INNOVATE

Uncover how leaders design, adapt, measure, and reimagine their organizations to navigate change and drive sustainable progress.

24

Innovate Through Design Thinking

Can You Build To Meet Real Needs?

Organizations that foster a strong design thinking culture see a 56% higher return on investment (ROI) and 75% increased customer loyalty.

IBM Institute

Hope Is Something You Can Design

I (Reda) still remember the father's voice, firm but trembling, when he pulled me aside after a school event. He looked me in the eyes and said, "I just want my daughter to go to college. That's why we came here. That's what I was hoping for in this country, an opportunity." He wasn't asking for special treatment. He wasn't even asking for help. He was expressing a quiet, almost fragile hope that this new beginning in America could lead his children somewhere safe, somewhere possible.

I was working as a refugee family liaison for Springfield Public Schools, supporting students who had recently arrived from conflict zones in Iraq, Jordan, and Syria. Many of them had missed years of school. Some 10th and 11th graders hadn't been in a classroom since they were in 3rd or 4th grade. Some had never stepped foot in a formal school at all. From an academic lens, the challenge was staggering. But what struck me most wasn't the lack of background knowledge or the gaps in reading. It was the silence. The distance. The way they sat through the school day like guests at a table where they weren't sure if they were welcome.

I spent the first few weeks listening to the students, the parents, the teachers, and sometimes to myself. They shared stories of growing up in refugee camps, where school was a luxury, not a guarantee. I heard about long winters without electricity. About siblings lost. About starting over, again and again. One student told me, "I'm not smart like American kids." Another asked, "How can I go to college if I don't even understand what this country is all about?"

The more I listened, the clearer it became. This wasn't a problem I could solve with tutoring or translated handouts. The students didn't just need academic support. They needed to see something they couldn't yet imagine. They needed a vision of what their life could look like in the future.

So I started small. I launched an afterschool club as a space for connection. I invited guests that included teachers, school leaders, and community members who could speak to their experience. I wanted the students to see that there were adults who cared, who noticed, and who believed they belonged. But still, I sensed something was missing. That's when the idea came to me. What if we left the school altogether?

I organized two field trips. The first was to the University of Massachusetts Amherst. I reached out to a student club on campus and asked if they would host us. They didn't hesitate. When my students arrived, they were greeted in their own language, given a campus tour by undergraduate and graduate students who understood their story. Some had also arrived in the U.S. as immigrants or refugees. Many had struggled to adjust. But they had made it. They were thriving.

The second trip was even more ambitious. We went to Yale University. I knew it might seem out of reach, but I wanted these students to step foot somewhere elite. I wanted them to feel the gravity of possibility. When we arrived, I watched them take in the architecture, the lecture halls, the students rushing by with backpacks and coffee. They didn't look out of place. They looked curious. They looked inspired. And that's when everything shifted.

That spring, four seniors applied to college, more than any year prior. Two were admitted to UMass Amherst. Another built up the courage to apply to Ivy League schools. And years later, one student who went on to become a dentist reached out to me. "That trip," he said, "was the first time I believed I could be someone."

What I learned in that role reshaped how I see leadership. When we design solutions based only on the surface-level problems, academic gaps, low test scores, attendance, we miss the real barriers. The deeper need wasn't tutoring. It was a sense of belonging and vision of a hopeful future. And that's what design thinking is about. Not guessing what people need. Not offering what's most efficient. But listening, learning, and creating experiences, systems, and products that meet real needs for real people.

PRINCIPLES

Principle 1: Walk in Their Shoes

The most meaningful solutions emerge when teams take on the perspectives of the people they're designing for. Although empathy may not be a common term in workplace vocabulary, it is a critical practice that shifts focus from solving temporary problems to creating improved experiences.

Leonard and Rayport (1997) coined the term empathic design to describe how innovation often begins when we observe what users do, not just what they say. They point out that people frequently adapt to flawed systems without recognizing the need for change, often rationalizing issues instead of identifying them. Studying behavior in natural settings can uncover workarounds, emotional signals, and friction points that traditional interviews may overlook.

Jack O'Donoghue (n.d.) offers a range of practical tools that extract what others are encountering: user shadowing, contextual inquiry, diary studies, journey maps, and storytelling. These approaches help teams stay immersed in the realities of those they serve. They synthesize data and become touchpoints for reflection as teams identify critical needs.

Knapp, Zeratsky, and Kowitz's (2016) *Sprint* model supports perspective-taking by grounding work in user needs, beginning with gathering expert insights and mapping the problem from the user's point of view. Throughout the process, from sketching solutions to testing prototypes with real users, teams are encouraged to step outside their own assumptions and design based on how others experience the problem. This structured approach ensures that decisions are driven by empathy and direct user feedback, not internal bias.

A classroom example illustrates what this looks like in action. In an IDEO (2012) project, a second-grade teacher talked with students as he physically lowered his own viewpoint to match theirs. He learned that bulletin boards were too high for them to see and cubby areas felt crowded and too unorganized to even try to keep neat. After redesigning the space based on their feedback, he saw a shift in both engagement and ownership. The improvement wasn't about new tools. It was about changing the current setting to match the perspective of the users.

To lead with empathy is to see challenges through the eyes of those most affected. It requires spending time in the environments where the real work and real struggle take place. When leaders commit to observing, listening, and learning with intention, they uncover the true nature of the problem. And in doing so, they design solutions that are not only effective, but grounded in respect, relevance, and real need.

Principle 2: Frame the Picture Correctly

Framing the right problem takes diagnostic empathy to the next level. It is the cornerstone of meaningful innovation. Too often, teams rush to solve the most visible issue, only to realize they've missed the deeper challenge. In design thinking, reframing is an intentional act that requires a disciplined pause to ensure efforts address root causes, not just symptoms.

Tim Brown (2009) explains that in design thinking, "The best designers don't just solve problems, they redefine them." This requires an uncommon but purposeful interlude to immerse in user experiences, identify hidden tensions, and look for signals beneath the surface. Leaders who frame challenges too narrowly risk building elegant solutions to irrelevant problems.

Berger (2014) adds that breakthrough solutions often come from asking a better "Why?" before moving to "How?" When teams learn to question the framing of the problem itself, they open the door to deeper impact.

A real-world example comes from the Stanford d.school's Neonatal Incubator Project. Initially, the challenge was framed as: "How can we make hospital incubators more affordable?" But fieldwork in rural Nepal revealed the true need. By reframing the challenge to find out why incubators were not helping babies, they could then ask, "How might we keep newborns warm in rural areas?" Mobility was the key. The team designed the Embrace infant warmer, a low-cost, portable solution that directly addressed the real barrier (Brown, 2009).

Put this principle into practice. Have different team members write the problem statement three different ways. One version should be based on currently held beliefs, one based on user observations and input, and one that flips the lens entirely (e.g., from teacher-centered to student-centered). Share them to determine the best next steps.

Principle 3: Ask Bold Questions That Challenge the Status Quo

Design thinking is a human-centered approach to problem-solving, and asking questions is at the heart of it. In fact, the quality of the questions you ask often determines the quality of the insights and solutions you uncover. These questions should disrupt inertia, uncover blind spots, and open the door to more meaningful solutions. They're not a brainstorming warm-up, they're a way to surface assumptions that have gone unquestioned for too long.

Berger (2014) describes these as "beautiful questions" that are ambitious, actionable, and designed to challenge what's always been. He believes that discernment often comes when we adopt a beginner's mind and use observations, not assumptions, to spur inquiry. Leaders who ask, "Why do we do it this way?" or "What would happen if we did the opposite?" often discover that many self-imposed constraints are lifted.

Edmondson (2012), in *Teaming*, adds that learning organizations rely on environments where it's safe to question norms. She explains that innovation requires people who are willing to name doubts, challenge the group's thinking, and test new directions. Silence, she warns, is not neutrality but a barrier to growth.

Knapp, Zeratsky, and Kowitz's *Sprint* model (2016) demonstrates how the use of effective questioning can move an organization from stagnant status quo to meaningful transformation. On Day 1, teams are asked to identify "sprint questions." These are challenging, thought-provoking questions that push against preconceived notions which have shaped their thinking. The goal is to uncover hidden assumptions and probe deeply with genuine curiosity to reach the heart of the problem.

One example comes from Hawaii's public school system, where a district team shifted the conversation from "How can we raise test scores?" to "Why are students disengaged?" That single question changed everything. Instead of layering on more interventions, they co-designed entirely new learning models grounded in student and community voice (IDEO, 2012). It didn't just improve performance. It reshaped the purpose of school.

Asking bold questions isn't about being provocative. It's about being honest. It's what happens when leaders care enough to disrupt what no longer serves and are brave enough to imagine what could.

Principle 4: Prototype Before Launch

Building prototypes is another way to truly understand and meet needs. Prototypes create a simple, testable version of an idea, product, or solution. They allow a test group of intended users to try out the product or idea before it is officially introduced to all. This allows teams to gather feedback and respond to problems while still in the design stages.

Brown (2009) stresses that prototyping and testing are essential tools for reducing risk. They are not tools for validating certainty. "Prototypes should be created early and often," he writes, "not to perfect an idea but to learn about it." Even rough, incomplete versions built on whiteboards, paper, or slides spark insights that can't be accessed through discussion alone.

Ash Maurya (2012) in *Running Lean*, encourages leaders to replace the question, "Will it work?", with, "What am I trying to learn?" The experimentation becomes a pathway to insight.

Knapp, Zeratsky, and Kowitz (2016) offers a structure for this learning loop. In addition to the steps mentioned above, teams build a testable version of their idea. Then they observe real users interacting with this prototype. Watching users struggle, ask questions, or ignore features often reveals more than months of planning. Maurya concludes that you must "validate before you build." If your solution can't survive early contact with users, it should be rethought and redesigned.

One powerful example came from a health records application team that launched a clickable prototype. Within hours, user testing revealed that people couldn't find the core navigation feature. That feedback saved the team from investing months into a flawed interface. Similarly, in IDEO's design work with clinics, a prototype for a new patient intake form was tested directly with nurses. One confusing question led to rewording and layout changes, small refinements that led to clearer, more accurate responses (IDEO, 2012).

Prototypes offer a practical way to test strategies, programs, or communication tools before full implementation. By piloting an early example with a small group that represents the intended audience, teams can gather meaningful feedback and make informed adjustments, thereby leading to more effective and well-received outcomes.

Principle 5: Choose Your Team

Innovation isn't the product of one person with a whiteboard. It's the outcome of diverse minds working side by side, each holding a different part of the problem, each contributing something others can't see by themselves. "Design is a team sport" means that the process is richer, faster, and more honest when collaboration is built in from the start.

Brown (2009) describes design thinking as a deeply collaborative process, rooted in cross-functional teams. He emphasizes that innovation is stronger when people from different disciplines share ownership of the work. This mix of perspectives prevents narrow solutions and brings lived experience into the design room. It's not individual brilliance but constructive variance that sharpens good ideas.

Edmondson (2012) expands on this in her research on teaming. Unlike traditional teams with fixed roles and structures, teaming happens dynamically. People come together quickly, across departments or roles, to solve problems in fast-changing environments. She highlights that real teaming requires psychological safety, humility, and a willingness to learn from others.

Once again, Knapp, Zeratsky, and Kowitz (2016) shows what this looks like in practice. Each sprint brings together a decider, designer, user expert, and strategist who work side by side for five days. The sprint compresses hierarchy and expands contribution. Long committee meetings are replaced by focused collaboration with equal voices and shared purpose.

A real-world example comes from IDEO's education design work in Maryland. A team of educators co-designed curriculum with parents, students, and community members to reflect their school's lived experiences. The result was stronger materials and a stronger school community. When people collaborate to co-create solutions, they're more likely to believe in and sustain them (IDEO, 2012).

The importance of collaboration can't be overstated. Building a diverse design team that includes voices from across roles and experiences, leads to more thoughtful, inclusive solutions. Whether redesigning a schedule or launching a new support system, the act of designing together invites deeper understanding, creativity, and shared ownership.

FROM ONE LEADER TO ANOTHER

Dr. Carol Birks

Superintendent of Allentown School District and Recognized National Education Leader

As heard on Othman's Leadership Podcast, Episode 40

We Cannot Design from Our Desks—We Have to Be in the Community

When Dr. Carol Birks became Superintendent of Allentown School District, she entered a system deeply rooted in history and hope, but burdened by distrust from years of top-down decisions. She knew her first move wasn't to roll out initiatives, but rather to listen. "We conducted listening tours, held town halls, met with elected officials, parents, and students. We asked: 'What's going well? What do we need? What should we stop doing?'" Over 9,000 community members responded. One visible result? Students successfully advocated to eliminate a district-wide uniform policy, a move that symbolized that their voices mattered. "It was about them seeing themselves reflected in the decisions," she said.

Rather than rely on surveys alone, Dr. Birks designed multiple human-centered touchpoints like Coffee with Birks and Real Talk with Birks, where every staff member had access to open dialogue. "We needed to re-humanize leadership," she said. "Teachers, clerical staff, everyone deserves a seat at the table." These routines became embedded rituals where people shared real feedback and helped shape direction. Birks didn't just practice listening. She practiced what she called "Level 3 Listening," a skill honed during executive coaching training. "You listen for not just what is said, but for values, pain points, and possibility. That's how you design from trust."

One of the most strategic co-design efforts she led was the development of a district-wide vision and strategic plan. This was not created by consultants, but by the community itself. "We didn't just tell people what we were going to do, we built it together," she said. More than 100 stakeholders, including board members, students, and families, co-created that roadmap. "They now feel ownership because they helped shape it," she reflected. That buy-in laid the foundation for long-term sustainability. "The work has continued, even as we've taken on more challenges, because the foundation is ours, not mine."

And the results of that empathy-led innovation have been tangible. Under Birks' leadership, Allentown opened the first public dual-language immersion school in the county, launched school quality reviews to identify equity gaps and realign resources, and restructured the system into Network Improvement Communities to support continuous learning across schools. "We found one school had 50 more positions than another that actually had greater needs," she said. "So we made the hard decision to rebalance. That's what equity looks like in action." Her district also earned national partnerships with Digital Promise and Verizon Innovative Learning

Schools, providing 24/7 connectivity and digital tools that opened doors for innovation, creativity, and student voice.

Dr. Birks reminds us that innovation doesn't start with ideas, it starts with inclusion. "You don't innovate in isolation. You innovate by standing in the shoes of those you serve," she said. Her story is a blueprint for empathy in action: if you want lasting change, co-create it with the people who will carry it forward.

STRATEGY IN A SKETCH

Design Thinking helps leaders shift from solving the wrong problem quickly to solving the right problem empathetically and effectively. It guides teams through five phases that concentrate on real human needs. This approach is especially powerful when traditional top-down solutions fall flat, and when leaders want to co-create with the end users. The magic of this framework lies in how it slows the impulse to fix and sharpens the ability to notice what matters.

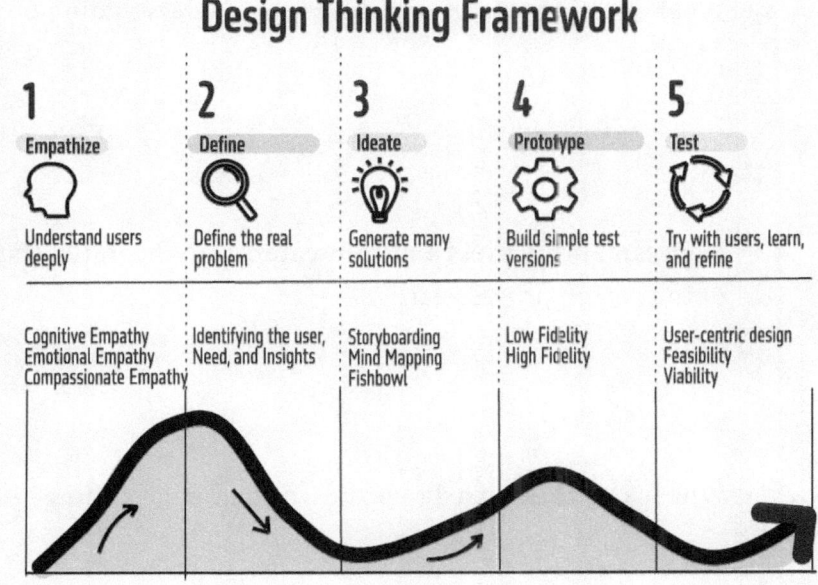

Based on Tim Brown's framework in Change by Design (2009).

MAKE IT YOURS

- How can I incorporate observation into needs analysis?

- What assumptions are built into our solutions?

- What questions could reveal a deeper understanding of the problem?

- How can I bring users and co-creators into the initial stages of the design process earlier?

- What's one idea I need to prototype before launching?

25

Innovate Through Evaluation

Can You Prove the Value You Deliver?

You need a goal that's both inspiring and concrete—aspirational so it motivates, but quantifiab:e so you know when you've arrived.

Christina Wodtke

The District-Wide Rollout That Almost Fell Flat

It was a large urban district with a clear goal: implement a new, system-wide practice that would support student growth across every classroom in every school. The training rollout was impressive with hundreds of teachers trained, slide decks delivered, and all boxes checked on the implementation list. At first glance, the district was ready to celebrate. The post-training report showed 95% of teachers had completed the modules, and survey responses were "mostly positive." But something felt off.

I was in a leadership role at the time, watching closely. I noticed something small but telling. In the "additional comments" section of the post-survey, where most people usually leave it blank, a handful of teachers had taken time to write notes. One wrote, "I've been using these strategies for years so it's not clear how this training helps me grow." Another said, "There was no space to practice. Just theory and slides." These could've been interpreted simply as complaints but when we looked deeper, we realized that the schools reporting the strongest implementation weren't doing it because of the training. These were veteran teachers who had brought their practices with them from their previous districts and had been teaching this way for years, so of course they were implementing the program successfully and with fidelity. It had nothing to do with the training. And the other respondent represented a group that needed more than what was provided. The assumptions were flawed and therefore, the evaluations were incomplete and inadequate.

That's when something powerful happened. At a districtwide leadership meeting, the superintendent boldly stood and named the problem, "Completion doesn't equal impact. We said we were building skills, but we only measured attendance. That's on us."

From there, everything shifted. The team began building better feedback loops with quick check-ins, focus groups, and classroom visits. Instead of tracking compliance, they started measuring teacher confidence, student engagement, and how often the new strategies showed up in real conversations. The story of impact began to change, not because the training suddenly improved, but because the evaluation finally asked the right questions and measured the important criteria.

PRINCIPLES

Principle 1: To Measure Success You Need To Know What It Looks Like

The goal of evaluation is to measure success. But you first need to know what success looks like. Too often, organizations launch programs, initiatives, or training and much later, scramble for data to justify their initiatives. They don't even know what "good" equates to, so how can they measure it? The foundation of strong evaluation is a shared definition of success that is clear, measurable, and mission-aligned. According to the Association for Talent Development, organizations that consistently measure whether objectives are met, and use evaluation to identify areas for improvement, outperform those that don't. Yet fewer than half collect data on business impact, not because it doesn't matter, but because it wasn't defined at the start.

This is where the W.K. Kellogg Foundation's Logic Model becomes essential (W.K. Kellogg Foundation, 2004). A logic model is a planning tool that helps leaders connect their inputs, activities, and outputs to the desired short, medium, and long-term outcomes. By mapping the intended change process before launching an initiative, teams create alignment across purpose, actions, and evidence. When used early, the model becomes a shared language that clarifies where you're going and how you'll know when you get there.

This principle also follows the first of the four disciplines of execution mentioned in the book by the same name. Step one is to define a Wildly Important Goal (WIG). As McChesney, Covey, and Huling (2022) write, WIGs help organizations "narrow the focus" to what matters most and measure from there. Framed as "from X to Y by when," a WIG forces clarity and accountability. The same logic applies in evaluation. If you want meaningful metrics, start with meaningful goals. Here's how to apply it:

1. Ask the Right Question First: "What change are we trying to make, and for whom?"

2. Sketch a Simple Logic Chain: What resources are we investing? What activities will happen? What short and long-term outcomes should follow?

3. Align Early: Before a project launches, gather stakeholders to agree on success indicators that are both qualitative and quantitative.

Defining success provides something to evaluate. Evaluation provides the insight needed to measure progress and inform strategic adjustments.

Principle 2: Use Both Quantitative and Qualitative Metrics

Not everything that can be counted counts, and not everything that counts can be counted. Effective evaluation isn't about choosing between numbers and narratives. It's about using both to see the whole picture. Quantitative data shows scale, trend, and alignment. Quantitative metrics like completion rates, test scores, or Return On Investment, offer the hard data leaders crave. But without the context of qualitative insight like focus group stories, interviews, or observational notes, the data can feel hollow or misleading. Qualitative data reveals experience, belief, and meaning. The Association for Talent Development reports that while most organizations track qualitative measures like participation and satisfaction, few gather data on behavior change or performance impact. High-performing organizations, on the other hand, were more likely to integrate interviews and individual productivity measures for a complete perspective.

Eric Ries, the author of *The Lean Startup* (2011), popularized the phrase, "vanity metrics", a term now used widely. Vanity metrics make you feel good. Actionable metrics tell you what to do next. That's why data collection must always begin with the question: What decision will this help us make? Without a clear link to action, even the most sophisticated measurement tools fall flat.

Ash Maurya (2012), also warns against "vanity metrics," data that looks good but offers no insight. He promotes a "Lean" evaluation that requires both exploratory (qualitative) and reporting (quantitative) data to validate assumptions and guide improvement.

This balance is codified in the Kirkpatrick Four-Level Evaluation Model (Kirkpatrick & Kirkpatrick, 2006), which calls for four levels of assessment:

- Level 1: Reaction (e.g., surveys, interviews),

- Level 2: Learning (e.g., tests, self-assessments),

- Level 3: Behavior (e.g., observations, manager feedback),

- Level 4: Results (e.g., retention, impact metrics)

At every level, a combination of metrics strengthens accuracy and actionability. Level 3, for example, often relies on qualitative feedback to explain whether, and why, behavior change occurred after training.

When evaluation includes both cognitive and emotional data, it generates meaningful insight. Effective evaluations go beyond measuring actions to explore outcomes such as application, reflection, and mindset shifts. By examining what participants took away, how they applied their learning, and what perspectives changed, organizations can uncover the deeper impact that spreadsheets alone may not reveal.

Principle 3: Incorporate Metrics into Movement

Evaluation is only one step. Real improvement comes from applying what the evaluation reveals. Too often, leaders gather data that looks good in a report but has no bearing on what actually gets better. Whether you're launching a district-wide initiative or refining a leadership program, impact isn't measured by what you collected, it's measured by what you changed. That shift requires building a system where data moves, informs, and reshapes decisions in real time.

In 2013, authors Croll and Yoskovitz gave us a blueprint for embedded measurements for action.

First, map out where feedback will be gathered along the way, not just at the end. Second, focus your metrics on movement and track implementation and improvement, not just attendance or satisfaction. Third, build in a process to act on what you learn and create regular check-in points where teams review insights and make adjustments in real time. Feedback becomes a loop instead of a line.

In a later publication, the same authors expand on the concept of actionable metrics by recommending a triangulation approach to build the system before the initiative begins. Start with questions:

- What are we trying to improve—and how will we know?

- Which numbers reflect progress—and which voices explain it?

- Where might we be over-relying on one lens?

Then, intentionally map data collection according to the Kirkpatrick Four-Level Evaluation Model (Kirkpatrick & Kirkpatrick, 2006). For example: after professional learning, send a short reaction survey (Level 1) and hold a focus group. Next, embed skill checks or reflective journals to assess learning (Level 2). After that, use peer observation or coaching notes to track behavior shifts (Level 3). And finally, measure downstream results (Level 4) through attendance, engagement, or student performance.

This principle is also about building smarter metrics. The Kirkpatrick Model reminds us to move beyond Level 1 satisfaction scores, which reveal opinions and not outcomes. The real value lies in Level 3 and 4 data. Are learners applying what they learned? Is performance improving? According to Brynjolfsson and McElheran (2016), organizations that embed feedback into decision-making processes consistently outperform their peers in innovation and productivity. The data becomes a steering wheel, not a rearview mirror.

Peter Drucker once wrote, "Planning is not an event. It is the continuous process of strengthening what works and abandoning what does not... through systematic feedback" (Drucker, 2008). It's a warning against static metrics and a call to embed evaluation into the rhythm of how learning happens. This idea is reinforced by the ATD 2025 report, which found that high-performing organizations integrate multiple feedback sources throughout the learning cycle, not just at the end. Timely data allows for mid-course corrections rather than postmortem regrets.

Done right, evaluation becomes evidence for adaptation, execution, and successful outcomes.

Principle 4: Communicate the Value You Create

High-impact leadership and learning initiatives don't just deliver results and make those results visible. Yet in many organizations, value goes unnoticed simply because it isn't communicated clearly, consistently, or compellingly. To maximize influence, leaders must go beyond measurement to translate data into a story that stakeholders understand, trust, and act on.

Peter Drucker argue that true organizational success is reflected in "changed lives and changed conditions." (Drucker, 2008). But unless those changes are framed in a way that resonates with investors, executives, or frontline teams, the impact may be missed entirely. Communicating value involves more than sharing numbers. It must include professional "storytelling," audience awareness, and strategic framing.

ATD's 2025 report on evaluating learning reveals the communication gap. Only 30% of organizations report using learning data to inform business decisions, and just 25% effectively share impact with external stakeholders. High-performing organizations do it differently. They use dashboards, scorecards, and tailored briefings to make data accessible and actionable for leaders while also celebrating wins with learners and teams.

Wodtke (2016) emphasizes the motivational power of transparency. OKRs and team scoreboards track outcomes, but as importantly, they help people stay connected to purpose. When individuals see how their efforts contribute to larger goals, engagement deepens.

To communicate value effectively:

1. Tailor the message to the audience, whether it's a board member, a learner, or a department lead.

2. Share before and after snapshots to reveal growth or change.

3. Use visuals like dashboards, infographics, and charts to simplify and highlight meaning.

4. Tell stories that humanize the numbers and bring your impact to life.

When others can see the difference you make, and understand how you make it, they're more likely to support, invest in, and advocate for your work.

FROM ONE LEADER TO ANOTHER

Dr. Alaina Szlachta

Academic-turned-entrepreneur | Author of Measurement and Evaluation on a Shoestring
   As heard on Othman's Leadership Podcast, Episode 42

Measure What Matters

When Dr. Alaina Szlachta thinks about the challenges of measuring impact in schools, she starts with a deficit. "What's the problem you're trying to solve?" she asks. "If you're implementing a new curriculum or training, there's probably some gap… something that's happening that we don't want to be happening." She used the example of implementing the Responsive Classroom framework to support social-emotional growth and academic engagement. But instead of jumping to results, she invites leaders to get curious about the domino effect. "What's the first thing that needs to change before the larger deficit improves?" That upstream indicator, the thing most likely to move the needle, is what leaders must learn to track.

Most new programs in schools launch with good intentions but not always with clear evidence to support the initiative. "The question of measuring impact… it's not a one-size-fits-all," said Szlachta. A common mistake? Starting with the solution instead of the problem. "If you want to know what success looks like, it's really a full-circle feedback loop. The reason we brought this curriculum in is because we discovered this consistent deficit." She urges leaders to focus on what keeps them up at night. "Go ask your superintendent, 'what are the biggest deficits that you're worried about right now?' That's the data that we want to look at." The deficit isn't just a statistic, it's the north star that defines whether your efforts are working or wasting time and resources.

Before you roll out a new curriculum or program, identify the core problem it's meant to solve. "What's the gap that we're trying to solve for? What's the deficit? What's the problem?" Szlachta asked. "There's probably going to be data that superintendents and principals are looking at... a consistent deficit in our student population or something with teacher performance." That clarity transforms wishful thinking into measurable action. "The curriculum or initiative is only worth doing if there's a real deficit and you believe the solution can realistically fill it." She emphasized the need to ground decisions in evidence, not hope. "Make sure whatever the curriculum or the initiative is... evidence-based. It's not just that somebody has a hunch, because sometimes those hunches can be very expensive."

Once implementation begins, monitor who's showing up and how. "We look at completion and participation rates. The teachers are obviously having to facilitate the curriculum. Are they doing it in the way that we expect? Are the students participating?" These early indicators matter because "if people aren't engaging in the initiative, well then there's no change." In event-based learning like professional development sessions or keynotes, engagement is often the best data available. "Sometimes what we want to accomplish is simply to make people feel good... to give them new ideas or help them think differently." Whether the format is training, curriculum, or coaching, "you've got to be honest; what can we realistically accomplish in one hour, or two hours?"

Between participation and long-term change, there's often a quieter signal, a growth indicator that reveals if progress is happening. "Think of it like a domino," Szlachta explained. "We know the deficit... but what's the thing that evolves on the way to that long-term deficit hopefully being improved?" For example, when evaluating an Social Emotional Learning (SEL) curriculum, she advises identifying "an indicator that we want to monitor, like an SEL score. We evaluate our youth before the curriculum rolls out, then track those scores at the beginning, middle, and end of the school year." This middle metric helps leaders adjust in real time. "If we're not seeing a change in that growth indicator, then we know that the deficit won't change."

Even the best initiative fails when it's not delivered as intended. That's where fidelity comes in. "We also have to track our teachers... are they implementing it in the way in which the designers want them to?" She warned that too many leaders overlook this. "If they're deviating from it, then we can't say for certain that it was the curriculum that made the difference." Fidelity must be measured, not assumed. "You literally have a fidelity score, it's 100%, it's 50%, and the challenge is figuring out how do we measure that?" Whether through spot checks, debriefs, or rubrics, leaders need to protect the integrity of the design if they want reliable outcomes.

What Szlachta wants K–12 leaders to remember is that evaluation must become a routine part of the program. "Most people don't do it because we don't have the muscles. We lack the practice." Her advice? Start now. "Use your personal life as a sandbox. Measure something small. Build the habit." More than anything, she hopes leaders will stop chasing quick wins and start asking better questions. "Don't ask, 'what do we want to accomplish?' Ask, 'what's the deficit? Where do we lack support?'" Because in the end, she says, "It's not about proving value just to justify the spend, it's about learning what works so you can actually serve your students better."

STRATEGY IN A SKETCH

Kirkpatrick's model equips leaders to evaluate more than just impressions. It helps you track the ripple effect of any initiative that's meant to change practice. The framework guides you through four levels: participants' initial reactions, what they actually learned, how their behavior shifts over time, and the real-world results that follow. It works for training, curriculum rollouts, SEL programs, and anything where you're asking people to think or act differently. The model's power lies in how it reframes success. Many leaders stop at surface feedback and assume that high attendance or positive comments equate to impact. But real value lives further up the pyramid where learning leads to lasting behavior.

Kirkpatrick's Four Levels of Evaluation

The model outlines four sequential levels for evaluating training or leadership development initiatives from surface reaction to measurable results. Each level builds upon the previous one.

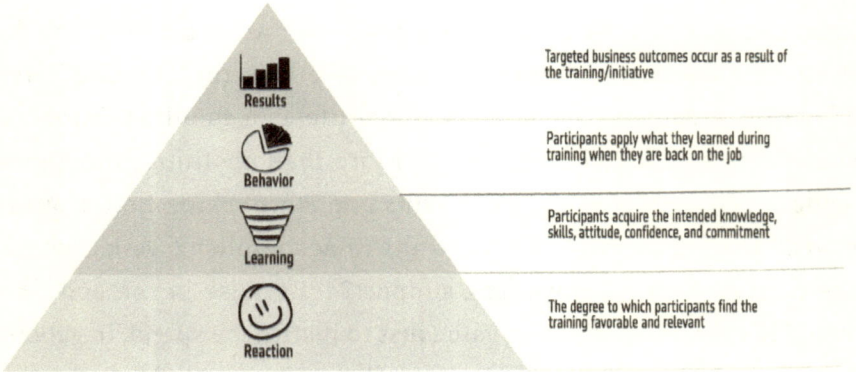

Results — Targeted business outcomes occur as a result of the training/initiative

Behavior — Participants apply what they learned during training when they are back on the job

Learning — Participants acquire the intended knowledge, skills, attitude, confidence, and commitment

Reaction — The degree to which participants find the training favorable and relevant

Based on Kirkpatrick and Kirkpatrick's Four Levels of Evaluation (2006).

MAKE IT YOURS

- What specific outcomes am I trying to achieve through this initiative and how will I know if I've succeeded?

- Am I capturing both the numbers that prove impact and the stories that explain it?

- How am I continuously using evaluation insights to inform decisions?

- How can I best communicate value in a way that resonates with stakeholders?

26

Innovate Through Knowledge Management

How Do You Capture and Share What You Learn?

Organizations with strong learning cultures where knowledge is regularly shared and applied are 58% more likely to meet their business goals, compared to those without.

Association for Talent Development.

What Left With Them

At a technical high school in the Northeast, two flagship programs, the Culinary Operations and Applied Automotive Systems, were discontinued within the same academic year. In both cases, the programs didn't fail because of performance, funding, or enrollment.

They vanished because the knowledge behind them walked out the door.

Both programs had been led for decades by expert instructors who retired within months of each other. Their systems, partnerships, and routines were never formally documented. In Culinary, the instructor had built a local network of restaurant partners that offered externships and job placement for graduating seniors. The student-run café provided meals for district events and generated revenue. Yet when the teacher left, there was no transition protocol, no written process, no contact list, no instructional guide. The café shut down. The internships dissolved.

In Automotive, the instructor had developed an internal training sequence that progressed from safety checks to diagnostics and real-time repair simulations. He'd also maintained long-standing vendor relationships for parts and supplies. But his curriculum, procedures, and purchasing systems existed only in his head. New hires arrived without a roadmap. Within months, performance stalled and district funds were redirected.

No "knowledge capture" interviews were conducted. No exit memos. No team transitions. The programs had been treated as individual competence, not institutional capability. As a result, years of hard-won expertise disappeared, and two thriving pathways for students closed without a successor.

This isn't a story about retirement, it's a story about perpetuation. When schools fail to embed knowledge into their systems, they become vulnerable to loss at every point of transition. Knowledge management isn't a luxury for central office teams or Fortune 500s. It's a leadership responsibility in every program, department, and building. If a simple end-of-year exit interview or transition playbook had been in place, those two programs might still be running and students might still be benefitting from the legacy that was never passed on.

PRINCIPLES

Principle 1: Build Knowledge into the Workflow

When the bell rings at 2:15, the real learning often begins for the adults. Teachers linger in doorways comparing strategies. A principal walks back to her office replaying a hard parent conversation. But what happens to all that insight? In many schools, it evaporates because there's no system to catch it. Knowledge gets lost not from lack of value, but from lack of design.

The Association for Talent Development (2024) defines Knowledge Management (KM) as a system for getting the right knowledge to the right people at the right time to drive action. Yet while 85% of organizations agree KM is essential, only 43% train staff to use it effectively. The message is clear: people value knowledge but haven't built the pathways to sustain it. High-performing teams do it differently. They stop treating knowledge as an add-on and start embedding it into the actual work.

In education, that shift might look like what one instructional leadership team did in a mid-sized urban district. Instead of sending professional development surveys after workshops, they closed each session with a "3-2-1 transfer" protocol which included three key takeaways, two actions for their team, and one insight to bring up in their next department meeting. Every teacher knew what they learned on Wednesday would shape how their team worked on Thursday. No extra forms required. Just integrated action.

To embed knowledge into your own workflow, start with the following moves:

1. Map the moments where insight already happens, like coaching debriefs, walkthroughs, or grade-level meetings.

2. Design microstructures, quick routines or templates, that turn those moments into catalysts for shared knowledge. For example, use, "One thing I'll try, one thing I'll tell" as a standing closing round.

3. Capture learning from unique experiences. When staff return from conferences, site visits, or specialized training, build in the habit of having them create a short written brief, a 90-second video, or a 3-slide share-out.

4. Use existing meetings for capture and cascade. Instead of asking people to log insights later, build reflection and sharing into what's already on the calendar.

If learning isn't captured, it can't spread. When knowledge lives in real conversations, routines, and planning decisions, it becomes more than something you store, it becomes something you live.

Principle 2: Build a Culture of Contribution

In one school, teachers arrive earlier than normal every Thursday. It's not mandatory, they choose to come because that's when they take time to share ideas. The first five minutes of each meeting are reserved for "wins and warnings." These are quick stories of what worked and what didn't. It's not performative. It's honest. A principal shared the impact. "Once we built that habit, people stopped guarding their lessons and started growing them."

Knowledge doesn't spread by accident but through purposeful people. The most effective leaders shape cultures where sharing what you know is safe, expected, and rewarding. However, the disappointing statistic according to the Association for Talent Development (2024), is that less than half of organizations assign clear responsibility for knowledge sharing, and even fewer offer guidance on how to do it. In the absence of structure and safety, sharing becomes optional, and most people opt out.

So what does it take to grow a culture of contribution? First, it starts with psychological safety. Edmondson (1999) established that teams learn more when members feel safe to speak up and take interpersonal risks. Building on this, Gagné et al. (2019) found that employees are more likely to share knowledge when they're autonomously motivated. That means admitting what didn't work, spotlighting team learning, and treating every insight as a shared asset. Second, it requires visible norms where sharing is the standard operating procedure. One district built a system where instructional rounds always ended with a "Knowledge Relay." Each observer shared one takeaway, then named one colleague they'd share it with. Once again, no follow-up forms required, and no portals to access. Just structure that caused positive ripple effects.

Principle 3: Turn Data into Direction

Most organizations aren't suffering from a shortage of information but rather from information overload. Climate surveys, walkthrough trends, achievement data, and community feedback all pile up. The real challenge isn't collecting more, it's turning what you already have into something useful. Without a clear system for reflection and interpretation, details become overwhelming. Leaders must follow the question, "Did we capture it?" with, "Did it change what we do?" Data is a catalyst for judgment, alignment, and strategy. The Association for Talent Development (2024) emphasizes that Knowledge Management must go beyond documentation to support "decision making, analysis, and continuous improvement" in daily operations. The shift from capture to application requires leaders to embed reflection into how their teams plan, prioritize, and adapt. Without it, you may have data, but not insight.

One high school built this mindset into their routine by ending every instructional leadership meeting with three prompts: What patterns are emerging? What surprised us? What decisions need to be made? These responses were logged in a running document for ongoing reference. Over time, this became a living system where teachers entered key moments from their own practice. The insights directly shaped mid-year professional development and schedule shifts. As ATD notes, reflection is what makes knowledge "trusted, valued, and consumed, "not just stored (Association for Talent Development, 2024).

To build a system that turns data into knowledge and action, consider these moves:

- Build reflection into existing rhythms. Quarterly is not frequent enough. It must be every week. Use meeting time to ask, "What are we learning?" and "How will this change our next step?"

- Move beyond raw data to patterns and tensions. What keeps showing up? What's the root cause?

- Use "insight loops" to track decisions back to the knowledge that informed them. When insights drive action, people begin to see the value of contributing what they know.

It's easy to mistake information for intelligence. But insight requires more than data collection. It requires intentional systems to make sense of the information. Knowledge must be managed so that it makes a positive influence on what your team does next.

Principle 4: Make Knowledge Easily Discoverable

When do people really need knowledge? They need it in the middle of their work when it is most applicable. Gottfredson and Mosher (2011) described this with the Five Moments of Learning Need framework. This model of learning happens at the start of a new role or during a training session but equally important, it happens afterwards, whenever people face a real situation that demands judgment and action.

The framework identifies five distinct moments when learning is essential. When (1) someone is learning something for the first time; (2) when they want to deepen or expand their knowledge; (3) when they need to put learning into practice; (4) when they must adapt to new ways of doing familiar tasks; and (5) when problems arise and they must troubleshoot unexpected challenges (Gottfredson & Mosher, 2011). The right resource is needed immediately when navigating a new digital platform, when handling an unfamiliar concern, or when interpreting assessment results. The challenge of Knowledge Management is ensuring that in the moment of need, someone can actually find information and use it to help.

Research reinforces the importance of making information easy to find. Nonaka (2007) argued that organizations thrive when they convert tacit knowledge like personal experiences and insights, into explicit documents that can be shared and accessed later. Leonard and Rayport (1997) cautioned that knowledge has little organizational value unless it is identifiable and retrievable. And Garvin, Edmondson, and Gino (2008) showed that high-performing "learning organizations" go beyond storing information; they design systems where insights are easily retrieved and applied across teams. In other words, knowledge that is too hard to find may as well not exist.

One district learned this lesson the hard way. After investing heavily in professional development, they discovered that teachers rarely revisited the resources. The problem was accessibility. Handouts were buried in email attachments, slide decks scattered across personal drives, and videos hidden behind expired links. Teachers stopped looking because finding what they needed took too much time. The district's pivot was simple but powerful. They created a single "Knowledge Hub" organized around real moments of need. Resources weren't listed by date of training but tagged by the problem they solved ("How do I structure small-group math?" or "How do I handle student safety concerns?"). Suddenly, knowledge wasn't a static archive but a living library people could use.

To make knowledge findable in your own setting, consider these moves:

- Design for search, not storage. Label and tag resources by the problems they solve, not the event where they were created. A binder called "August PD" gathers dust; a folder called "Strategies for Student Engagement" is desired like gold.

- Build continuity into transitions. Require short "knowledge briefs" when staff attend conferences, finish projects, or step into new roles. Store them where others can quickly retrieve them.

- Leverage simple technology. You don't need enterprise platforms. Even a shared Google Drive, if well-structured and consistently updated can become a powerful retrieval system. What matters is usability, not complexity. Important Note: Be sure to have a system in place that keeps information updated and relevant.

- Make it part of onboarding. New staff should be oriented not just to policies, but to the knowledge systems that capture "how we do things here." Introduce the system and allow the new hire time to practice while help is available.

The real test of a knowledge system isn't how much you've stored, it's whether people can find what they need when it matters most. A leader's job is to close the gap between what your organization knows and what your people can use. When knowledge is findable, your team spends less time reinventing solutions and more time applying proven strategies for impact.

FROM ONE LEADER TO ANOTHER

Dr. Rachel Teague

Senior Knowledge Management & Training Director, Southern NH University
   As heard on Othman's Leadership Podcast, Episode 17

Keeping What Leaders Can't Afford to Lose

When Dr. Rachel Teague began experimenting with knowledge transfer at her university, she knew the stakes were high. Too often, when experienced staff retired or left, decades of hard-won expertise vanished overnight. To test whether it could be captured, she launched a small pilot program focused on knowledge retention. That's when she met Cathy. Cathy had built a teacher preparation program from scratch, running it almost single-handedly for twenty years. As retirement approached, all of that experience with the accreditation requirements, state policies, and the unwritten rules of team dynamics, lived only in her head. Week after week, Rachel sat with her, recording conversations and gathering notes until she had what she jokingly called the Cathy Handbook. When leaders saw it, they realized Cathy was doing the job of four people. That single moment forced them to restructure the budget to prevent collapse. The lesson was clear: when knowledge walks out the door, organizations lose far more than they realize.

Teague's initial focus was to cultivate an environment grounded in dialogue and understanding. "We want to be able to foster a culture that is open to sharing. Make it the norm to have conversations." In addition, she further integrated "the emotional intelligence factor, the willingness to teach and to share, and to learn." This was especially important after conferences and trainings which often ended with insights beneficial only to those who attended. By deliberately spreading knowledge, individual takeaways became collective understanding.

Mindset mattered just as much. Too often, organizations are plagued by what Teague calls the "never enough time syndrome." Employees believe they're too busy to document their work, and leaders pay the price later. "It's a huge cost in knowledge, because you have all of this great information, especially if it's been a long-time employee with intricate knowledge that might be valuable to somebody down the line." Rachel experienced this firsthand. "When I left the university for a little while, I documented everything for everybody, and I still managed to forget some super random things." A few weeks later, she was still fielding texts about obscure problems only she had ever solved. The gap showed how fragile undocumented knowledge really is. Her solution: normalize quick documentation through check-ins. "Most organizations do annual reviews. I'd propose quarterly check-ins... write down the different daily pieces that you do, the different activities, meetings, responsibilities. What's changed? What's still yours? What has been passed on?" Even small updates keep teams from reinventing the wheel or forgetting small but important tasks.

The next step was to find tools that made the information easy to access. For Teague, it was SharePoint. "I've built a SharePoint repository... one folder for general knowledge that anybody can access, and another with sensitive information, shared only with a few people so it's not always just in the hands of one person." When she built handbooks, they didn't replace training, they enhanced it. "This is not a training tool. It's something to help support your learning and your work." By creating layers of access, leaders ensure that what is secure in one person's head becomes usable for others. Done well, repositories and handbooks don't sit idle; they give successors both confidence and context as they step into complex roles.

In the end, Knowledge Management is a human practice. "When you take those words out, just have it sink in that it's the people that are the most important aspects of any of these topics." Teague often reminds leaders that they are already practicing Knowledge Management. "You are probably doing more than you realize, whether it's through a water cooler conversation, a quick Teams Catch Up, or sharing a recipe your grandmother made with your child." And it doesn't stop at work. In her own home, she and her spouse keep a spreadsheet of passwords, doctors, and bills, shared with family members in case of emergency. It's a reminder that knowledge, when left undocumented, leaves loved ones vulnerable. "Knowledge management is not just for the professional doing the work at the workplace; it is also personally taking the time to document some of the stuff that might not seem terribly important to you, but believe me, from a firsthand experience, it's incredible."

Knowledge management, Teague concludes, is the quiet leadership practice that prevents chaos. It protects institutions, equips teams, and honors the people who have poured years into their work. And most importantly, it reminds us that every act of sharing keeps knowledge alive.

STRATEGY IN A SKETCH

The After Action Review (AAR) is a deceptively simple tool with transformative power. It helps teams turn everyday work into a source of collective learning. Rather than waiting for formal evaluations or end-of-year reviews, AARs prompt reflection in the moment through four core questions that surface insight and opportunity. The strength of the tool lies in the contrast between intent and reality, what you planned versus what actually happened. From there, the conversation shifts to root causes and actionable learning. A common mistake is turning the AAR into a performance review instead of a curiosity-driven dialogue with candid reflection on communication, roles, and preparation. When used consistently, this loop builds a culture where thoughtful insight is routine and learning is shared.

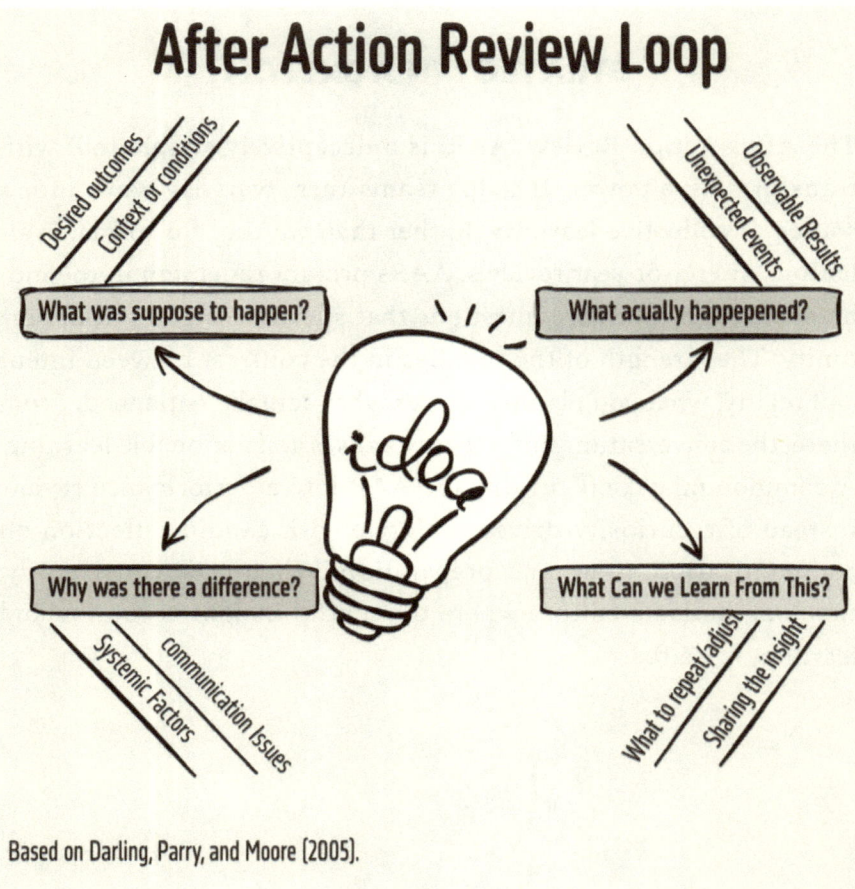

After Action Review Loop

Based on Darling, Parry, and Moore (2005).

MAKE IT YOURS

- How is knowledge currently captured, synthesized, and acted upon in my organization?

- What routines or tools can I build into our existing workflows to help teams reflect, analyze patterns, and make insight-driven decisions together?

- Are we turning what we learn from data, feedback, and professional development into specific changes in practice, or are we simply storing it?

- How easy is it to find information when staff needs it quickly?

27

Innovate Through Systems Thinking

How Do You Build Comprehensive Structures?

The performance of a system depends on how the parts interact, not on how they perform separately.

Russell Ackoff

The Silence Wasn't the Problem

It started with one email. Then another. Then four. An elementary school principal had just hired a much-needed team member to support students with intensive behavioral needs. This role had been vacant for months, and the gap had stretched her staff to the edge. Two of her team members were carrying double the caseload. They were tired. Students were waiting for services. And now, finally, an offer was accepted by a qualified candidate. It was time for the

Human Resources Department to exercise due diligence and make it official.

The administrator made the hiring decision but had no control over when the new person would start, what documentation was needed, and who would coordinate the onboarding process. More emails. More silence. Days turned into a week. She followed up. Still nothing. In the meantime, she couldn't create a schedule, introduce the new hire to their responsibilities, or inform the rest of the team. Two staff members continued to do the work of three. Students with urgent needs remained unsupported. And she, the leader, couldn't do the basic preparation that would allow her new team member to start strong.

She wasn't asking for a favor. She was asking for a workable system. But silence had become a normal part of the culture. Unfortunately, this wasn't the first time she had this experience. It was, in her words: "the norm. It seems if people don't like your question, they simply ignore it. Or, instead of explaining the delay, they leave you in limbo. Maybe they were waiting for the background check to come back. Couldn't someone send a quick email? It's so very unprofessional!"

No one was officially told not to respond. There were no memos encouraging neglect. But systems don't always speak in policies. Sometimes, they speak in patterns. And the pattern here was to wait, follow up, hope, follow up, follow up, follow up, and give up.

When a new superintendent joined the district that spring, she announced she would be holding office hours for staff to share ideas, concerns, and feedback directly. The idea was well received. But what surprised many was how quickly a common request emerged: "Can you create a districtwide policy that requires responses to emails within two business days?" It was a plea for structure.

The superintendent realized that unreturned emails were a symptom of a larger systemic problem that could only be resolved with a holistic approach. Instead of sending an email about emails, she thought about the information provided by Senge (2006) and Sargut and McGrath (2011). She needed to zoom out and start noticing the recurring loops that held them in a detrimental pattern. She began a process of analysis and problem-solving that focused on interrelationships between the Central Office and staff. She knew she needed to emphasize patterns, feedback loops, and system dynamics to uncover root causes, anticipate unintended consequences, and design sustainable solutions. In this case, she knew the problem would be solved by naming the loop, mapping the process, and rethinking the structure. She asked, "Who owns onboarding communication? What's the guaranteed timeline for response? What backup systems kick in if one person is unavailable?" More importantly, she wanted to reinforce that every staff member deserves timely and clear communication. Theirs was a complex educational environment. By using Systems Thinking as the guiding lens, everyone understood how to build a structure that would drive desired organizational behavior.

PRINCIPLES

Principle 1: See the Whole: Shift from Parts to Patterns

Systems Thinking demands what Senge (2006) calls a "shift of mind." This is the solution-oriented outlook that moves from reacting to events to seeing the hidden patterns and structures underneath them. Instead of solving parts in isolation, systems thinkers study how feedback loops, mental models, and time delays interact over time. They ask what's reinforcing the behavior, not just how to stop one incident.

Sargut and McGrath (2011) make a critical distinction between complicated and complex systems. Complicated systems, like building a car, can be broken into parts and optimized. But complex systems, like educational institutions and other organizations, aren't predictable. You can't just fix one part and assume the rest will follow. Solving low achievement with more professional development, or fixing burnout with a one-time wellness day doesn't work if deeper causes like incoherent priorities or lack of adequate staffing, stay unaddressed.

Fortunately, Systems Thinking is a tool you can put into practice. Leaders start by mapping patterns over time instead of reacting to snapshots. Senge's (1994) "iceberg model" is one practical entry point. It begins with naming the event:"Our reading scores dropped". Next comes naming the pattern:"Scores dipped every time curriculum shifted". And observing the structure follows: "We have no long-term curriculum strategy", with the final discovery of the underlying mindset: "We believe new programs fix old problems." This simple disciplined process reveals leverage points that matter.

Try these moves:

- When something goes wrong, don't just ask what happened, ask what's happening again and again.

- Practice systems mapping with your leadership team. Draw causal loops or storyboards to explore ripple effects.

- Before launching a new initiative, ask what structure created the old outcome and what assumptions still live in the system?

Seeing the whole is about seeing the whole picture and analyzing recurring reactions. It's how leaders move from chasing symptoms to reshaping systems. Because when you see the loops that caused the knots, you untangle the organization.

Principle 2: Design for Flow, Not Control

When an urgent decision takes four committee meetings, six months, and three signatures to move forward, something's broken. People may be trying but the system isn't designed to move. In too many schools and nonprofits, the instinct to create order leads to layers of oversight, rigid protocols, and unnecessary approvals. The process feels safe. But it slows everything down and in complex environments, speed and responsiveness are survival skills.

Systems Thinking shifts design for control to design for flow. Jeff Sutherland (2014), co-creator of *Scrum*, argues that high-performing teams are built around the flow of value, not job titles, silos, or hierarchy. Agile systems use short feedback loops, small-batch work, and shared goals to keep progress visible and adaptable. People closest to the work make decisions, adapt quickly, and stay aligned through purpose, not permission.

Senge (1994) reinforce this with a systems lens. They write that learning organizations evolve by empowering those within through trust, reflection, and distributed decision-making. When leadership pushes every decision up the chain, the system stalls. When flow is built in, the organization becomes dynamic, not reactive.

This doesn't mean removing structure. It means building a smart structure:

- Push transparency: Make goals, priorities, and decision rights visible to everyone, not just leaders.

- Design routines that adapt: Use short cycles like weekly team huddles or sprint check-ins to keep work flowing and blockers surfaced early.

- Audit approval chains: Determine where control is slowing momentum. What would happen if you removed a layer.

Leaders who design for flow build organizations that breathe. Information moves. Decisions don't wait. Innovation doesn't need permission slips. Where speed is critical, effective systems minimize oversight and maximize smooth performance.

Principle 3: Use Feedback Loops to Learn and Adapt

What's the problem with rolling out a new intervention with energy and urgency? Nothing unless no one determined if the last one worked and why or why not. Without structured feedback, each new initiative becomes another shot in the dark. Leaders act on impulse, not insight. And the staff often suffer the consequences.

Systems don't improve by accident, they improve through feedback. Senge (2006) calls feedback the heartbeat of Systems Thinking. It's how we understand what's working, what's not, and what to adjust. But not all feedback is created equal. Systems thinkers pay attention to reinforcing loops which escalate patterns, and balancing loops which stabilize them. When leaders see these loops clearly, they stop reacting to symptoms and start redesigning the system.

Agile frameworks like Jeff Sutherland's "Scrum" operationalize this idea. Sutherland and Sutherland (2014) built feedback into every layer: daily stand-ups, sprint reviews, and retrospectives are structured pauses to inspect, adapt, and improve - while the work is still in motion. Croll and Yoskovitz (2013) sharpen this approach with the idea of a One Metric That Matters (OMTM). This feedback loop tracks the right signal at the right time to know when to pivot or persist.

Senge (2006) reminds us, "Learning cannot be imposed; it can only be encouraged and supported by structures that reward reflection, inquiry, and dialogue." It is important to gather user feedback before investing heavily. Teams fast-forward into the future by gathering reactions, and refining policies based on what they learn. The result is faster decisions, lower risk, and better ideas.

Systems thinkers reinforce this approach. Senge (1994) caution that system-wide changes made too soon can create confusion, resistance, and unintended harm. Instead, they advocate for small, localized experiments, what they call "safe-to-fail" probes, that provide feedback before larger implementation. These small moves generate early wins, surface blind spots, and inform better long-term design.

To build feedback loops that guide smart decisions, try these three-steps:

1. Zoom In: What signals are we already getting but not fully listening to? Review the daily experiences of student behaviors, staff frustrations, and missed deadlines. These are not noise; they're feedback.

2. Create the Loop: Where does feedback go, and how fast? Set short, predictable feedback routines like five-minute closing reflections at staff meetings, weekly student check-ins, or quick parent pulse surveys. Choose one and make it stick.

3. Close the Gap: What changes because of what we learn?

Make adjustments visible. Post a "You said, we did" summary. Shift a policy and name the reason. The fastest way to build a feedback culture is to show that voices move the system.

Principle 4: Prioritize High-Leverage Actions, Not Quick Fixes

Painting over a water stain hides it for a short time but eventually the problem bleeds through. This is also the case with providing a quick but temporary fix to an underlying organizational issue. Systems Thinking challenges leaders to go deeper. Senge (2006) describes the concept of compensating feedback: when you push hard on a symptom, the system pushes back because its underlying structure remains unchanged. Training, rewards, and mandates won't result in lasting improvement if the system itself resists the change. To shift outcomes, you must shift the conditions producing them.

Senge's Fieldbook (1994) offers powerful system archetypes like "Shifting the Burden" and "Fixes That Fail." They help leaders diagnose recurring patterns and determine if the intervention is easing discomfort or solving the real issue? When burnout is met with a staff lunch instead of revisiting workload and priorities, you've shifted the burden. The pattern will return.

This is where high-leverage actions matter most. They aren't big, flashy solutions. They're the smallest actions with the greatest impact, the ones that create ripple effects across the system. Sutherland (2014) encourages teams to regularly reflect, test, and learn where small adjustments drive meaningful change. These decisions emerge by observing patterns, surfacing root causes, and intervening at the right pressure point.

To lead with leverage, ask:

- What pattern do I see, not just what problem do I feel?

- What structure might be producing this outcome again and again?

- What's the smallest action I could take to shift that structure?

Quick fixes are tempting, especially when pressure is high. But they rarely hold. High-leverage actions are harder to spot, but they shape what lasts. Systems don't change when we push harder, they change when we intervene smarter.

Principle 5: Architect for Resilience, Not Just Efficiency

In the pursuit of streamlined operations, many organizations chase efficiency above all else. But systems designed only for speed and precision often become brittle and unable to absorb shocks or adapt to change. Resilience, by contrast, is the ability to sustain performance and bounce back stronger after disruption. Leaders who architect for resilience build systems that bend without breaking.

Peter Senge's Systems Thinking framework warns against treating organizations like machines that can be perfectly tuned (Senge, 2006). Real systems are dynamic, full of interdependencies, feedback loops, and time delays. Ironically, the pursuit of maximum efficiency often removes the very buffers like slack time, cross-training, or reflection, that organizations need to adapt. As Senge et al. (1994) argue, resilient organizations invest in learning capacity, not just output.

Sargut and McGrath (2011) make a related point: complex systems are unpredictable, so traditional "best practices" often fall short. Their research encourages leaders to build systems that can evolve under stress by emphasizing diverse thinking, distributed decision-making, and real-time feedback over rigid control structures.

Scrum offers a practical example. With its short sprints, cross-functional teams, and constant iteration, it embeds resilience into the work. Sutherland and Sutherland (2014) notes that these agile rhythms equip teams to respond and pivot without unraveling.

Architecting for resilience means shifting from "just-in-time" to "just-in-case." It means building flexible structures, prioritizing well-being, and fostering collective sense-making when things go wrong. It's about designing for durability in a world that rarely follows the script.

To build resilience into your system:

- Leave room for reflection and slack: Every minute scheduled to the brim is a system waiting to break. Build in time to pause, learn, and reset.

- Distribute ownership: Resilient systems don't rely on a single leader. They're designed so others can lead when it counts.

- Plan for the stretch: Ask, "How will it hold under pressure? Who will absorb the shock?"

Designing for resilience is about leading with foresight. Because what keeps a system running includes how flexible it can be. Resilient systems don't just survive change, they absorb it, learn from it, and come back stronger.

FROM ONE LEADER TO ANOTHER

Jose Escribano

Assistant Superintendent of Community Engagement, Family Empowerment and Partnership, Springfield Public Schools
As heard on Othman's Leadership Podcast, Episode TBD

See the System Before You Fix the Process

When Jose Escribano took on oversight of the enrollment department at Springfield Public Schools, he quickly realized there was a problem, but it wasn't what others had come to believe. "Everyone thought the enrollment team was just behind," he recalled. But when he looked closer, what appeared to be a backlog turned out to be a systems failure. "We had 100 kids enrolled in preschool, but 600 others waiting for special education evaluations," he said. These children were referrals from early intervention, logged into one system but invisible in others, leaving them stuck in limbo. "Special Ed. had no idea these students were showing up in enrollment, and enrollment didn't know they needed to be evaluated." That discovery shifted everything. Escribano's big picture view spurred him to do more than just fix a form. He united departments, aligned timelines, and redesigned how information flowed across the district. Systems Thinking, he learned, starts with asking, "How does this decision affect the whole?"

Escribano's years of experience shaped the mindset that drove his success. In Family Systems Theory, every member influences the whole," he explained. That training shaped how he saw schools, not as departments, but as interdependent parts. "If you want change to stick, you can't act like you know everything. You need to understand how people interact, how they feel, and where the friction lives." That human-first lens, he believes, is often missing. "A process isn't a system," he cautioned. "A system is how processes interact with each other and with people." That insight turned his leadership into a practice of mapping interactions, gathering honest feedback, and listening beneath the surface. "I like the iceberg model," he said. "Because what's visible, the data, timelines, or reports, is just the tip. If you want lasting change, you need to understand what's underneath."

Still, the work is never quick or perfect. "Complex systems take time to untangle," he said. "But if you rush it, you'll miss key voices, and the system will collapse under pressure." To avoid that, Escribano gives every initiative a clear timeline—and a humble title. "Everything's a pilot," he said with a smile. "When people hear 'pilot,' they relax. They know we're learning, not just launching." That approach builds psychological safety and makes feedback more honest. And feedback, he believes, is non-negotiable. "It doesn't matter if I created the system. If someone points out a better way, I have to be open to changing it. That's leadership."

For Escribano, Systems Thinking is a critical responsibility. "If our systems don't work, our students suffer," he said plainly. "In my district, that's the difference between breaking the cycle of poverty or not." "Explain to me," is his favorite verse. He repeats it frequently because it opens the door to honest dialogue. "It's not judgmental," he explained. "It's just curiosity. And curiosity is where Systems Thinking starts."

STRATEGY IN A SKETCH

The Iceberg Model invites leaders to stop reacting to surface-level events and start investigating the hidden systems beneath them. It breaks complexity into four levels so leaders can trace difficulties to their root causes. This model is especially powerful when the same issue keeps resurfacing. For instance, rather than responding to another staff resignation as an isolated event, a Systems Thinker looks for patterns in exit interviews, then examines workload policies and unspoken norms that expect unpaid overtime. The biggest mistake leaders make is staying at the top of the iceberg and firefighting events without investigating what enables them. The strength of this tool lies in moving from a specific event to notice ongoing patterns, identify organizational structures, and understand the mindset that blocks progress.

The Iceberg Model

Systems thinkers dig for patterns and reshape the structures — and mindsets — that create them

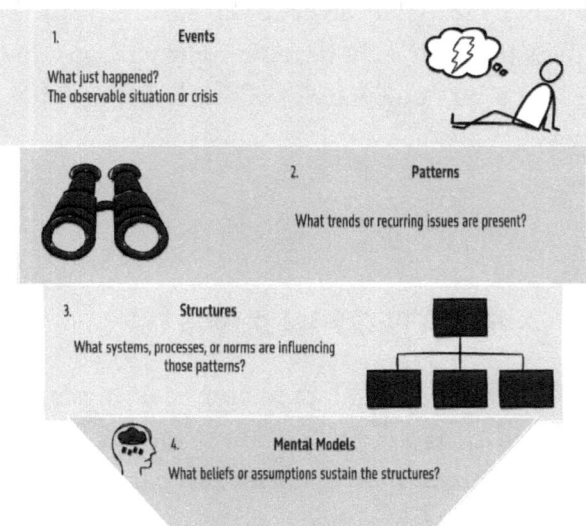

1. **Events**

What just happened?
The observable situation or crisis

2. **Patterns**

What trends or recurring issues are present?

3. **Structures**

What systems, processes, or norms are influencing
those patterns?

4. **Mental Models**

What beliefs or assumptions sustain the structures?

Based on Donella Meadows' systems thinking framework in Thinking in Systems (2008).

MAKE IT YOURS

- What patterns are driving behavior? Do they reflect what we truly value? Have I been treating them as isolated problems instead of a systemic issue?

- Where in my team or organization is control stalling progress, and how could I redesign for smoother flow?

- What feedback loops currently exist in my organization, and how quickly do we act on what we learn?

- What small initiative could I pilot now to validate a bigger idea or direction?

28

Innovate Through Inclusion

How Do You Build A Structure That Values Every Voice?

Diversity is being invited to the party; inclusion is being asked to dance.

Verna Myers

When the Pictures Say Yes, But the Culture Says No

The company's website made a promise: "Our commitment to diversity and inclusion ensures a welcoming environment for all families and staff."

Those words appeared on every platform: LinkedIn, Instagram, printed brochures. They celebrated Black History Month, recognized religious holidays, and highlighted cultural appreciation days. Anyone visiting their social media would think it was the kind of place where everyone belongs. But what Nadia experienced told a different story.

She was a teacher in one of the company's school-based programs and by every metric, she was excelling. The classroom environment she created was warm, creative, and visibly joyful. She poured energy into her lessons, designed immersive activities, and built deep relationships with her students. She didn't need a formal observation to know her impact. She could see it in the students' faces and ironically, she could see it in the company's own Instagram account. That's where her work kept showing up. The bulletin boards in the photos, the student projects on display, the classroom setup were all hers. Her classroom was the most featured in the region. The internal company portal regularly featured "Shoutouts" from site directors and leaders celebrating staff. Every week, the same names were praised and sometimes it was only for small contributions. But her name? Never mentioned. Never tagged. Never recognized... Nadia was also the only staff member at her site who wore a Hijab.

At first she thought it was her imagination but what she began to notice was hard to ignore. Colleagues looked the other way when they passed in the hall. Even though she greeted them, she was met with silence. Even her own director avoided acknowledging her contributions during team meetings. One week, after Nadia single-handedly coordinated a student-led learning showcase that drew in parents and community members, her director praised the event but attributed its success to "the whole team." The group shifted uncomfortably and quickly changed the subject. No one looked her in the eye.

She worked harder. She helped others more often. She tried to be extra friendly and accommodating. Nothing changed. It wore her down slowly. By the time she gave her two weeks' notice, she was barely sleeping. She told a friend, "It's not that they said cruel things to me. It's that they ignored my very existence." That's what broke her. Not one moment but the accumulation of small exclusions. The purported public commitment to diversity made the silence sting more.

Inclusion isn't what's printed on a brochure. It's who gets credit. It's who gets acknowledged. It's who gets greeted in the hallway. What Nadia experienced wasn't a failure of messaging. It was a failure of messaging practiced through the culture of the organization. And culture lives in daily interactions, not in hollow proclamations.

PRINCIPLES

Principle 1: Encourage Authentic Speech

Earlier in this book, we explored the concept of psychological safety emerging as the engine of trust and performance in collaboration and high-performing teams. Here, we revisit it through a different lens: its role in building truly inclusive teams. Inclusion does not stop with diverse representation alone. It materializes when dissimilar people can speak honestly, raise dissenting views, and take risks without fear of disproportionate penalty.

Amy Edmondson (2019) defines psychological safety as the shared belief that it is safe to take interpersonal risks. Without it, silence becomes the default, especially for those who feel marginalized. Inclusive leadership begins with listening deeply and noticing who is consistently silent or sidelined. Roberts (2023), in the article Where Does DEI Go From Here?, uses the term "Voice Equity" to ensure that all team members, not just the loudest or most senior, have the opportunity to influence decisions, share insights, and be heard. Leaders who practice Voice Equity ask not only, "What's being said?" but also "Who's not speaking and why?" This shift from content to participation ensures that diverse perspectives are surfaced and acted upon. Voice-centered inclusion is the intentional design of team environments that promote equitable participation, enabling all members, regardless of identity, role, or status, to speak, be heard, and influence outcomes. It is grounded in psychological safety and structured dialogue, where speaking up is encouraged and valued as essential to team learning, trust, and innovation (Edmondson, 2019)

Research shows that when leaders actively encourage open dialogue, normalize vulnerability, and reframe mistakes as learning opportunities, underrepresented voices are more likely to contribute. Roberts (2023), argues that Voice Equity is essential to the workplace freedoms of being and becoming. Marginalized team members often engage in code-switching, performative conformity, and identity suppression just to "fit in." This lack of authenticity diminishes their impact, causes disengagement, and results in the loss of collective intelligence.

To lead with Voice Equity, organizations must go beyond open invitations to speak. Leaders should actively track whose voices are present, use intentional meeting designs that equalize airtime, and regularly ask, "Whose perspective haven't we heard yet?" These actions signal that participation is an opportunity for inclusion, innovation, and shared success.

Inclusion thrives when leaders raise the quality of engagement. Protecting the freedom to speak ensures that equity is a daily experience. When leaders make psychological safety the bedrock of inclusion, they create conditions where innovation is no longer limited to the confident few, but unlocked from the varied and diverse intelligence of the whole.

Principle 2: Cultivate Collective Growth

Inclusion is not simply inviting various backgrounds to the table. More importantly, it is ensuring that once they arrive, they grow, contribute, and co-create. Collective growth means that teams are not only diverse but are transformed by that diversity. When performance is paired with learning as the core goals of inclusion, teams shift from competing individually to evolving together.

Amy Edmondson's *Teaming* (2012) makes a compelling case that innovation isn't born from individual brilliance but from messy, adaptive collaboration across boundaries. Successful teams embrace failure, explore opposing ideas, and treat every interaction as a learning opportunity. Inclusive leaders fuel this kind of teaming by actively elevating diverse voices because they understand that innovation depends on the tension and synergy between differing perspectives.

Liz Wiseman's concept of "multipliers" adds another layer to this principle. Multipliers amplify team intelligence by asking thoughtful questions, assuming others are capable, and framing challenges as shared opportunities for discovery (Wiseman, 2017). In this view, inclusion discovers, "What can we learn from this person?" rather than "How do we include them?" Diversity becomes a dynamic source of insight, not just a demographic checkbox.

Frei and Morriss (2023), in 10 Reasons Why Inclusion Is a Competitive Advantage, reinforce that learning-centered inclusion is more than noble, it's strategic. Research shows that inclusive teams make better decisions 87% of the time and are more likely to meet financial targets. Why? Because cognitive diversity invites challenge, reduces blind spots, and strengthens collective sense-making.

Simon Sinek's *Leaders Eat Last* (2014) underscores how trust and safety lay the groundwork for this kind of collective development. When people feel psychologically and emotionally protected through empathy, shared purpose, and genuine investment from leaders and peers, they're more willing to take risks, accept feedback, and grow. Inclusion fuels learning, and learning deepens inclusion.

To cultivate collective growth through good times and bad, leaders must design team experiences that prioritize reflection, feedback, and exploration. Failure is a reality and those involved should be treated fairly, and the team should be accustomed to sharing the lessons learned. As Roberts (2023) explains, this attentiveness creates the "freedom to fail," since equitable inclusion cannot exist when some individuals are penalized more severely for mistakes than others. Feedback should be mutual and frequent. Innovation sessions should focus on "What did we learn?" instead of "What went wrong?" Inclusion, then, provides the fertile ground where diverse talents can take root and grow into collective success.

Principle 3: Build Inclusion Into the Structure

Inclusion cannot be left to chance or goodwill, it must be systematically built into the very architecture of how teams operate. When inclusion is embedded into structures, routines, and tools, it becomes not only expected but inevitable. This principle focuses on replacing passive inclusion efforts with active, repeatable practices that empower all members to contribute meaningfully, regardless of role or identity.

Daniel Coyle, in *The Culture Code*, explains that successful teams thrive on a foundation of safety, shared vulnerability, and purpose (Coyle, 2018). These cultural cues are not spontaneous, they're deliberately encoded into team rituals. Practices like structured check-ins, "safe-to-fail" ideation rounds, and rotating facilitators reinforce team norms that invite participation and normalize risk-taking. These routines make the culture visible and repeatable, helping teams move from intention to action.

In cross-functional or cross-cultural environments, inclusion must go beyond individual relationships. *In Cross-Silo Leadership*, Ernst and Yip (2019) describe how formal structures like role rotation, cross-boundary mentorships, and inclusive governance models create bridges across divides of expertise, function, and identity. Leaders who invest in these structural pathways help prevent silos and status hierarchies from muting diverse voices. It's not enough to say, "Your input matters." Systems must show that it does.

In the article The Power of Small Acts of Inclusion, Muragishi, Aguilar, Carr, and Walton (2024) show how simple routines reshape group dynamics. They show how routine behaviors like ensuring everyone speaks before decisions, naming unseen contributions, and using inclusive language have cumulative effects. They promote small design changes like using round-robin brainstorming, and silent-start journaling to disrupt status-based silence and shift teams from hierarchical to inclusive, allowing people to participate fully without needing to dominate. These small actions, when embedded structurally, reduce social risk, affirm value, and make participation a shared expectation. Over time, they help create a rhythm where inclusion is less about personalities and more about process.

According to a Deloitte study cited in The Value of Belonging at Work (Carr et al., 2019), employees with a strong sense of belonging are 56% more likely to show improved performance and 50% less likely to leave. But belonging is not just being included in the room, it's about being invited to participate in what is going on there. Micro-inclusion practices like tracking speaker airtime, rotating roles, and building structured feedback loops uncover hidden contributions and elevate unseen talent.

In the article The False Dichotomy of Merit and Inclusion, Praslova (2025) explain that well-designed systems can protect fairness without sacrificing excellence. Structural inclusion practices like blind reviews, equitable speaking turns, and role-sharing expose overlooked talent and invite wider contribution. It moves evaluation from charisma to capability, and leadership from default to design.

To apply this principle, leaders can use tools like the Circle Process or Liberating Structures to design meetings where every voice matters. They can rotate team roles among facilitator, notetaker, and timekeeper to share power and visibility. Most importantly, they can audit team rituals with a systems lens. Who speaks first? Who decides? Who gets the follow-up? The answers often reveal where equity breaks and where inclusion can begin. Ultimately, inclusive teams don't just hope for the contribution of all, they expect it. When leaders shift from good intentions to intentional design, inclusion stops being something we remind people to do and becomes the way we work.

FROM ONE LEADER TO ANOTHER

Dr. Miko Nino

Assistant Vice President for Adult and Online Education at Rhode Island College
As heard on Othman's Leadership Podcast, Episode TBD

Give People a Voice, Not Just a Seat

He still remembers the first time he realized what it truly meant to give someone a voice. Before his career in online learning and higher education, Dr. Miko Niño was a conference interpreter. One day, at a community event, residents were speaking to local authorities about issues that mattered to them. Many didn't speak English, so he was there to interpret. "One guy... gave his opinion, and when he was closing his comment, he said, 'But nobody listened to me because I'm a minority.'" As he prepared to translate, "everybody turned to look at me, and it was a realization that, for the first time, that person was going to have a voice." Immediately, Nino understood that his role was not only to interpret but to be "a platform, a mechanism, a device to give a voice to somebody who never had that opportunity." From that moment on, he began actively noticing those in the room who weren't being heard.

One of the biggest mistakes leaders make about inclusion, Nino explained, is that "we take it for granted." Leadership often comes with privileges, and "we make an assumption that everybody feels welcome or included." That's why he deliberately looks for those "who might not be feeling that they belong to the team or to the conversation." For him, inclusion means ensuring "everybody has the opportunity to have a seat at the table, regardless of their backgrounds," and double-checking that the intent to include is actually inclusive in practice.

Nino also warns about subtle ways exclusion creeps in. "When you don't ask the right people questions, you only talk to the top, and that's a way of leaving people out." True inclusion requires "hearing their voice" directly, whether through open forums, surveys, or town halls. But more importantly, he says, "people are tired of providing feedback and nothing is done about it." His rule is simple: "Always make sure you're listening and applying what you hear, using that feedback for improvement." Without that, trust erodes, and voices go silent.

In his own teams, Nino has built systems to prevent that silence. As director of online learning, he created a strategic plan where "everybody had equal participation" and understood "the value they brought to the team." He avoided only meeting with senior staff, making sure "everybody was part of major decisions." In meetings, he set expectations early: "We want to hear from everyone, so in the interest of time, I'm going to be playing the role of moderator here. Don't take it personally." For those hesitant to speak publicly, he introduced gamification software with live polls and QR codes, allowing team members to share thoughts completely anonymously during the meeting. He ensured confidentiality and respect for privacy, creating an environment where people felt safe to contribute. Along with one-on-one and other private channels, these tools ensure involvement. "You have to find more than one way to make sure people participate, because people have different preferences for different reasons."

Nino's approach is anchored by a phrase he first heard as a Special Olympics volunteer: "There is a place for everyone." He believes "everyone has unique values and unique skill sets," and that too often "people are misplaced." His job as a leader is to "get to know them and listen to them," then "place them in a place where they're going to excel." That belief shapes how he reorganizes teams, rewrites roles, and builds environments where "with the right coaching and respect, people add so much value" to their lives, others' lives, and the organization.

STRATEGY IN A SKETCH

Liberating Structures offer leaders a way to design conversations with high participation and high inclusion. This framework shifts teams out of patterns where a few voices dominate and others disappear. Instead of relying on open-ended discussion or top-down decisions, these microstructures like 1-2-4-All, "create predictable ways for everyone to think, speak, and shape what happens next. 1: Each person reflects on a question or challenge alone for about 1 minute. 2: People pair up and share their thoughts with one other person for about 2 minutes. 4: Each pair joins another pair, and builds on each other's ideas for about 4 minutes. All: The small groups share insights, patterns, or key takeaways with the larger group.

The model helps you surface quiet wisdom, reduce superficial participation, and challenge the myth that louder means smarter.

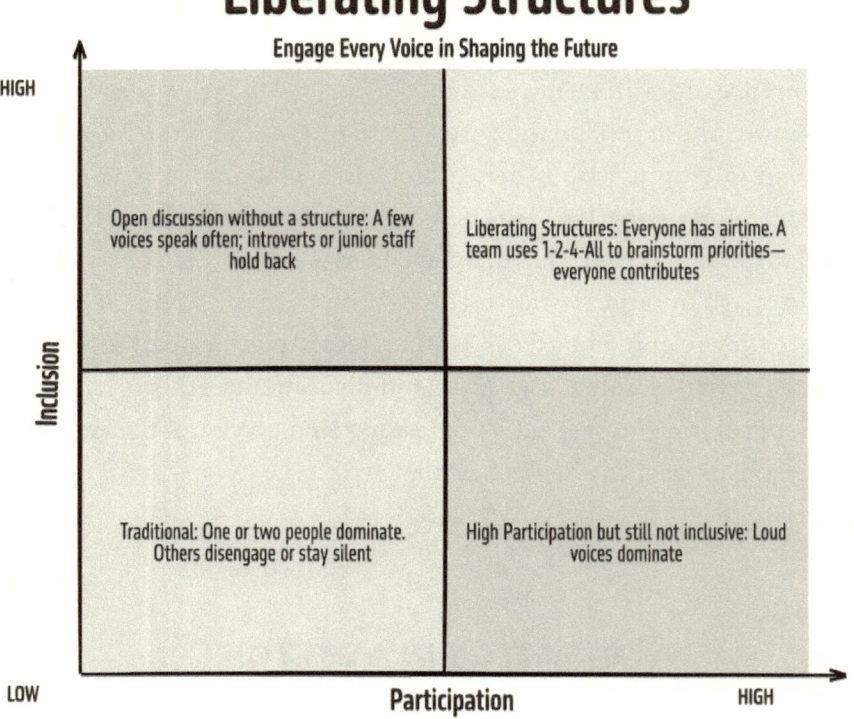

Based on Lipmanowicz and McCandless's Liberating Structures framework (2013).

MAKE IT YOURS

- Whose voices are consistently heard and whose are missing or overlooked?

- How have I made the diversity of my team into a dynamic source of insight and learning?

- What routines or structures do I have in place to ensure everyone has a chance to contribute meaningfully?

29

Innovate Through Performance Improvement

How Do You Raise the Bar Without Burning People Out?

A bad system will beat a good person every time.

W. Edwards Deming

Raising the Bar Without Breaking the Team

Linda owned a small early learning center that served children ages one through five. Her program had grown steadily over the years, and parents often described it as a warm, family-like environment. On the surface, things looked good. Classrooms were full, staff members showed up on time, and there were no complaints from families. But behind the scenes, Linda was exhausted. Quality varied from one classroom to the next, lesson plans were inconsistent, and communication with parents wasn't where it needed to be. Licensing reports had flagged her for documentation gaps, and staff turnover was quietly rising.

When we first met, Linda admitted she was torn. "They're good people," she said. "I don't want to push them away. But I can't keep running around fixing everything myself." She had a natural gift for seeing the best in her teachers, but she struggled to turn those insights into clear expectations. She wanted performance to improve but feared that being direct would make her staff feel criticized.

Linda asked me for a few quick strategies she could try, but I knew that wouldn't be enough. If she wanted real improvement, we had to dig deeper. Over the next three weeks, we worked through a gap analysis. Where did she want her staff to be? Where were they now? And how did those gaps connect to the drivers of her business: parent satisfaction, enrollment growth, and licensing compliance? Step by step, Linda described what she was seeing. As I listened, I noticed she often slipped into talking about her teachers' strengths, the creative way one teacher engaged toddlers, the patience another showed with transitions, and the organizational skills of her lead teacher. We mapped those strengths onto the goals of the center, and Linda began to see a new possibility. What if she used strengths not just to affirm people, but to raise their performance?

As we role-played a conversation with her lead teacher, Linda named what she valued. "You're so gifted at consistently creating a calm process for student transitions." Then she added, "I'd love to see that same structure carried into your parent communication. Families need that consistency, too." For the first time, she realized feedback didn't have to feel harsh. It could be a bridge between her appreciation and her expectations. Linda's eyes lit up. "I can do this," she said.

Five weeks later, we met again. Linda was glowing. "Three out of our four performance indicators have already improved," she reported. Parent satisfaction scores had risen as communication became clearer. Lesson plans were more consistent, with teachers taking ownership instead of waiting for Linda to fix problems. Licensing compliance had improved as staff followed procedures with greater confidence. The only lagging area was staff attendance, but even that, she noted, was beginning to trend upward as morale improved.

What mattered most was how different Linda felt in her role. She was no longer carrying the entire weight of the center on her shoulders. Her staff began saying things like, "Now I know exactly what she expects, and it feels good to be able to accomplish it." Parents noticed the change, too, and began complementing the improved communication. The word spread. New families began inquiring about enrollment. For Linda, the biggest win wasn't just the numbers, it was the culture. She had discovered how to improve performance without demands or threats, but by connecting feedback to strengths and tying expectations directly to purpose.

Linda's story shows what performance improvement really looks like when done well. It isn't about pushing people harder, it's about helping them see how their best qualities can improve results and create a team that grows stronger, more confident, and more resilient.

PRINCIPLES

Principle 1: Manage Energy As Well As Time

Great leaders elevate performance by fueling the energy that sustains focus, resilience, and momentum. Most conversations about productivity revolve around time, how to schedule it, protect it, and stretch it. But to elevate performance without pushing people toward burnout, leaders must manage energy as strategically as they manage time. The distinction is simple but powerful. Time is finite; energy is renewable. As Schwartz, Gomes, and McCarthy (2010) argue in *The Way We're Working Isn't Working*, sustainable high performance comes from supporting the physical, emotional, mental, and spiritual energy of employees.

Energy management begins with a mindset shift. Humans are not machines that can be programmed to operate 24 hours a day, 7 days a week. The most productive people work in cycles, alternating between focused effort and deliberate recovery. Micro-breaks and walking meetings can increase productivity. Deep work sprints followed by rest can dramatically improve output without increasing hours. As Schwartz, et al. note, even elite athletes train in intervals, because quality performance is developed by short bursts of strenuous activity followed by rest to repair. Yet, many workplaces expect uninterrupted output, leading not to excellence but to exhaustion.

Emotional energy is just as vital. Mortensen and Gardner (2017), in The Overcommitted Organization article, explain how constant multitasking across teams depletes both emotional and cognitive bandwidth. The cost? Lower performance and well-being. Leaders can protect energy by clarifying expectations, reducing low-value meetings, and fostering psychological safety.

Most importantly, leaders must model energy stewardship themselves. That means setting boundaries, taking meaningful breaks, and honoring their own rhythms. When leaders treat energy as a strategic asset they signal to their teams that excellence doesn't come from agonizing intensity, but from intentional, rhythmic, and renewable strength.

Principle 2: Celebrate Small Wins And Consistent Gains

In high-pressure environments, leaders often equate performance with pushing harder, expecting more, and constantly moving the target. But sustainable improvement doesn't come from relentless pressure. It comes from momentum. When leaders recognize modest gains and steady improvement, they unlock motivation and performance. This principle prioritizes progress over pressure and builds a culture where small wins fuel big impact.

Kouzes and Posner (2017), in *The Leadership Challenge*, reinforce the need for "generating small wins" to sustain commitment and engagement. They note that incremental achievements clarify direction, build confidence, and make excellence feel attainable. When people see progress, even small progress, they're more likely to stay engaged, take initiative, and stretch their capacity.

Matthew Syed's *Black Box Thinking* (2015), echoes this idea when he explains that marginal gains consisting of a series of small, continual improvements lead to breakthrough outcomes. By focusing on one area at a time, testing and adjusting based on feedback, teams improve faster than they would through pressure alone. The *Organizational Performance Improvement* whitepaper (ATD, 2018) supports this finding. The report shows that organizations addressing root causes with focused, incremental solutions, rather than broad, high-pressure initiatives, achieve more consistent results. It also highlights that performance efforts aligned with clear business priorities, rather than vague aspirations, are far more likely to drive lasting impact.

Encouraging small wins also protects people's energy. As Wiseman (2021) notes in *Impact Players*, standout contributors are the ones who advance work consistently, not those who exhaust themselves or others. They simplify complexity, take the next right step, and help others do the same. This steady rhythm creates lasting traction. Leaders can reinforce this by celebrating progress as much as outcomes, modeling and rewarding learning behaviors, and making incremental improvement the norm.

Principle 3: Implement Feedback Systems People Trust

Most organizations say they value employee feedback, but their systems tell a different story. Leaders launch annual engagement surveys, gather piles of data, and then silence follows. Employees are left to wonder whether anyone read their responses, or worse, whether their input was rejected. Over time, silence breeds cynicism. Instead of motivating performance, feedback systems become a source of disengagement and distrust.

At its best, organizational feedback is a growth engine. When employees see that their input is recognized and acted upon, they engage more fully, innovate more often, and sustain higher performance. Gallup's (2024) research shows that employee disengagement costs the global economy $8.8 trillion annually, with U.S. engagement at a 10-year low of just 31%. One major cause is broken feedback loops - systems that ask but never answer. In contrast, when organizations design feedback processes that provide follow-through, employees develop trust that their voice matters and their effort has impact.

Champagne (2025) has spent decades researching how surveys can be transformed from a compliance activity into a system that builds loyalty and drives performance. His "Survey Conversation" method rests on three core drivers of engagement: my voice was heard, my advice made an impact, and I can see how my ideas compare to others. To activate these drivers, Champagne (2014, 2025) recommends replacing one-time, 50-question surveys with a cadence of short, bite-sized surveys with only three or four questions. These are launched in waves, for example, ask on Monday, share preliminary results on Wednesday, and close the loop by Friday. This fast cycle gives employees a chance to see their input in real time, compare perspectives with colleagues, and feel the momentum of change. Most importantly, leaders don't just share what was collected, they explain the action that will follow. Feedback loops are closed by telling people: "Here's what we heard. Here's what we can act on. Here's what we can't change right now, and why." Transparency is as powerful as agreement. Even when leaders cannot implement a suggestion, employees trust the process when leaders are candid about limitations.

Champagne's work echoes broader research on feedback loops. Syed (2015) shows how industries like aviation improve by analyzing errors without blame. They are systems designed for learning, not fear. Similarly, Kouzes and Posner (2017) found that leaders who connect feedback to shared values and aspirations increase openness and growth. The ATD (2018) *Organizational Performance Improvement* report emphasizes that feedback must be built into implementation phases, not bolted on as an afterthought. But Champagne adds something essential: the architecture of trust. Feedback becomes developmental only if employees see the loop closed, the action explained, and the progress reported. Without these design features, feedback systems collapse into fear: "What will they do with my answers?" or futility: "Why bother? Nothing changes."

To bring this principle to life in your organization:

- Ask fewer, better questions: Keep surveys short, targeted, and meaningful.

- Share results immediately. Post interim findings while the survey is still open to spark participation and transparency.

- Close the loop. Tell employees what will change, what cannot, and why.

- Show progress over time. Report periodically on how feedback has been implemented.

- Avoid survey pitfalls. Don't ask about things you can't change (Champagne, 2014).

When organizations design feedback as a system rather than an event, they don't just gather opinions, they fuel performance. Employees who see their voice leading to action are more loyal, more innovative, and more committed. In Champagne's studies (Champagne, 2025), completion rates soared when employees trusted the process. Nearly 90% of respondents said they wanted to complete more surveys when they saw that their input was valued and acted upon

Closing the loop is more than good survey practice. It is a leadership commitment to growth over fear, dialogue over silence, and transparency over assumption. Leaders who design feedback systems people trust create performance cultures built on confidence, clarity, and continuous improvement.

Principle 4: Match Strengths With Responsibilities

One of the most sustainable ways to elevate performance is to ensure that people are doing work that energizes them. When leaders align tasks with individual strengths, what Patrick Lencioni calls "working genius," they tap into discretionary effort, reduce burnout, and build lasting capacity. This principle could be called, "Align Genius to Work" because it is about optimizing performance through alignment, not pressure.

In *The 6 Types of Working Genius*, Lencioni (2022) outlines six distinct modes of contribution: Wonder, Invention, Discernment, Galvanizing, Enablement, and Tenacity. Each person has two areas of "genius" where they thrive, two areas of "competency" where they can contribute but tire quickly, and two areas of "frustration" that drain energy. Leaders who assign responsibilities based on people's genius zones see greater fulfillment, efficiency, and resilience. These natural inclinations unleash unrestricted effort, reduce friction, and elevate both morale and results. In contrast, consistent misalignment leads to friction, fatigue, and disengagement, no matter how talented the individual.

Dayna Williams (2023) cautions that misalignment between roles and capabilities doesn't just frustrate individuals, it destabilizes entire systems. In sales organizations, she found that companies often placed "farmers" in roles that required "hunters," creating cycles of underperformance and wasted effort. The parallel in schools is clear: when we assign tasks that don't align with a teacher's or leader's strengths, inconsistency and burnout follow. Matching genius to responsibility is a safeguard against systemic cracks.

Wiseman (2021) found that top performers sustain their energy not by doing more, but by doing work that both energizes them and uplifts others. They reduce drama, focus on what matters most, and model calm amidst chaos. High-impact contributors also concentrate on where they can add the greatest value, often behind the scenes or in overlooked spaces, aligning their effort with their unique abilities. Leaders who recognize and reward this kind of contribution create conditions where initiative and energy multiply.

The Leadership Challenge by Kouzes and Posner (2017) adds another layer. Empowering others to act is a hallmark of effective leadership. That starts by understanding what people do best, and then stepping back. Strength-based leadership doesn't ignore weaknesses; it designs for interdependence, where one person's genius fills another's frustration.

To apply this principle:

- Use tools like MBTI Team Report, Working Genius, or or internal strengths mapping to identify individual energy zones.

- Create team maps that visualize strengths and skills, exposing gaps and overlaps.

- Regularly ask, "What kind of work gives you energy?" and

"Where do you feel most effective?"

When people operate in their genius zones, work gets done better, faster, and with greater joy. Leaders who align genius to work build sustainable, productive organizations.

Principle 5: Use Learning to Power Performance

In many organizations, learning is treated as an emergency intervention as a response to underperformance, disengagement, or burnout. But learning after it is needed is often too late. The real opportunity lies in making learning a daily habit, a built-in rhythm that fuels growth, strengthens resilience, and sustains high performance. This principle invites leaders to shift from occasional training to ongoing development embedded in the flow of work.

Williams (2023) also warns against what she calls "Band-Aid" solutions that promise quick results but fail to address deeper structural needs. These reactive fixes might generate short-term activity, but the same performance gaps reappear because learning is not embedded in daily practice. Schools face the same danger when professional development is treated as an isolated event rather than a rhythm of growth.

Syed (2015), contrasts closed-loop systems, where mistakes are hidden and repeated, with open-loop systems that use errors as fuel for improvement. Industries have reduced failure rates dramatically by treating every misstep as a learning opportunity. When teams adopt learning in real time, not just in crisis, they build short-term recovery and long-term capacity.

Kouzes and Posner (2017) reinforce this mindset in *The Leadership Challenge*. They argue that exemplary leaders "model the way" by being learners themselves. They foster psychological safety, enabling teams to reflect, experiment, and try new ideas without fear. In these cultures, learning is a daily expectation tied to performance, purpose, and shared growth.

The *Organizational Performance Improvement* white paper (ATD, 2018) further affirms that the most successful interventions are ongoing, not one-time fixes. Learning that is directly tied to solving real problems and reinforced over time is retained. Especially during times of change, consistent learning routines help teams adapt without feeling overwhelmed. Learning, in this view, is readiness.

Wiseman (2021), in *Impact Players*, identifies the desire to learn as a defining trait of high performers. They aren't "know-it-alls," they're "learn-it-alls." These individuals seek input, test solutions, and share insights across teams. When organizations reward this behavior, they grow talent and cultivate a culture where improvement compounds.

To apply this principle, leaders can normalize daily debriefs, weekly reflection questions, and microlearning nudges. A cadence of small learning moments keeps teams sharp and agile because in a learning culture, growth isn't the medicine after the crisis, it's the healthy practice that prevents it.

FROM ONE LEADER TO ANOTHER

Amol Mandalaywala

Assistant director for learning and development, EY Consulting
  As heard on Othman's Leadership Podcast, Episode TBD

Fit to Perform is a Mindset a Design Challenge

For Amol Mandalaywala, performance improvement begins with a mindset. "When I think about performance improvement, I really talk about more than just managing people. It's really about managing people to enable performance." He calls it a "fit to perform mindset," a way of asking not just whether people are doing their jobs, but whether the conditions around them are setting them up to thrive. "It's not about pushing harder. It's about removing obstacles and ultimately optimizing capability."

That perspective shaped one of his most revealing consulting experiences. A business owner approached him with what seemed like a straightforward problem. The sales team's performance was slipping. "The obvious might be, oh well, let's talk to the sales team and figure out what sales strategy they're using." But Mandalaywala decided to go deeper. He met with the team, mapped their processes, and tested their product knowledge. "It became obvious that I didn't think the sales team had a problem doing what was expected of them." The real problem, he discovered, was downstream. "Once it got to production, traffic slowed down. Items were not being shipped to clients on time. And that's why performance was actually slipping."

In that situation, Mandalaywala learned that performance gaps are not always where they first appear. "The first thought was, oh, the salespeople are not doing their job well. Therefore, we must upskill them, we must retrain them. But that may not be necessary." Looking at the whole system matters. "Whatever one part of the system is doing, it has downstream impacts on other parts. And maybe something can't autocorrect itself. We've got to figure out where that is."

Understanding the difference between skills, capabilities, and motivation is just as critical. "If they have the knowledge and they have the skills, then what is the problem? Is it the system? Do we have a capacity problem? Do we have an incentive problem? Do we have something else going on?" For Mandalaywala, skills are tactical - the ability to use a tool, follow a process, complete a task. Capabilities are broader. "When you learn a skill and you are now thinking, okay, how can I apply it in a different context? Well, now you are building a capability." Motivation, meanwhile, must be considered in context. "Yes, motivation is an issue for some people. But if you are truly invested in promoting that 'fit to perform' mindset, you are going to take away obstacles that inhibit performance and really enhance everything so they can get the job done."

Designing solutions with that lens often means focusing less on training and more on creating perspective. In the case of the sales–production–logistics breakdown, Mandalaywala recommended job rotations so employees could experience other units. "Let's get somebody from logistics to sit in production. Let's get someone from production to sit in logistics for six weeks. Let's get somebody from sales, also, to sit in both of those units." The goal was understanding. "Once they understood how each block is interconnected to really deliver for the company and the client, then perhaps they would understand the benefits of cooperation and collaboration."

This attention to systemic solutions also applies to learning design. "The new challenge in identifying gaps is really technology. We always will have a gap." Instead of constantly chasing the newest tools with endless reskilling, Mandalaywala focuses on building long-term capability. "If we foster and nurture certain capabilities... it will be a lot easier to design a learning solution that has a longer shelf life." For him, performance improvement is not about overwhelming people with generic programs. "If you force people into a solution that is all-encompassing, we are going to expect mediocre results. And that, to me, is detrimental. We are tarnishing ourselves."

Sustaining performance, he says, requires deliberate review and ongoing dialogue. "Performance is not a one-and-done thing. You have to regularly review performance. You use data, you use feedback, and you use observation." Leaders must also communicate transparently about external pressures, whether tariffs, economic shifts, or industry disruptions. "You've got to see where exactly changes are happening in the system. And data, feedback, and observation are the tools to help guide how you're going to assess that."

Conversations with employees are part of that process, but not just to check it off a to-do list. "How do you feel about your work today? Oh, I feel really great. Wonderful. Then everything seems fine. Your performance has been great. We're done. Is that really valuable? No." Real conversations require trust and authenticity. "Not only does the individual contributor need to share vulnerabilities and concerns, but the leader must also demonstrate empathy. They should live those values. You can't say it's safe to share anything and then later on say, well, that really wasn't appropriate."

Mandalaywala also acknowledges the resistance leaders face, particularly from high performers. "The problem with high-performing individuals is that they don't see a need to change because they are focused on outcomes. But if the products are going to change, then so is your job. If you are resisting change because you're high performing, that is shortsighted." His strategy is to clearly explain what is changing and why it matters, even for those already suc- ceeding.

In the end, his philosophy comes back to a leadership mindset. "It should never be about self as the individual. It's really about the collective, whether it be the team, the business unit, or the entire organization." Leaders, he believes, must see themselves as architects. "You are creating the environment to allow people to continually perform better." That is the essence of performance improvement: not squeezing more out of people, but building the conditions where they are truly fit to perform.

STRATEGY IN A SKETCH

The ATD Performance Improvement Model helps leaders uncover what's really causing underperformance before rushing to solutions. Instead of guessing what's broken or defaulting to more training, this model urges you to slow down and investigate. What's the goal, what's the gap, and what's getting in the way? It guides you through a sequence of targeted analyses, each one designed to sharpen your understanding and ensure that any intervention is backed by real insight. Used well, this model saves time, prevents waste, and builds credibility by aligning every decision to results.

ATD Performance Improvement (HPI) Model

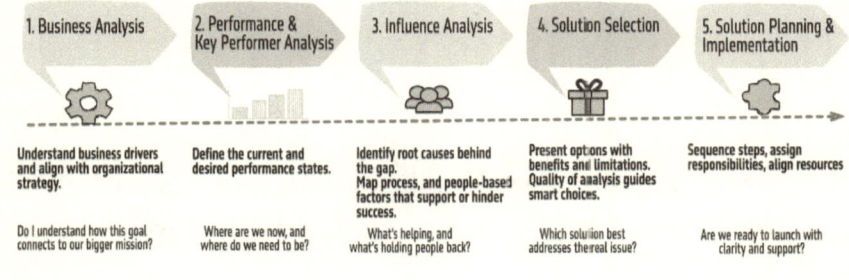

1. Business Analysis	2. Performance & Key Performer Analysis	3. Influence Analysis	4. Solution Selection	5. Solution Planning & Implementation
Understand business drivers and align with organizational strategy.	Define the current and desired performance states.	Identify root causes behind the gap. Map process, and people-based factors that support or hinder success.	Present options with benefits and limitations. Quality of analysis guides smart choices.	Sequence steps, assign responsibilities, align resources
Do I understand how this goal connects to our bigger mission?	Where are we now, and where do we need to be?	What's helping, and what's holding people back?	Which solution best addresses the real issue?	Are we ready to launch with clarity and support?

Note: Use data to guide decisions. Conduct formative and summative evaluations to ensure effectiveness. What worked, and how do we know?
Common traps: Failing to define success metrics before launching solutions

Based on ATD's Talent Development Body of Knowledge (2nd ed., 2024).

MAKE IT YOURS

- Where is my team overextended? What energizing rituals or rhythms could I build in this week?

- What small, meaningful progress have I overlooked that deserves recognition and reinforcement?

- How might I redesign feedback to inspire trust that action will follow?

- Am I aligning responsibilities with each team member's unique strengths, or just assigning based on availability?

- What am I doing daily to model a learning mindset and make improvement part of the culture, not just a crisis response?

30

Innovate Through Data Storytelling

How Do You Show What It Means and Why It Matters?

The challenge is not to collect the data, but to make sense of it and tell a story.

Hans Rosling

The Night the Data Came Alive

At first, the room was quiet. Parents sat with folded arms. Teachers leaned back in their chairs. Board members watched, waiting. It was the first community night hosted by the district's new superintendent. The event had been promoted as a night of transparency, a time to "review the data together." Some arrived curious. Others arrived skeptical. All had low expectations based on previous presentations.

The superintendent stood in front of the room and shared the numbers. Test scores. Graduation rates. Attendance trends. But then, he surprised everyone. He explained what the numbers actually meant. Rather than letting data points sit on a slide, he brought them to life. He shared the context behind each shift, why a dip happened in one school, why a rise in graduation rates should still be interpreted with care, and why certain subgroups showed unexpected trends. He used fictitious student names to walk the community through real-world examples. Each story preserved confidentiality but revealed the deeper truth that there were real people behind these numbers. And that changed everything.

As he moved from raw numbers to meaning, the atmosphere lightened. Parents leaned in. Teachers nodded. What started as a spreadsheet began to feel like a shared journey. And then, he went a step further. He outlined what would happen next and who was responsible. "This is what my cabinet will focus on in the next quarter. Here's what I'm asking principals to do. Here's how families can help. And here's what success will look like." Instead of dumping data, he translated it into action. Everyone had a role. Everyone had a path forward.

The impact was tangible. That night sparked a revival. Within a month, the district's Parent Teacher Organization (PTO) gained five new volunteers. The annual climate survey, which had only received 158 responses the previous year, jumped to 240. More importantly, the narrative in the community began to change from frustration to forward movement. This wasn't just a well-run meeting. It was an example of data storytelling done right.

Most leaders know how to present numbers. Fewer know how to interpret them. Even fewer know how to weave them into a story that builds trust, invites ownership, and moves people toward action. That night, the superintendent put faces behind the data. He helped the community see what the numbers couldn't say alone.

PRINCIPLES

Principle 1: Reveal What Matters

Leaders often fall into the trap of presenting data as a sequence of charts, dashboards, or metrics, and assume that numbers alone will guide people to insight. But in today's crowded information landscape, facts alone seldom convey their full weight. Data storytelling is the practice of communicating data-driven insights through a structured narrative that integrates visual design, emotional resonance, and audience context to drive understanding and action (Knaflic, 2015). Data storytelling combines analytical thinking with storytelling principles to make data more memorable, persuasive, and actionable (Knaflic, 2015). The most effective communicators begin with the message that matters most, the "so what," and use data to support it.

Knaflic (2015) calls this "informing with intention." Bladt and Filbin (2013) put it more sharply: "Data without a narrative is noise." Their work at DoSomething.org showed that analysis alone didn't change behavior, meaning did. They replaced reporting everything they knew with highlighting what their audience needed to feel, understand, and do. The story, not the spreadsheet, drove engagement.

In practice, this means flipping the script. A school leader doesn't start with a dashboard on absenteeism. They begin with, "If the trend of absenteeism continues, 1 in 5 students may fall permanently behind." Only then do they share the supporting data. A nonprofit director doesn't open with donation charts, they open with, "One in three families can't afford heat this winter. Here's how our work is changing that."

Revealing what matters requires stepping into the mindset of your audience. What do they care about? What pressures shape their decisions? What insight will move them to act? When leaders lead with the "so what," they turn passive data into purposeful narrative. Ultimately, meaning first, metrics second is a strategy that transforms data from information into influence.

Principle 2: Shape Stories Around Audience Needs

Effective data storytelling must be developed within the context of audience experiences. Leaders often assume their message will resonate if the data is strong, but relevance is what drives engagement. A powerful story begins with empathy. It requires understanding your audience's values, concerns, and context so you can frame the data in a way that meets them where they are.

Roy (2022) highlights how today's audiences live in dynamic, fragmented "enclaves" where information flows differently depending on identity, affiliation, or need. In these spaces, the same set of facts can be interpreted very differently depending on how well they're framed. McKinsey research echoes this: leaders who succeed at change are often those who intentionally align their communication with both emotional and strategic concerns (Takai et al., 2024).

Consider the absenteeism example. If a principal is speaking to teachers, the story must connect to classroom realities: "I know many of you are struggling to support students who are frequently absent. Today's data helps us identify which students are most at risk and what support systems can help you help them." For families, the story shifts: "We know how much you care about your child's future. This data shows that missing even two days a month can set students back. Together, we can reverse this trend." Same numbers, different approach.

The nonprofit case illustrates the same principle. To field staff: "You're on the ground every day seeing the impact of energy insecurity. This data helps us target the families most at risk this winter and ensure we respond in time." To donors: "We're seeing one in three families in this city who are at risk of heating insecurity. With your support, we can keep children warm this winter." By changing the angle, the leader ensures both groups not only hear the message but also see their role in it.

The heart of data is how it is framed. Leaders who translate serve as sense-makers rather than mere messengers. They anticipate what their audience values, the pressures they navigate, and the language most likely to inspire commitment. By translating rather than simply transmitting, leaders craft messages that inform and endure."

Principle 3: Use Visuals To Clarify Data

Once you've identified the message and shaped it for your audience, the next step is to bring it to life visually. Design is important. It is how you help people process, remember, and act on what they see. When visuals and narrative align, they sharpen meaning and spark emotion. When they compete or overwhelm, the message gets lost.

Building on Knaflic's (2015) call for intentional communication, good design removes clutter, highlights what matters most, and guides the eye through the story. Sandosham (2024) adds that emotion is carried not only in words but also in visual choices. Colors, icons, and layout can elevate a message from passive to persuasive. In short, design carries the story.

Consider absenteeism. A typical dashboard might show average attendance by grade. But to design for impact, a principal could show a single bar chart of how many students miss more than 10% of school days, paired with the image of an empty desk. A red callout reads: "1 in 5 students is on track to fall behind." The visual emphasizes urgency.

In the nonprofit example, a thermometer-style progress bar communicates funding gaps far more powerfully than a pie chart. A map shaded with warming colors makes heating insecurity visible across neighborhoods, turning an abstract number into a scene people can feel.

Design should always match intent. Are you aiming to alarm, inform, or inspire? Choose a visual that symbolizes and amplifies your message. In practice, this means telling the story once in words and/or numbers, and again in pictures. When language and imagery reinforce each other, the message reaches further and resonates longer.

Principle 4: Organize the Story

Even the most compelling insights and visuals can fall flat if they're not organized well. That's why great data storytellers rely on narrative frameworks. These clear, logical patterns help audiences follow the journey from problem to insight to action. Barbara Minto's Pyramid Principle (2009) is a classic example of how this can work. Start with the "governing thought" and then gather supporting evidence beneath it in a logical flow. Similarly, the SCQA framework (Situation, Complication, Question, Answer), used by McKinsey and other firms, provides a repeatable way to build stories. What's the context? What tension has emerged? What critical question does it raise? And what answer are we proposing?

Here's how SCQA would apply to the absenteeism example:

1. Situation: Student attendance has historically remained stable.

2. Complication: Over the last two years, chronic absenteeism has doubled.

3. Question: Why is this happening, and what's the risk if it continues?

4. Answer: Our data shows that 1 in 5 students now misses enough school to jeopardize academic progress. We must act quickly to implement early interventions.

Likewise, in the nonprofit example:

1. Situation: Our organization has consistently provided heating assistance.

2. Complication: This year, rising costs left one in three families at risk.

3. Question: How can we close the gap and serve everyone?

4. Answer: We have raised 70% of our goal. A final campaign push focused on the hardest hit areas can ensure no family is left in the cold.

A well-structured story should always culminate in a call to action that is simple, direct, and compelling. What should the audience do next? How can they help? What role can they play? A framework like SCQA sets the stage for understanding, but it's the call to action that ensures the story ends with commitment.

FROM ONE LEADER TO ANOTHER

Dr. Laurie Shanderson

Founder and CEO of Accreditation Insights
   As heard on Othman's Leadership Podcast, Episode TBD

Let the Data Lead the Story

Dr. Laurie Shanderson traces her appreciation for data back to graduate school. While working at a pain management clinic, she began tracking outcomes for patients. "I remember the information found in that data being so powerful, the patterns it revealed, the anomalies that surfaced, the insights that could be drawn." That early project, she says, was "a good entrée into understanding data and the potential it holds to change thinking."

Years later, as an undergraduate, she sat in on a doctoral presentation about an island community's health during and after monsoon season. At the time, the conclusion seemed obvious: "Of course you're going to have less weight and less health." But she sees it differently now: "It's really important to look closely at the data, because it may point to something unexpected. You gain power from having information."What did she learn that was different from the "of course" info? These early experiences shaped her belief that data's true value lies in its ability to challenge assumptions and open new possibilities.

That belief has become a disciplined practice. For Shanderson, every data story begins with accuracy and completeness. "A strong data story includes having reliable and valid information. It needs to be timely, relevant, and appropriate." Even imperfect datasets can be valuable if you "understand the limitations, fill in any gaps, and make corrections so you can draw conclusions." Without integrity at the start, she warns, the story will collapse under scrutiny.

Her commitment to integrity also means resisting the temptation to bend data to fit a preferred narrative. "We want data to fit the story we want to tell instead of letting the data tell the story." She urges leaders to "be careful to stay honest about the data, what it means, and how it can be interpreted." This honesty, she notes, is most importantly, ethical, but it is also strategic because decisions built on distorted evidence rarely last.

She saw the power of this approach during a national discussion on the 90-credit bachelor's degree. "You can talk about that from a theoretical standpoint, but when you look at the actual data relative to outcomes, you begin to think differently about it." Considering financial, accreditation, teaching, and standards data revealed new opportunities: "If you've earned at least 90 credits, there should be some credential. Those credits have value to offer the workforce." The conversation shifted from a technical policy debate to a recognition of learning as an asset to the student and employer.

This same principle applies to leading change of any kind. "You shouldn't make a change without having a need to make the change, and that documented need can be found by looking at the data." Whether launching a new program or retiring an old one, she relies on "feedback in the data that shows we need to do something different." Data becomes both the reason for action and the evidence that builds buy-in.

Sometimes, the insights are as practical as knowing your audience. At a conference for podcasters, participants debated whether more people watch podcasts or listen to them. "Many of us were trying to figure out how to get our podcasts live with video, but the data showed people listen more than they watch." Audio-only formats allowed for flexibility when "gardening, cooking, and exercising," in ways video could not. Without that data, leaders might have invested in changes their audience didn't actually want.

For Shanderson, the lesson is simple and enduring. "Using data is very powerful. It's not biased, and there's no judgment with it. It is what it is." Her challenge to leaders is to approach every dataset with openness: "Be curious about the information you're looking at. Don't go in thinking you already know." When leaders let the data lead, their stories carry credibility, invite buy-in, and inspire change.

STRATEGY IN A SKETCH

Cole Nussbaumer Knaflic's framework transforms data from a report to a revelation. It guides leaders through six essential moves that start with understanding your audience and end with telling a clear, compelling story. This tool matters most when your goal isn't just to inform, but to influence. The power of this framework lies in how it blends design and empathy, reminding you to ask: What does my audience need to see, understand, and do? The most common mistake? Thinking the data speaks for itself. It doesn't. You do. This model helps you turn numbers and words into a story that promotes trust, sparks action, and makes insight impossible to ignore.

Cole Nussbaumer Knaflic's Storytelling with Data

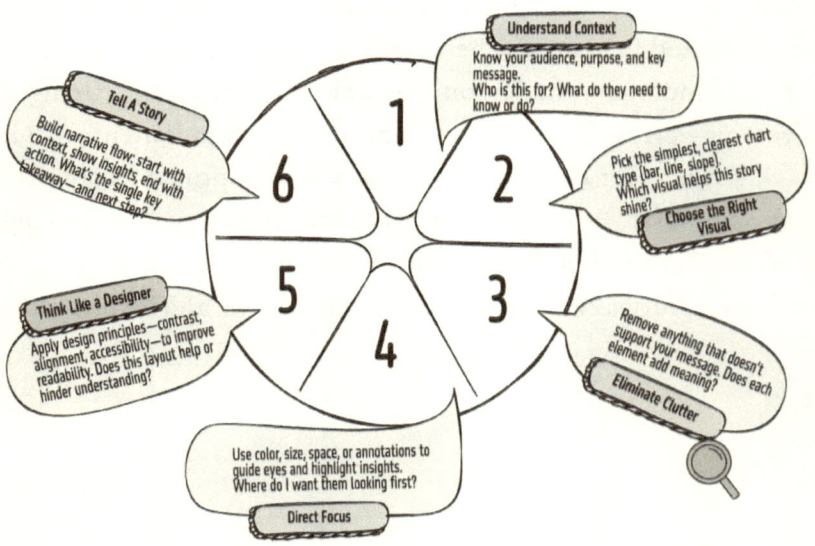

Based on Cole Nussbaumer Knaflic's book Storytelling with Data (2015).

MAKE IT YOURS

- Begin with the "So What" - What is the single most important insight my audience needs to walk away with, and why does it matter to them?

- Build the Bridge - How can I tailor my message to align with the specific outlooks, concerns, language, and priorities of my audience?

- Design for Impact - Does my visual design highlight the key message clearly and emotionally, or is it competing with it?

- Structure the Story - Have I organized my data story using a clear framework that guides my audience from understanding to action?

- Deliver for Action - What tone, story, or personal example can I use to make my message memorable and inspire action?

31

Innovate Through Branding

How Do You Become a Brand People Want to Join?

Your brand is what people say about you when you are not in the room.

Jeff Bezos

When Narrowing Your Focus Expands Your Impact

Layan was one of the most determined people I had ever met. For years she worked in the medical field, known for her precision and compassion. But her heart kept tugging her in another direction, toward children, and the dream of building something that reflected her values. So she left her career and poured her savings, her energy, and her passion into opening an Early Learning Child Care center.

From the beginning, her commitment was undeniable. The classrooms were spotless. Learning corners were thoughtfully designed. She spent late nights planning lessons, tweaking activities, and making sure each detail reflected her vision of quality. Parents who enrolled loved it, and the children were engaged and happy. By every measure of excellence, Layan was doing everything right. But the numbers told a different story. Enrollment remained flat. Calls were rare. Some months, only a handful of tours came through. For all the love and detail she poured into her center, the seats stayed empty.

The problem was in the structure itself. Layan had opened her doors to children ages two through six. On paper, it made sense to cast the widest net. In practice, it meant constant exhaustion. Toddlers needed diaper changes, sensory play, and close supervision. At the same time, older children needed structured pre-literacy and math foundations. Every night she sat at her kitchen table rewriting lesson plans, trying to bridge a gap that was just too wide. She was serving everyone and yet, in a way, serving no one fully.

The turning point came when she attended marketing training through the Western Massachusetts Professional Development Center. In one session, the facilitator said something that struck her: "If you try to stand for everything, you end up standing for nothing." For the first time, she thought about her center not just as a place for children, but as a brand. And branding meant clarity. Who was she here to serve? What did she want to be known for? That's when it clicked. From the very beginning, what she had dreamed of wasn't a general center for every age. It was creating rich, high-quality learning spaces for three and four year-olds. Those were the years when children's curiosity exploded, when language took off, and when early social skills formed. This was the age group she connected with most deeply and where she wanted to concentrate her efforts.

So, she made the counterintuitive move to narrow her enrollment. Instead of advertising for children aged two to six, she announced her specialty with ages three and four. Friends warned her the move risked failure. But within months, the opposite happened. Parents began calling and visiting. One mother told her during a visit, "I scheduled this tour because you specialize in this age group. I wanted my child in a place designed just for her."

For the first time, Layan felt relief. She wasn't stretched across impossible demands anymore. She was pouring her energy into the very space she had once dreamed of, and now families saw it too. Soon, she had something she never thought possible - a waiting list. By narrowing her focus, Layan's excellence was on display. Families weren't just enrolling their children in a program, they were joining a promise, one she could now deliver with confidence and joy. Layan discovered that once her brand's positioning was clearly defined, its narrative communicated itself with clarity and impact.

PRINCIPLES

Principle 1: Stand for Something But Not for Everything

One of the easiest traps for school leaders is trying to be everything for everyone. In the name of inclusivity, many districts water down their identity until no one is sure what they actually stand for. But branding that tries to cover every base causes confusion. A strong school brand emerges when you take a stand for something specific, something that sets you apart in a crowded landscape of options.

Research on branding shows that clarity, not breadth, builds loyalty. Miller (2017) reminds us that "the customer is the hero, not your brand." That means families don't choose a school because of how much it talks about itself, they choose the one that names their hopes and positions itself as the place to help fulfill them.

Likewise, Ries and Trout (1993) argued that marketing is "a battle of perceptions, not products." The most successful organizations win because they're perceived as clear, focused, and first in something. Dib (2016) reinforces this, warning leaders that "trying to target everyone in reality means you're targeting no one." The tighter the focus, the stronger the pull. Bailey (2010) builds on this by arguing that branding without coherence is empty. Using a "candy bar" classroom experiment, he shows that people don't respond to louder claims or broader appeals; they respond when what you offer matches what they actually want. Coherence is the alignment between your stated promise and the lived experience families encounter.

For K–12 leaders, this means translating research into a promise that parents, students, and staff can feel. A magnet school might brand itself as "The place where every student learns through real-world projects." A district might declare, "A safe place where every newcomer belongs by the first week." A high school might embrace, "We prepare leaders by connecting classrooms to careers." Notice that each is specific enough to be memorable, testable, and repeatable. When teachers, parents, and students can state the brand promise in ten words or less, your brand is alive, not just on a brochure, but in the culture.

The main point here is that a diluted promise is untrustworthy. If you want your school or district to attract and retain the right families and teachers, you must take a stand. Don't aim for broad appeal, aim for clear resonance. Write down in one sentence what your school stands for, then ask your staff to repeat it. If they can't, your brand isn't clear yet. Strong brands are built on a focused priority.

Principle 2: Guide Your "Customer"

Many school leaders fall into a branding trap by making themselves the star of the story. The message becomes "Look at our programs,"

"Look at our test scores," or "Look at our facilities." But in truth, families, students, and staff don't join a school because of its résumé. They commit to a place where they see themselves growing. The strongest brands flip the script and don't boast, they guide.

Donald Miller's book *Building a StoryBrand* offers a simple but powerful reminder to always position your customer as the hero and your brand as the guide (2017). For schools, that means parents are the heroes who want safety and opportunity for their children, teachers are the heroes who want to thrive in a supportive environment, and students are the heroes who want belonging and purpose. Your job as a leader is to be the trusted guide who helps each audience move closer to what they value most.

Sabri Suby, in *Sell Like Crazy* (2019), sharpens the point by saying nobody really cares about your brand story until they believe you understand their problem. Great educational leaders start by naming those problems out loud, sometimes better than parents or staff can themselves. For example, a principal might say, "We know how hard it is to balance your child's academic progress with their mental health. That's why we designed our advisory program to support both." On a district level, a superintendent might frame their role as guide by saying, "We understand families want schools that prepare students for the workforce right here in our community. That's why we built partnerships with local employers to create internships and career pathways." Both examples show how the brand message shifts from self-promotion to empathy and guidance.

Joey Coleman (2018), in *Never Lose a Customer Again*, adds that people rarely remember what you promoted, but they do remember how you made them feel. When families sense empathy, when teachers feel supported, and when students believe the school cares about their journey, your brand becomes part of their identity. It's not about clever messaging; it's about genuine guidance that shapes perception and builds loyalty.

Rick Bailey (2010), *Coherence: How Telling the Truth Will Advance Your Cause*, defines coherence as a reciprocal process in which audiences express their hopes and needs, while leaders shape their message in response to them. For schools, this means families and staff must "co-hear" the brand. A brand that guides without listening risks becoming another self-promotional slogan. A brand that guides by listening creates loyalty rooted in truth.

Every leader should ask the following questions. What kind of guide am I? Am I showing up with empathy, clarity, and a plan or just repeating the party line? Perception becomes reality. Families and staff don't gravitate toward the school that is technically the "best"; they choose the one that makes them feel understood. The strength of your brand lies in positioning yourself as the guide who empowers others to become who they aspire to be.

Principle 3: Strengthen Your Brand Through Ongoing Experiences

Most people think the job ends when students enroll and new hires sign a contract. But great leaders with great brands know that's just the beginning. The "after" is where trust is either confirmed or broken. It's the experience people remember, talk about, and share. And unfortunately, it's where many schools and districts drop the ball. They celebrate the win of enrollment, new staff, or a first-day orientation, then disappear, leaving families, teachers, or students to figure things out alone.

Stengel, Lamberton, and Favaro (2023) indicate that focusing only on quick-win "performance marketing" leads to diminishing returns, since acquisition costs rise over time without brand loyalty to sustain them. The same dynamic is true in education: if parents or teachers feel abandoned after the initial welcome, the cost of regaining their trust, or replacing them, soars. A strong "post-sale" experience is what anchors the brand, reducing the need to constantly re-sell your school's value.

Coleman (2018), bluntly admonishes organizations that put all their energy into the chase and neglect the relationship. He notes that 20–70% of new stakeholders disengage within the first 100 days because no one follows up or makes them feel valued. Schools often make the same mistake. A new family might receive a warm welcome at registration but hear nothing for weeks afterward. A new teacher may be given a laptop and a handbook, but little support in navigating school culture. The result? Early enthusiasm fades into frustration.

Your brand includes the ongoing experience. It's your real branding force. When families are surprised by thoughtful touches like a principal sending a handwritten note after the first month of school, or when a district checks in with new hires weekly during their first semester, trust deepens. Peer recommendations and a positive reputation are a result of how people feel after they've interacted with you. That "after" impression travels further than any advertising budget.

McKinsey researchers show that personalization is accessible because tools now exist to make every customer, client, or family feel like a priority (McKinsey & Company, 2021). Schools can use the same principle by segmenting newsletters for families of new students, sending timely updates during key transitions, or creating welcome events that extend beyond day one. The most effective districts align short-term communication wins with long-term brand-building, creating a sense of continual belonging rather than a one-time transaction.

Al Ries and Jack Trout (1993), in *The 22 Immutable Laws of Marketing*, remind us that "marketing is a battle of perceptions, not products." When families and staff perceive your school as generous, consistent, and caring after they've joined, trust compounds. Dib (2016) makes the same case: the "after" phase of business is where repeat customers and brand advocates are born. The same is true for schools: loyal families become your recruiters, committed teachers become your ambassadors, and students themselves carry your brand story into the community.

In education, the enrollment, the hiring, or the first-day handshake is not the finish line. It's the starting point of a real relationship. That's where brand loyalty is born, and where your quietest marketing through thoughtful follow-up, authentic care, and lived-out promises, resonates the loudest.

FROM ONE LEADER TO ANOTHER

Dr. Rick Bailey

The Founder of RHB Consulting | Author of Coherence: How Telling the Truth Will Advance Your Cause (and Save the World)
As heard on Othman's Leadership Podcast, Episode TBD

Tell the Truth About Who You Are

When Dr. Rick Bailey explains branding, he doesn't start with logos or taglines, he starts with the importance of trust. He tells the story of walking into a Target store and spotting what looked like a Tiffany crystal bowl, tucked behind the housewares and marked at $7.99. The turquoise box, the shine, and the display all seemed enticing, but it didn't add up. "It was incoherent for Tiffany to be at Target, incoherent for an $800 bowl to cost eight bucks, incoherent that there wasn't more hoopla about the deal," he recalled. When things don't add up, people start doubting. "Coherence builds trust.

When it's missing, there's no transaction." For Bailey, that's what branding is - the alignment of truth, message, and perception.

He saw this play out with Agnes Scott College in Georgia. The institution had history, loyal alumni, and a mission rooted in women's education, but its brand had grown stale. "They were not defining themselves in a way that enthused people, even the people that worked there," Bailey explained. Too often, leaders try to mimic others, like the colleges that claimed to be "the Harvard of the Midwest," a label that sounded prestigious but rang hollow. "We'd laugh and say, 'You're not even close to Harvard.'" Instead of pretending, Bailey urged institutions to tell their real story, flaws and all. His team even developed a worksheet with 100 questions, answered it for Harvard, and then asked clients to do the same. "It forced clarity." At Agnes Scott, that clarity came through three guiding questions: What's true about us? What do we say is true? What do others believe is true? From there, the "Summit Curriculum" emerged, guaranteeing every first-year student a global experience and leadership mentorship. The focus was specific, the design was authentic, and the brand was believable. "They went from struggling to being ranked the most innovative college in America," Bailey shared.

Branding grows strongest when continually reviewed, refreshed, and reinforced. Rick described a moment of personal reckoning at his own firm when he realized that, across thirty years of hiring, he had failed to build a diverse team. Although his brand spoke of inclusivity, he admitted that without intentionally excluding anyone, he "hadn't been proactive" to make it a reality. At a companywide retreat, he confessed this truth to his staff. "It was embarrassing, but necessary." The vulnerability shifted culture, signaled a new commitment, and reshaped the firm's brand from the inside out. An organization's values are most powerful when reflected in daily practices. Bailey offers four S's: Share your vision so people can picture it, Spell out expectations so they know how to deliver, Sweat the details because the brand lives in the specifics, and Serve as a model so people see values in action.

He also pushed back on the obsession some leaders have with becoming a "household name." "Why do you want to be one?" he asked. "Your market isn't everybody." Instead of trying to be everywhere, he advised leaders to identify exactly who needs to know them and why. Without knowing your audience or your current position, even the clearest vision becomes a shot in the dark. He illustrated this with a GPS story: while driving in Boston, his screen flashed, "seeking third satellite." "That's what it's like when you don't know where you are, you can't get to where you want to go."

Bailey often recalls the college president who told him, after working through this process, "Thank you. You held up a mirror." That, he says, is the essence of branding: not crafting spin, but reflecting the truth so clearly that people can see themselves in it. "Leaders need the courage to stop hiding and start owning their brand," he said. Whether you're leading a school or a company, branding is about making your truth visible. "Do the work to be confident in the truth. Then you won't need a script. You'll just need your story."

STRATEGY IN A SKETCH

The Brand Key Model helps leaders uncover what their organization truly stands for and why it matters. At its core, the framework moves branding beyond slogans or surface marketing by walking you through nine elements: origin story, values, audience insight, benefits, reasons to believe, competitive frame, personality, emotional payoff, and brand essence. Together, these pieces act like a compass, pointing your school or district toward a clear identity. The power of the model lies in where it begins and ends. It starts with deep insight by naming what your people really need, and finishes with essence, the two or three words that capture your promise.

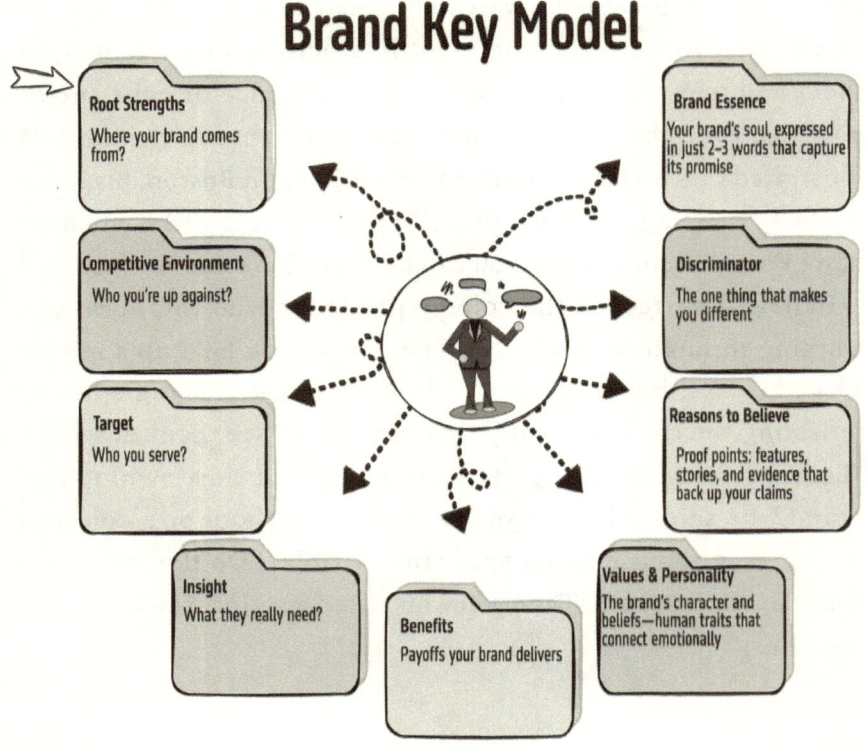

Brand Key Model

Root Strengths
Where your brand comes from?

Brand Essence
Your brand's soul, expressed in just 2–3 words that capture its promise

Competitive Environment
Who you're up against?

Discriminator
The one thing that makes you different

Target
Who you serve?

Reasons to Believe
Proof points: features, stories, and evidence that back up your claims

Insight
What they really need?

Benefits
Payoffs your brand delivers

Values & Personality
The brand's character and beliefs—human traits that connect emotionally

Unilever's Brand Key model (1990s)

MAKE IT YOURS

- What do I stand for? What does my organization stand for? Write one sentence to answer each question.

- Am I marketing my features or the transformation my audience truly wants?

- What are my ongoing activities that consistently reinforce my brand promise and deepen trust?

32

Innovate Through Journey Mapping

What Does the Experience Look Like Through Others' Eyes?

If there is any one secret of success, it lies in the ability to get the other person's point of view and see things from his angle as well as your own.

Henry Ford

Carlos Wasn't in the Room, But He Changed It Anyway

Carlos wasn't a consultant or a coach. He wasn't a principal or a policymaker. He was the maintenance guy at the compound where Jonathan lived, a friendly, hard-working man who liked to chat while fixing the occasional leak or outlet. Every time Carlos came by, he shared a small story, something about his wife, a neighbor, or someone at church. And every story ended the same way: "People need help." It wasn't a complaint, just an understanding of reality.

As he tuned in, Jonathan started seeing what Carlos meant. Although he was an administrator, he also enjoyed teaching as an adjunct professor. One evening, a Master's Degree candidate quietly shared that she had been taken by ambulance from her school the week before. She had been in excruciating pain but refused to call out of work. "If I miss a day, the kids fall behind," she said. Her body was giving signals, but her sense of responsibility wouldn't let her step away. A few days after that, Jonathan received an email from a former colleague asking him to serve as a reference. She had left the district five years earlier. When he followed up, she shared that she had spent the past few years battling breast cancer and was finally ready to return to the classroom. This was a teacher who used to arrive before the bell and stay long after dismissal, someone who gave everything to the work, even while carrying an invisible battle she hadn't shared until now.

It was in a district-level meeting where Jonathan decided to share his new insight. It was a tense setting, the tone was sharp, and participants were quick to blame. People weren't "stepping up." Others weren't "meeting the moment." There was a lot of talk about what was missing, so Jonathan decided to ask questions that might get to the root causes of the problems: What help do people really need? What would their journey look like if we outlined it?

The group caught on and word spread. Administrators started to realize that decisions made without understanding the people they affect are unproductive. When someone questioned why teachers weren't filling out a form or attending a training, they changed the narrative. "Before we try to fix them, let's follow them. Where are they coming from? What does that moment feel like from their perspective?" Eventually, Jonathan redesigned meeting structures so that outcomes included support. The team began identifying not only what they wanted people to do, but what those people needed from them to do it well.

For Jonathan, "help" became a leadership design principle. It meant identifying what people truly needed so their experience improved, their outcomes rose, and their sense of belonging deepened. He approached systems by tracing the lived reality of the people they were meant to serve.

Carlos never sat in on a strategy session. But his words did. Because of him, Jonathan no longer starts with solutions. He starts with someone's story and builds from there. That's the kind of leadership he practices, and the kind of change he helps others create.

PRINCIPLES

Principle 1: Gain insight for impact

In the realm of innovation and leadership, the capacity to see through others' eyes creates a key differentiator. Journey mapping is a method for visually representing the experiences of a person across key stages or touchpoints with an organization. It captures their actions, emotions, and interactions to highlight pain points and opportunities for improvement. Effective leaders don't just collect feedback; they immerse themselves in the lived experiences of those they serve. Perspective-taking dismantles assumptions, surfaces hidden barriers, and ensures solutions are grounded in reality.

Zander and Zander (2000) remind us that perceptions are not facts. They are stories shaped by bias and mental shortcuts. Leaders who fail to test these scripts risk making decisions based on the abstract rather than reality. Liedtka and Ogilvie (2011) extend this by identifying empathy as the first step in human-centered innovation. When leaders truly understand frustrations, workarounds, and unspoken needs, they design solutions that are practical and personal. Without this shift in perspective, innovation often defaults to organizational convenience rather than human need.

Hall (2017) pushes this even further, arguing that the insights that drive big-picture change rarely emerge in brainstorming sessions, but are more likely found in hallway conversations, subtle frustrations, and unspoken hesitations. The leader's task is to stay relentlessly aware of the small, messy, emotional inevitabilities that shape daily life. This is where insight leads to innovation.

Recent research reinforces the point. Bisht et al. (2024), found that customer loyalty and employee engagement are more strongly tied to emotional connection than technical performance alone. People don't just remember what was said or done as much as they remember how it made them feel. The emotional resonance of feeling seen, supported, and safe becomes the anchor of trust and connection. Leadership, then, is deeply relational, rooted in empathy and presence.

This concept is evident in schools. A superintendent who shadows a first-year principal for a day will likely notice things a dashboard never reveals: the tension of back-to-back parent meetings, the exhaustion of navigating policy shifts while managing student behavior, and the small but powerful wins that keep principals going. That experience changes the leader's understanding and, more importantly, their decisions. Instead of rolling out another initiative from a distance, they can design supports that coalesce with the real journey their principals walk each day. Direct insight into the daily experience of others ensures leadership decisions that are informed, empathetic, and effective.

Principle 2: Use Journey Mapping to Uncover What's Really Happening

Perspective-taking is the mindset, but mindsets don't shift systems on their own. Leaders need a structured way to capture and communicate what others are really experiencing. That's where journey mapping comes in. It transforms empathy into a concrete tool for change.

Mapping the lived experience is a powerful leadership practice that shifts focus from assumptions to insights. Journey mapping makes a diagram come alive by inviting leaders to step inside the user's world and document what someone actually experiences while moving through a program, process, or initiative. Rather than analyzing systems from the outside, journey mapping flips the lens. It captures how the system feels from the inside.

According to Gibbons (2018), a robust journey map includes several key elements: the person whose journey you are mapping, the scenario, the phases, user actions, the thoughts and emotions at each stage, and the insights or opportunities that emerge. This structure reveals not only what is happening but also what it feels like to be on the receiving end. The subsequent map serves as a catalyst for systems-level change grounded in lived reality.

The evidence is compelling. Lucidchart (n.d.) reports that 94% of organizations using journey mapping improved service delivery, while 91% saw measurable improvements in outcomes. In education, where new initiatives often create friction instead of flow, journey mapping helps leaders close the gap between strategic intent and day-to-day reality. Liedtka and Ogilvie (2011) reinforce this by positioning journey mapping as essential in the "empathize" and "define" stages of design thinking, where leaders uncover unmet needs, emotional undercurrents, and unspoken behaviors often invisible in spreadsheets or project plans. Dundon echoes this in *Seeds* of *Innovation* (2002), reminding us that breakthrough ideas emerge when leaders are willing to "see the system from the inside out."

For schools, the application is straightforward. A principal might map the journey of a new teacher's first year, from onboarding and classroom setup to evaluation and professional development. Such a map might reveal excitement in August, fatigue in November, and isolation in February, patterns that data alone might not expose. With this insight, leaders can anticipate where teachers need extra support, build in timely encouragement, and redesign the system to reduce friction points. In the same way, a superintendent mapping a parent's journey through enrollment might discover that the most stressful moment is not choosing a school but navigating confusing paperwork and deadlines. Addressing that moment can transform frustration into accomplishment. By mapping the lived experiences of teachers and families, school leaders can proactively address challenges, provide meaningful support, and create smoother, more empowering journeys for everyone they serve.

Principle 3: Design to Delight

Journey mapping uncovers the friction and emotions others carry, but awareness alone doesn't change culture. The next step is designing responses that fix problems and also create moments of delight. Designing to delight means creating systems, experiences, and supports that move past surface-level problem solving to design experiences that spark emotional engagement, build loyalty, and signal that people are truly seen and valued. According to Bisht et al., (2024) delight happens at the intersection of joy and surprise, when expectations aren't just met but exceeded in ways that feel thoughtful, human, and unexpected.

Traditional leadership often defaults to functionality: what fits the schedule, what meets the requirement, what checks the box. But compliance rarely inspires commitment. McKinsey's global research shows that organizations embedding delight into their service delivery see measurable improvements in retention, referrals, and even revenue. Customers who felt delighted, not just satisfied, were significantly more likely to return, recommend, and emotionally connect with the brand (Bisht et al., 2024).

The lesson is significant in the world of education. Schools often design experiences for efficiency rather than emotion. Yet emotional resonance is what transforms initiatives from obligations into movements. Liedtka and Ogilvie (2011) remind us that delight doesn't require flashiness; it requires alignment with people's unspoken needs. For instance, a district that redesigns its parent enrollment process to include clear, multilingual communication and a warm welcome not only reduces confusion but also builds relationships. Or consider a principal who surprises staff with handwritten notes during the toughest month of the year, not as a mandated program, but as a personal gesture of care. These small, thoughtful actions can turn transactional experiences into transformational ones.

Gibbons (2018) reinforces that delight is not accidental, it's a design outcome rooted in empathy and insight. It comes from anticipating moments of friction or uncertainty and responding with care, clarity, and creativity. When students, parents, or staff feel supported in those moments, especially when they didn't expect it, they experience reassurance, belonging, and a deep sense of trust in the school community.

Lucidchart. (n.d.) pushes us further, reminding leaders that designing for delight builds stronger systems while also building stronger relationships. Delight, in this sense, is the natural outcome of empathy and mapping. It transforms compliance into commitment and turns initiatives into movements. Leaders who consistently design for delight not only meet needs but also build trust, loyalty, and a culture people want to belong to.

FROM ONE LEADER TO ANOTHER

Dr. Ryan Rosiello

Manager of Leadership Development, United Natural Foods, Inc
As heard on Othman's Leadership Podcast, Episode TBD

Design Every Step of the Journey

"We leveraged journey mapping to really help us understand the experience of participants that are going through our leadership development programs so we can design the best experience possible for them." For one senior-level program, the stakes were high. "These are people that we're really investing in, that we want to stay at our organization and to make the biggest impact possible." That meant nothing could be left to chance. "We really mapped out all the different experiences - welcoming them into the program in a very warm and exciting manner, kicking off the program with a very special note, the content that they're learning, the networking that they're doing, hearing from the guest speakers, what it looks like when they put some of these skills into practice, and then, of course, long term, really making sure that they not only go through the program but they feel empowered to sustain what they're learning." The payoff was clear. "We got such great feedback afterwards... And so that's how we could really tell that participants got a lot out of the program."

When it comes to designing any leadership journey, Rosiello always starts with purpose. "I always recommend starting with charting your objectives, really making sure that you're clear on what you want to achieve with the program." Those objectives need to include both sides of the experience. "One is what they should learn as part of the program. The other part of it is getting an understanding of what you want them to feel after they go through the program." For him, the emotional journey is just as important as the intellectual one. "When we go through a journey, there are a lot of emotions. And ultimately, when you are mapping out an experience, you want to take that into consideration so you can build something that impacts both elements."

Equally critical is stepping into the participant's shoes. "As we were facilitating this to some of our senior leaders, one of the things that we really tried to do is sit in on the experience and observe what was happening." His team deliberately rotated roles so they could "sit down as part of the crowd and take it in almost as a participant." That act of immersion is what keeps design grounded in reality. "What does it feel like to go through some of the simulation or activities, what does it look like to be trying to do some of the networking and relationship building?"

Feedback then drives improvement. "Some of the data collection techniques that I always recommend for folks include using focus groups, interviews and surveys." Each tool adds something unique. "Focus groups, you get some really good, unique insights. Interviews, you can really go deep. Surveys are good too, when you need to collect just a broad understanding from a whole group of people." Resisting bias, however, is a necessary part of the process. "What resonates from my point of view as opposed to the participant? What's going to resonate most with them?" To avoid distortions, Rosiello insists on "staying true to the data, and trying to identify some of the common themes that you're hearing from those data collection mechanisms."

Rosiello also reminds leaders to widen the circle. Feedback should include "a direct report, a customer, the participant's manager, and Human Resources, too," since each perspective reveals how the program affects not just the learner but those around them. Over time, this commitment to multiple lenses ensures growth. "The biggest thing to do is to make changes. And whenever you make changes, document what you did and why." He calls this practice "a record of evolution" that prevents stagnation and keeps programs fresh. His closing advice is powerful. "Get something down on paper for when you start to think about what the experience looks like. Sometimes getting started is the trickiest part. When you have it as a starting point, to have it out there visually, and it makes the whole rest of the process a lot easier than trying to come up with it all in your head."

STRATEGY IN A SKETCH

The Experience Map, as described by Kalbach (2021), is a strategy tool that helps leaders see the full story of a person's journey by connecting behavior, emotion, systems, and gaps to drive meaningful change. Its purpose is to align internal processes with the real, lived experience of the people those systems are meant to serve. Rather than just listing tasks or responsibilities, this framework reveals where intentions break down, whether through confusion, delays, isolation, or miscommunication, so leaders can act with insight, not assumption. The value of this tool lies in its ability to make the invisible visible and bring empathy into operational decision-making.

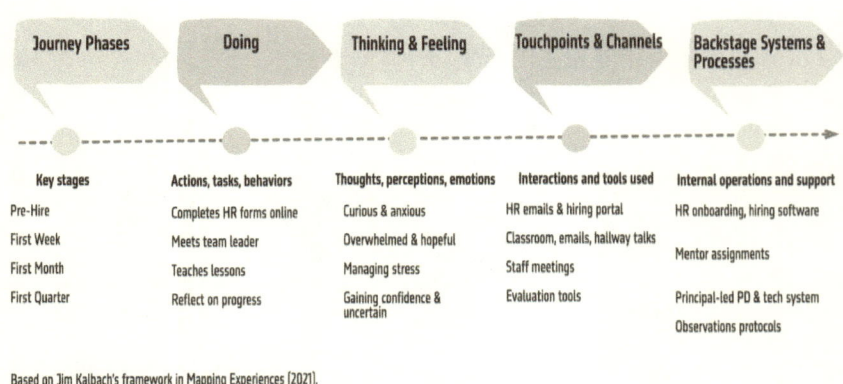

Experience Map
Insights for Alignment – Where to Improve, Fix, or Design Better

Journey Phases	Doing	Thinking & Feeling	Touchpoints & Channels	Backstage Systems & Processes
Key stages	Actions, tasks, behaviors	Thoughts, perceptions, emotions	Interactions and tools used	Internal operations and support
Pre-Hire	Completes HR forms online	Curious & anxious	HR emails & hiring portal	HR onboarding, hiring software
First Week	Meets team leader	Overwhelmed & hopeful	Classroom, emails, hallway talks	Mentor assignments
First Month	Teaches lessons	Managing stress	Staff meetings	
First Quarter	Reflect on progress	Gaining confidence & uncertain	Evaluation tools	Principal-led PD & tech system
				Observations protocols

Based on Jim Kalbach's framework in Mapping Experiences (2021).

MAKE IT YOURS

- Who can I shadow (a parent during enrollment, a new teacher in their first month, or a student navigating multiple classes) and document what surprised me about their experience?

- What critical journey (student transition from middle to high school, parent communication during IEPs, or teacher onboarding) will I map with phases, pain points, and emotions? Who will I share it with to ask where we can do better?

- What is one friction point from my journey map that I can redesign to delight the participant? (It could be as simple as replacing a confusing form with a guided conversation, or as meaningful as pairing every new teacher with a mentor who checks in weekly.)

33

Innovate Through Data & Analytics

Can You Turn Raw Data into Meaningful Insight and Action?

The greatest value of a picture is when it forces us to notice what we never expected to see.

John Tukey

Look–Think–Act in Action

Five math teachers gathered at Cedar Valley High School, each bringing stacks of student results, only to discover they were speaking different languages. The assessments weren't the same. The pacing was different. Even the units of study were misaligned, so a student excelling in one geometry class might be two units behind in another. When they tried to compare results, there was no common baseline. "It's like trying to diagnose the health of a patient when each doctor is using a different medical test," one teacher observed. English Learning staff were equally hamstrung. They couldn't support students effectively because there was no shared plan for what those students were learning. The leadership team had noticed the inconsistency, but no one had a clear map of why it was happening or how to fix it until Maria stepped in.

She had learned about action research and how it could help with this kind of complex, systemic challenge. Using the Look–Think–Act process, she began Cycle 1 by examining the current reality. She designed an open-ended survey and questionnaire that minimized bias by avoiding leading language and framing each one to let stakeholders speak from their own perspective. Questions included, "What obstacles do you face in aligning instruction? What's the impact on you and your students?" This stage was all about understanding the problem through the lens of those living it.

In Cycle 2, Maria moved to the "Think" phase by making sense of the data with the group. The patterns were unmistakable. There was no common prep time, no unified assessment calendar, and no meeting structure to turn good intentions into action. In a focus group, she facilitated the co-creation of a solution, testing each idea against the query, "Would this make our data more comparable and our decisions more reliable? The answer emerged in the form of a simple but powerful solution. It was a structure designed with weekly meetings, a clear agenda, equitable task distribution, and a shared Google Drive to store lesson plans, pacing guides, and common assessments.

Cycle 3 was the "Act" phase. Maria piloted the new structure over four weeks, guiding the team to meet consistently, open their time with a check-in, move through the agenda, and divide work so no one carried the full load. Google Drive became their single source, eliminating version confusion and lost files. By the end of the pilot, the group had a horizontally aligned geometry unit, a shared assessment calendar, and most importantly, data they could actually compare. When they looked at student performance together, the conversation shifted from, "We can't tell," to "Here's what's working, here's where we need to adjust."

And then the cycle began again - Look, Think, Act - to refine what they had built. The team reflected on what worked, adjusted their meeting norms, and planned how to expand the model to other courses. The process became a living example of what leaders can do when they stop treating data as static numbers and start treating it as a tool for collective learning. Maria didn't just help improve collaboration, she helped build a system that could keep improving itself.

PRINCIPLES

Principle 1: Start with the Right Question

Leaders often jump into data collection or dashboard-building without first asking the question that matters most: What problem are we trying to solve? The first and most foundational principle of effective data analysis is aligning inquiry with a clearly framed stakeholder need. Without a focused question, data is just a bunch of numbers. Data-driven leadership is the strategic practice of using structured, relevant, and actionable data to inform decisions, align teams, and drive continuous improvement across an organization. As Davenport and Harris (2010) emphasize, effective data-driven leaders make better decisions not by collecting more data, but by asking better questions and acting on evidence consistently.

In *The McKinsey Mind*, Rasiel and Friga (2001) stress that successful problem-solving begins with defining a structured, Mutually Exclusive, Collectively Exhaustive (MECE) issue tree - a tool that sharpens the problem and clarifies where to look. Instead of gathering a lot of data, the focus is on gathering the right data. Similarly, Ariker, Breuer, and McGuire (2014) warns against "mindless exploration of a big mountain of data." His research shows that organizations rarely suffer from a lack of information. They suffer from a lack of purpose in how they use it.

Warren Berger (2014), in *A More Beautiful Question*, reframes the leader's job as asking better, more catalytic questions. When leaders start with inquiry rather than assumptions, they shift the entire tone of the analysis. Questions grounded in a stakeholder's real-world context yield more relevant, useful, and actionable insights. Peter Drucker (2008) echoes this approach in *The Five Most Important Questions*, beginning with the deceptively simple, "What is our mission?" That one question alone reorients data work toward meaning, alignment, and decision-making that matters.

This principle is especially vital in education, where districts often collect volumes of attendance, testing, and discipline data without clarity on how it will inform change. Consider a private school facing declining high school enrollment. A reactive team might dive into numbers through the years and spreadsheets on demographic shifts. But a leader who starts with the right question might instead ask, "Why are families choosing other options, and what value do they believe they're missing here?" That reframing moves the analysis from surface metrics to deeper insights about community perception, program relevance, and student experience.

Another example would be a principal who notices a spike in student tardiness and is tempted to pull reports on bus schedules or attendance rules. But the sharper question might be, "What barriers are students facing before they even reach the door?" That question could open new avenues of exploration such as traffic congestion, inconsistent morning routines, or even feelings of disengagement with the school culture. These are important factors that numbers alone might never reveal.

Useful data starts with thoughtful, intentional questions. Because when the question is clear, data can spark transformation. Before inquiring about numbers or pouring through reports, pause and ask, "What is the question that truly matters here? Whose experience am I trying to understand? What decision do I need this information to support?" The quality of your question will determine the quality of your answer, and ultimately, the benefit of your data.

Principle 2: Use Frameworks to Guide Your Thinking

Before collecting data or diving into analysis, high-performing leaders pause to build a thinking structure. By organizing the problem before searching for answers, leaders reduce wasted effort, sharpen focus, and avoid the all-too-common "data trap" where they end up gathering too much, too little, or the wrong kind of information entirely.

Rasiel and Friga (2001) emphasize that elite consultants always begin with structure. Among the most useful tools are Mutually Exclusive, Collectively Exhaustive (MECE) issue trees. MECE issue trees are structured breakdowns of complex problems into smaller parts that don't overlap (mutually exclusive) and together cover all possibilities (collectively exhaustive). They help ensure clear, logical thinking and prevent gaps or duplication in analysis. Another structure often used are logic maps which show the step-by-step reasoning behind how data is gathered, what it measures, and how it connects to broader goals (Rasiel & Friga, 2001). They're essentially visual frameworks that link inputs, processes, and outcomes so you can see why a certain type of data is being collected and how it will be used.

Structure transforms a vague challenge into a roadmap for action. For example, if a district is experiencing declining enrollment, a structured breakdown might ask, "Are the causes academic, reputational, demographic, or competitive?" Each branch leads to a distinct data need and turns guesswork into targeted inquiry.

This method is reinforced in *Lean Analytics* (Croll & Yoskovitz, 2013), which urges leaders to define clear problem categories before even looking at a dashboard. They begin with a framework, using tools like Swim Lanes, logic diagrams, or hypothesis trees to clarify what must be true for a solution to succeed. In the context of data collection, swim lanes are a way of visually organizing processes to clarify who does what, when, and how data flows across different roles or systems. Each lane represents a person, team, or tool and shows their tasks, responsibilities, and data touchpoints, while the flow across lanes reveals where data is collected, transferred, or transformed, making it easier to spot gaps, redundancies, or bottlenecks. In short, swim lanes help ensure that data collection responsibilities are clearly defined and traceable across the workflow. Logic Diagrams are visual tools that map out the reasoning behind a process and show cause-and-effect relationships. And Hypothesis Trees are structured diagrams that break a central question or problem into a set of testable hypotheses and sub-hypotheses. Each branch represents a possible explanation, and the associated data points define what needs to be collected to confirm or reject it. This helps teams focus on evidence-based analysis rather than assumptions. These structures distill multifaceted issues to their essential drivers.

In practice, this means starting with a simple visual problem map. Consider again the challenge of declining enrollment. A district leader might organize the issue into four categories: (1) academic performance, (2) student experience, (3) parent perception, and (4) external competition. Beneath each, they might list sub-factors like test scores, program offerings, survey feedback, or competitor enrollment trends. This becomes the foundation for focused data collection and targeted stakeholder interviews.

McGuire, Ariker, and Roggendorf (2013) cautions that many leaders fall into the trap of chasing data without a plan which results in surface-level reports and missed insights. Structure is what prevents that drift. It ensures that every data point you collect is aligned to a decision you need to make. This is especially critical in K–12 leadership. Imagine a superintendent facing persistent gaps in math achievement. Instead of rushing to pull every assessment report, a structured issue tree might first break the problem into three buckets: curriculum alignment, instructional practice, and student support systems. Under each, the team can then identify specific data needs: alignment checks with state standards, classroom observation notes, and tutoring participation rates. That structure ensures the analysis doesn't just pile up more numbers but directly connects data to actionable drivers of student success. Once the structure is clear, teams can divide and conquer by assigning sub-questions, designing surveys, and gathering documents with precision. The structure itself doesn't solve the problem but it ensures you're solving the right one, in the right way.

Leaders should begin every inquiry with a clear map. Before collecting data, it is essential to define the categories of the problem, clarify the conditions that must hold true for a solution to succeed, and specify the decisions the data will ultimately inform. By structuring the investigation upfront, leaders shift from a scattershot search to purposeful, targeted analysis that drives insights leading to actionable solutions.

Principle 3: Collect What Counts

Once the right question is framed and the thinking is structured, the next step is to gather data, but not just any data. Leaders must resist the urge to collect everything available. Instead, they must intentionally pursue only the data that is most relevant to the question, reliable in quality, and likely to lead to applicable, decision-ready findings. The clarity of a decision is only as strong as the clarity of the data behind it.

Rasiel and Friga (2001), in *The McKinsey Mind,* reinforces that clean data is non-negotiable. Even the most sophisticated models will fail if they're fed inconsistent or inaccurate inputs. He urges organizations to adopt strong data hygiene practices like regular audits, clear data ownership, and rigorous validation protocols. In education, for example, attendance records, exit surveys, and enrollment reports must be consistently defined and accurately captured or they risk distorting the very story they're meant to illuminate.

Consider a district wrestling with declining high school enrollment. A reactive team might drown in a decade's worth of spreadsheets, wasting weeks combing through irrelevant details. A disciplined leader, however, narrows the lens to three critical data sets: (1) internal trends such as enrollment by neighborhood and grade level; (2) stakeholder signals like exit interviews and parent feedback and (3) external context like charter school growth or local demographic shifts. This tighter focus filters out distracting information and keeps the analysis anchored to the real drivers of decision-making.

Croll and Yoskovitz (2013) strengthens this case with the principle of the "One Metric That Matters." Their argument is straightforward: more data doesn't equal better decisions, pertinent data does. They emphasize that meaningful analysis depends on spotting patterns and directional shifts. A steady decline in 9th-grade enrollment. A spike in transfer requests after a new policy. These are not just statistics, they are signals. Effective analysts move beyond what is happening to uncover why it is happening, treating data not as an endpoint but as the beginning of deeper understanding.

The same lesson applies across K–12 leadership. Suppose a principal notices a steady dip in 5th grade reading scores. Instead of pulling every dataset available, the principal could hone in on three essentials: benchmark assessments by subgroup, student attendance patterns, and teacher assignment stability. Together, these reveal whether the issue is instructional, structural, or attendance-related, and is far more actionable than a hundred pages of general performance data.

This process doesn't demand advanced models. In fact, simple techniques often unlock the most actionable insights: year-over-year comparisons, segmenting by demographic or program, and visualizing trends through clear, accessible charts. Bersin et al. (2017), in McKinsey's *case study on people analytics*, highlight how organizations uncovered the root causes of attrition through basic correlations layered with employee interviews. Schools and nonprofits can apply the same approach—using numbers as starting points, then adding context and conversation to see the whole picture.

In the end, leaders don't need more data, they need the right data. Data that is relevant, clean, and connected to the questions that matter. Because information only becomes insight when it is focused, trustworthy, and purposeful.

Principle 4: Translate Insight into Action

The final step in the analytics journey is converting understanding into meaningful change. It's one thing to know what's happening. It's another to do something about it. This is where many teams stall. The analysis is complete, reports are generated, insights are shared... and then nothing changes. Impact doesn't come from knowing, it comes from acting.

Rasiel and Friga (2001) emphasize that insights only carry value when they inform real decisions. Clear communication, logical structure, and actionable recommendations are non-negotiable. If findings don't lead to change, they remain nothing more than interesting facts. McKinsey experts in Straight Talk About Big Data article explain the importance of embedding newfound knowledge into workflows, decision-making processes, and accountability systems to deliver real-world impact (Manyika et al., 2011).

Ariker, Breuer, and McGuire (2014) pushes further, arguing that data teams must operate as partners in change, not just producers of reports. Every insight should explicitly answer the question. "What will we do differently because of this?" That often requires rethinking roles, streamlining approval chains, and aligning incentives so that behavior reflects what the data reveals.

Take the example of declining high school enrollment again. Suppose the data shows families are leaving due to a lack of advanced academic programs. Insight alone doesn't change outcomes. Acting on it requires forming a cross-functional team to redesign course offerings, piloting new programs, and proactively engaging families with updates. Leaders must go further by assigning ownership. Who is responsible? What's the timeline? How will we measure progress? Without those commitments, the insight remains an observation instead of becoming a lever for improvement.

K–12 schools confront this challenge often. Imagine a district that uses survey data to identify low parent engagement in middle schools. Reporting the problem is not enough. The real test comes when the district creates action teams of principals, teachers, and parents to co-design communication routines, pilot family workshops, and track attendance at parent nights. Here, the insight sparks new behaviors, not just new slides for a presentation.

McKinsey's "insight-to-action loop" provides a practical structure:

1. Generate insight

2. Define the decision it supports

3. Assign ownership

4. Track the outcome

5. Revisit the data for learning (McGuire et al., 2013)

This loop transforms data from something you review into something you use. It also embeds continuous improvement and shared accountability into the process.

Insight gained from relevant data collection and analysis is a launchpad. It can close the gap between knowing and doing, and become a lever for shaping the future. A strong example comes from schools that treat transition years as predictive moments. Suppose a district discovers that families attending spring orientation sessions are three times more likely to enroll in the high school. That insight isn't just descriptive, it's predictive. Acting on it, the district could design targeted outreach to increase orientation attendance, track engagement, and measure resulting enrollments. If the pilot works, scale it. If it doesn't, refine and retest. Learn as you do, and do better because you learn.

McKinsey's Seven-Step Problem-Solving Process (Rasiel & Friga, 2001) offers a structure for embedding this mindset: define the problem, disaggregate it, prioritize key issues, analyze, synthesize, and communicate. But in future-ready organizations, the process doesn't stop at communication. It continues through cycles of experimentation, reflection, and redesign, what education researchers call "continuous improvement." Bryk et al. (2015), in *Learning to Improve*, show that school systems that thrive on evidence don't rely on one-time data reviews; they build routines where teachers, principals, and leaders regularly test small changes, learn from results, and adapt forward.

Data should do more than explain what already happened, it should shape what happens next. Too often, organizations get stuck treating data as a report card rather than as a compass. Predictive, adaptive leadership flips that script. It embeds data into culture so that inquiry, experimentation, and learning become daily habits. In this way, data isn't just backward-looking; it's forward-driving.

The goal is to create a data-smart culture that makes space for sense-making, distributes capacity across the system, and rewards experimentation. Predictive leadership adds the forward-looking edge, treating every metric as both a signal and an invitation to learn. Together, they move organizations from passive reporting to proactive shaping of the future.

FROM ONE LEADER TO ANOTHER

Debbie Richards

Chief Technology Officer, Creative Interactive Ideas
   As heard on Othman's Leadership Podcast, Episode TBD

Watch the Work Before You Read the Data

Debbie Richards didn't find her breakthrough in a spreadsheet, it came by watching someone struggle with a task. "I watched them complete this purchase order," she recalled. "They started filling in this form online. She's scrolling all the way across to the end of the line, and then she's going all the way back to the very beginning." When Richards asked why, the employee explained that the form didn't match the order of the paper document she was using. "That's a simple fix," Richards thought. "We either change the piece of paper or move that field on the online form." It was a perfect reminder of the importance of going to the source rather than the statistics.

Many leaders assume more data equals more insight but Richards disagrees. "The biggest misconception is that the more data they collect, the better the analysis is going to be." She described a client who had "all this wonderful data, but the information is incomplete. There's information that's missing. It doesn't correlate to exactly what we want to do." The result was a dashboard that looked impressive but lacked meaning. "You've got to build out that framework. The tool isn't going to magically produce something insightful. Humans still have to specify how you want that information to look."

To turn raw data into meaningful action, Richards encourages leaders to lead with inquiry. "You look at a number or some reports and I go, so what? What does this mean for us?" Whether reviewing course completions or onboarding outcomes, she insists data cannot just stop at customer surveys, it has to make an impact. Dashboards, she advises, should only come after goals are clear. "You've got to show how data relates to not just learning goals, but business goals." As she put it, "The number one way you can get people to give you what you want is to show them the 'what's in it for me."

Richards clearly articulates that data doesn't create change, people do. She has seen survey results mislead when participants "just want to get this done" and don't pay attention to what they enter. The key, she explained, is to "translate that into human stories, not just the numbers." Whether it's system logs, completion rates, or feedback forms, she insists leaders ask, "how does this impact people and their workflow?" Her tip is to use surveys and dashboards, but also to shadow the process, listen deeply, and put stories at the center of analysis.

For leaders ready to build better habits with data, her advice is simple: "Make sure you've got good clean data and that you're collecting relevant data." She has seen too many teams get "all wrapped up in the content" and wait until the end to ask what success looks like. "Think about data first. What's the information you need to make this successful?" And her reminder is timeless. "Just because something is working 'kind of' doesn't mean we should be keeping it." For Richards, data isn't about chasing metrics, it's about making smarter, more human decisions.

STRATEGY IN A SKETCH

This reflective inquiry model helps leaders turn raw data into decisions that matter. It breaks a finding into three steps: naming the evidence, interpreting its significance, and choosing the next step. While many teams rush from charts to solutions, this framework forces a pause so meaning doesn't get lost. It is especially powerful when data sparks confusion, defensiveness, or urgency. Instead of leaping to fixes, leaders guide the conversation with three questions regarding what's happening, why it matters, and how to respond.

What – So What – Now What

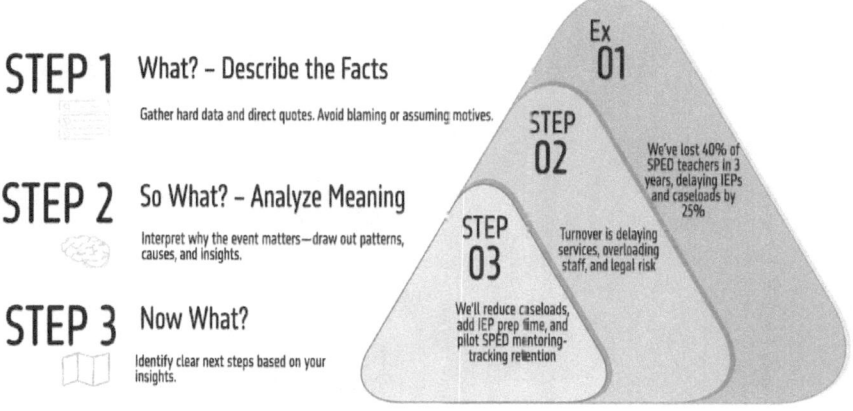

STEP 1   What? - Describe the Facts

Gather hard data and direct quotes. Avoid blaming or assuming motives.

STEP 2   So What? - Analyze Meaning

Interpret why the event matters—draw out patterns, causes, and insights.

STEP 3   Now What?

Identify clear next steps based on your insights.

Ex 01

STEP 02

We've lost 40% of SPED teachers in 3 years, delaying IEPs and caseloads by 25%

STEP 03

Turnover is delaying services, overloading staff, and legal risk

We'll reduce caseloads, add IEP prep time, and pilot SPED mentoring-tracking retention

Based on Borton's reflective model (1970), later applied in professional practice by Driscoll.

MAKE IT YOURS

- What is the core question I am trying to answer with data?

- Which structure would be best to use to organize the information I collect?

- When insight is gained, how will I embed it into the workflow and promote future action?

About the authors

Reda Othman

Reda's journey into leadership began in the classroom. As a math teacher, he was known for being "data-obsessed," proudly sharing his students' SAT growth at the end of each year. The numbers told a story of progress, but something was missing. He wanted to understand not just what students achieved, but why they learned, led, and behaved the way they did.

That curiosity led him to pursue a doctorate in leadership education. Just before classes began, an unexpected email landed in his inbox asking him to complete a personality assessment. Wanting to clear it from his to-do list, he clicked the link without much thought. Seventeen pages later, he was stunned. The report didn't just outline traits; it described him with a clarity he didn't have words for. "It named parts of me I couldn't name myself," he recalls. That assessment - the Myers-Briggs Type Indicator® (MBTI) - was the turning point.

The experience ignited a mission. Othman didn't stop at reading his own results. Determined to give others the same clarity he had found, he earned MBTI certification, advanced to become one of only three MBTI Master Practitioners in Connecticut, and went on to achieve the CPTD® (Certified Professional in Talent Development) designation.

Today, Dr. Othman is a performance strategist who blends psychological insights with talent development tools. His work begins with a deep needs analysis and builds toward strategic solutions that improve communication, collaboration, leadership, and organizational performance. He has partnered with Chicago Public Schools, the Massachusetts Department of Early Education and Care, and Holyoke Community College. He also hosts Othman's Leadership Podcast, where he interviews leaders from across industries to uncover practical lessons on growth, performance, and thriving at work.

At the core of all his work is a simple belief: when people understand themselves and others, they perform better, lead better, and achieve more.

Suzanne Shippee

Suzanne's dynamic professional career spans corporate leadership, education, and program development. With a foundation in business and a passion for education, Suzanne brings a unique blend of strategic thinking, operational excellence, and people-centered leadership.

She began her career in the corporate sector as a Regional Sales Manager for an international insurance company, where she led the sale of high-value computer systems. Her ability to connect strategy with execution was further demonstrated when she served as Program Manager for a groundbreaking initiative that integrated ideas from over 8,000 employees, resulting in organizational savings of more than $10 million.

Suzanne has also served as Recruiting, Selection, and Training Manager for new insurance agents, managing millions in premium dollars and overseeing a seven figure sales budget. She is the author of comprehensive recruiting and selection manuals, as well as a hiring workbook and procedural guide.

Her expertise extends to the academic world as well. Suzanne has been an adjunct professor in both business and teacher education, and an instructor for the preparation of professionals for industry certification. Her background in career guidance includes formal vocational and interest assessments to support individuals navigating career transitions.

In education, Suzanne has led at multiple levels - directing clinical experience programs for university students, hiring and managing supervisors, and training educational assistants. She has been instrumental in coordinating and implementing local, state, and federal mandates, and has served as coordinator and central office instructor for an international educational exchange organization.

Her work in character education and intercultural training reflects a lifelong commitment to values-based learning. As a research manager for a major university, Suzanne developed and delivered professional development workshops that strengthened instructional practice and deepened educational impact.

Suzanne holds two master's degrees: one in Education and another in Teaching English to Speakers of Other Languages (TESOL), which reflect both her deep content knowledge and her ongoing dedication to empowering learners and leaders across industries. While her professional journey has been rich and varied, Suzanne considers her most meaningful and rewarding role to have been raising her three remarkable children alongside her amazing husband, a role that now brings continued joy as she watches them all thrive and delights in the laughter and love of her grandchildren.

References

Abrahams, M. (2023). *Think faster, talk smarter: How to speak successfully when you're put on the spot.* Simon Element.

Achor, S., & Gielan, M. (2016, June 24). *Resilience is about how you recharge, not how you endure. Harvard Business Review.* https://hbr.org/2016/06/resilience-is-about-how-you-recharge-not-how-you-endure

Allen, J. R. (2024, May). *Sequencing instruction to reduce cognitive load. TD Magazine.*

Andersen, E. (2016, March). Learning to learn. *Harvard Business Review.* https://hbr.org/2016/03/learning-to-learn

Anderson, C. (2016). *TED Talks: The official TED guide to public speaking.* Houghton Mifflin Harcourt.

Ariker, M., Breuer, P., & McGuire, T. (2014, December). How to get the most from big data. *McKinsey Quarterly.* https://www.mckinsey.com/capabilities/quantumblack/our-insights/how-to-get-the-most-from-big-data

Association for Talent Development. (2017). *Microlearning: Delivering bite-sized knowledge.* ATD Research.

Association for Talent Development. (2018). *Needs assessments: Design and execution for success.* ATD Research.

Association for Talent Development. (2018). *Organizational performance improvement.* ATD Research.

Association for Talent Development. (2024). *Talent development body of knowledge (TDBoK™ guide)* (2nd ed.). ATD Press.

Association for Talent Development. (2025). *Knowledge management: A key function of the modern organization* [Research report]. ATD Research. https://www.td.org/product/research-report--knowledge-man agement-a-key-function-of-the-modern-organization/192503

Association for Talent Development. (n.d.). *Association for Talent Development* [Website]. https://www.td.org/

Bailey, R. (2010). *Coherence: How telling the truth will advance your cause (and save the world).* Function Press.

Bandura, A. (1977). Self-efficacy: Toward a unifying theory of behavioral change. *Psychological Review, 84*(2), 191–215. https: //doi.org/10.1037/0033-295X.84.2.191

Bandura, A. (1997). *Self-efficacy: The exercise of control.* W.H. Free-man.

Berger, W. (2014). *A more beautiful question: The power of inquiry to spark breakthrough ideas.* Bloomsbury.

Bisht, A., Ram, S., Giese, A., & Munawar, K. (2024, August 13). *Fueling growth through moments of customer delight.* McKinsey & Company. https://www.mckinsey.com/capabilities/growth-marketing-an d-sales/our-insights/fueling-growth-through-moments-of-cu stomer-delight

Bladt, J., & Filbin, B. (2013, March 27). *A data scientist's real job: Storytelling. Harvard Business Review.* https://hbr.org/2013/03/a -data-scientists-real-job-storytelling

Blanchard, K., & Johnson, S. (2015). *The new one minute manager.* William Morrow.

Bloom, B. S. (Ed.). (1956). *Taxonomy of educational objectives: The classification of educational goals. Handbook I: Cognitive domain.* David McKay.

Bock, L. (2015). *Work rules!: Insights from inside Google that will transform how you live and lead.* Twelve.

Borton, T. (1970). *Reach, touch, and teach: Student concerns and process education.* McGraw-Hill.

Brackett, M. A. (2019). *Permission to feel: Unlocking the power of emotions to help our kids, ourselves, and our society thrive.* Celadon Books.

Brett, J. M., Behfar, K. J., & Kern, M. (2006, November). Managing multicultural teams. *Harvard Business Review.* https://hbr.org/2006/11/managing-multicultural-teams

Brinkerhoff, R. O. (2003). *The success case method: Find out quickly what's working and what's not.* Berrett-Koehler

Brouk, T. (2018, November 7). To give a great presentation, distill your message to just 15 words. *Harvard Business Review.* https://hbr.org/2018/11/to-give-a-great-presentation-distill-your-message-to-just-15-words

Brown, B. (2012). *Daring greatly: How the courage to be vulnerable transforms the way we live, love, parent, and lead.* Avery.

Brown, B. (2021). *Atlas of the heart: Mapping meaningful connection and the language of human experience.* Random House.

Brown, T. (2009). *Change by design: How design thinking creates new alternatives for business and society.* Harper Business.

Bryk, A. S., Gomez, L. M., Grunow, A., & LeMahieu, P. G. (2015). *Learning to improve: How America's schools can get better at getting better.* Harvard Education Press.

Brynjolfsson, E., & McElheran, K. (2016). Data in action: Data-driven decision making in U.S. manufacturing. *Center for Economic Studies, U.S. Census Bureau.* https://www2.census.gov/ces/wp/2016/CES-WP-16-06.pdf

Buchdahl, H. (2024, April 19). *Author Talks:* William Ury on conflict negotiation. McKinsey & Company. https://www.mckinsey.com/featured-insights/mckinsey-on-books/author-talks-the-formula-for-successful-negotiation

Buckingham, M. (2007). *Go put your strengths to work: 6 powerful steps to achieve outstanding performance.* Free Press.

Burkeman, O. (2021). *Four thousand weeks: Time management for mortals*. Farrar, Straus and Giroux.

Buzan, T. (2018). *Mind map mastery: The complete guide to learning and using the most powerful thinking tool in the universe*. Watkins Publishing.

Byrne, R. (2006). *The secret*. Atria Books.

Carr, E. W., Reece, A., Rosen Kellerman, G., & Robichaux, A. (2019, December 16). The value of belonging at work. *Harvard Business Review*. https://hbr.org/2019/12/the-value-of-belonging-at-work

Center for Creative Leadership. (2017). *Feedback that works: How to build and deliver your message*. CCL Press.

Chamorro-Premuzic, T., & Ahmetoglu, G. (2024, August 6). A new approach to knowledge sharing within organizations. *Harvard Business Review*. https://hbr.org/2024/08/a-new-approach-to-knowledge-sharing-within-organizations

Chamorro-Premuzic, T. (2018, November 20). How to help your employees learn from each other. *Harvard Business Review*. https://hbr.org/2018/11/how-to-help-your-employees-learn-from-each-other

Champagne, M. V. (2014). *The survey playbook: How to create the perfect survey*. Embedded Assessments.

Champagne, M. V. (2025, August). *Keep your employees forever* [Conference presentation]. Training Magazine Network.

Chapman, G. D., & White, P. E. (2019). *The 5 languages of appreciation in the workplace: Empowering organizations by encouraging people*. Northfield Publishing.

Christensen, C. M., Allworth, J., & Dillon, K. (2012). *How will you measure your life?* HarperBusiness.

Clark, D. (2020, March 25). How to bounce back from rejection. *Harvard Business Review*. https://hbr.org/2020/03/how-to-bounce-back-from-rejection

Clear, J. (2018). *Atomic habits: An easy & proven way to build good habits & break bad ones*. Avery.

Clifton, J., & Harter, J. (2019). *It's the manager: Gallup finds the quality of managers and team leaders is the single biggest factor in your organization's long-term success.* Gallup Press.

Coleman, J. (2018). *Never lose a customer again: Turn any sale into lifelong loyalty in 100 days.* Portfolio.

Collins, J., & Porras, J. I. (1994). *Built to last: Successful habits of visionary companies.* Harper Business.

Collins, J. C., & Porras, J. I. (1996, September–October). Building your company's vision. *Harvard Business Review.* https://hbr.or g/1996/09/building-your-companys-vision

Community Tool Box. (n.d.). Chapter 8. Developing a strategic plan: Section 2. Proclaiming your dream: Developing vision and mission statements. University of Kansas. https://ctb.ku.edu/en/table-of-contents/structure/stra tegic-planning/vision-mission-statements/main

Coyle, D. (2018). *The culture code: The secrets of highly successful groups.* Bantam Books.

Croll, A., & Yoskovitz, B. (2013). *Lean analytics: Use data to build a better startup faster.* O'Reilly Media.

Cross, R., Dillon, K., & Greenberg, D. (2021, January 29). The secret to building resilience. *Harvard Business Review.* https: //hbr.org/2021/01/the-secret-to-building-resilience

Csikszentmihalyi, M. (1997). *Finding flow: The psychology of engagement with everyday life.* Basic Books.

Daniels, A. (2016). *Bringing out the best in people: How to apply the astonishing power of positive reinforcement* (3rd ed.). Mc-Graw-Hill Education.

Darling, M. J., Parry, C. S., & Moore, J. E. (2005). Learning in the thick of it. *Harvard Business Review, 83*(7/8), 84–92.

Davenport, T. H., Harris, J. G., & Shapiro, J. (2010, October). Competing on talent analytics. *Harvard Business Review.* http s://hbr.org/2010/10/competing-on-talent-analytics

David, S. (2016). *Emotional agility: Get unstuck, embrace change, and thrive in work and life*. Avery.

Deci, E. L., Olafsen, A. H., & Ryan, R. M. (2017). Self-determination theory in work organizations: The state of a science. *Annual Review of Organizational Psychology and Organizational Behavior, 4*(1), 19–43. https://doi.org/10.1146/annurev-orgpsych-032516-113108

Dewar, C., Keller, S., & Malhotra, V. (2022). *CEO excellence: The six mindsets that distinguish the best leaders from the rest*. Scribner.

Dib, A. (2016). *The 1-page marketing plan: Get new customers, make more money, and stand out from the crowd*. Successwise.

Doerr, J. (2018). *Measure what matters: How Google, Bono, and the Gates Foundation rock the world with OKRs*. Portfolio.

Drucker, P. F. (2008). *The five most important questions you will ever ask about your organization*. Jossey-Bass.

Duarte, N. (2012). *HBR Guide to Persuasive Presentations*. Harvard Business Review Press.

Duckworth, A. (2016). *Grit: The power of passion and perseverance*. Scribner.

Dundon, E. (2002). *The seeds of innovation: Cultivating the synergy that fosters new ideas*. AMACOM.

Dweck, C. S. (2006). *Mindset: The new psychology of success*. Random House.

Edmondson, A. (1999). Psychological safety and learning behavior in work teams. *Administrative Science Quarterly, 44*(2), 350–383. https://doi.org/10.2307/2666999

Edmondson, A. C., & Kerrissey, M. J. (2025, May–June). What people get wrong about psychological safety. *Harvard Business Review*. https://hbr.org/2025/05/what-people-get-wrong-about-psychological-safety

Edmondson, A. C., Jang, S., & Casciaro, T. (2019, May–June). Cross-silo leadership: How to create more value by connecting experts from inside and outside the organization. *Harvard Business Review*. https://hbr.org/2019/05/cross-silo-leadership

Edmondson, A. C. (2012). *Teaming: How organizations learn, innovate, and compete in the knowledge economy.* Jossey-Bass.

Edmondson, A. C. (2019). *The fearless organization: Creating psychological safety in the workplace for learning, innovation, and growth.* Wiley.

Enders, A., & de Haas, R. (2025, March 21). 5 techniques to build a more powerful speaking voice. *Harvard Business Review.* https://hbr.org/2025/03/5-techniques-to-build-a-more-powerful-speaking-voice

Ericsson, K. A., Charness, N., Feltovich, P. J., & Hoffman, R. R. (Eds.). (2006). *The Cambridge handbook of expertise and expert performance.* Cambridge University Press.

Ernst, C., & Yip, J. (2019, May–June). Cross-silo leadership. *Harvard Business Review.* https://hbr.org/2019/05/cross-silo-leadership

Eurich, T. (2017). *Insight: The surprising truth about how others see us, how we see ourselves, and why the answers matter more than we think.* Crown Business.

Ferrazzi, K., & Gohar, N. (2020). *Leading without authority: How the new power of co-elevation can break down silos, transform teams, and reinvent collaboration.* Currency.

Ferrazzi, K. (2020, November 17). Research: How virtual teams can better share knowledge. *Harvard Business Review.* https://hbr.org/2020/11/research-how-virtual-teams-can-better-share-knowledge

Flyvbjerg, B., & Gardner, D. (2023). *How big things get done: The surprising factors behind every successful project—from home renovations to space exploration.* Crown Currency.

Fogg, B. J. (2019). *Tiny habits: The small changes that change everything.* Harvest.

Fox Cabane, O. (2012). *The charisma myth: How anyone can master the art and science of personal magnetism.* Portfolio/Penguin.

Frei, F. X., & Morriss, A. (2023, October 10). 10 reasons why inclusion is a competitive advantage. *Harvard Business Re-*

view. https://hbr.org/2023/10/10-reasons-why-inclusion-is-a-c ompetitive-advantage

Friedman, S. D. (2009, May 8). The most compelling leadership vision. *Harvard Business Review.* https://hbr.org/2009/05/the-m ost-compelling-leadership

Gagné, M., Tian, A. W., Soo, C., Zhang, B., Ho, K. S. B., & Hosszu, K. (2019, July 19). Why employees don't share knowledge with each other. *Harvard Business Review.* https://hbr.org/2019/07/w hy-employees-dont-share-knowledge-with-each-other

Gagné, M., Tian, A. W., Soo, C., Zhang, B., Ho, K. S. B., & Hosszu, K. (2019). Different motivations for knowledge sharing and hiding: The role of motivating work design. *Journal of Organizational Behavior, 40*(7), 783–799. https://doi.org/10.1002/job.2364

Gallo, C. (2018, October 3). The art of the elevator pitch. *Harvard Business Review.* https://hbr.org/2018/10/the-art-of-the-elevato r-pitch

Gallo, C. (2020, January 6). What it takes to give a great presentation. *Harvard Business Review.* https://hbr.org/2020/01/what-i t-takes-to-give-a-great-presentation

Gallup. (2024). *State of the global workplace: 2024 report.* Gallup.

Garvin, D. A., Edmondson, A. C., & Gino, F. (2008, March). Is yours a learning organization? *Harvard Business Review.* https ://hbr.org/2008/03/is-yours-a-learning-organization

Gawande, A. (2009). *The checklist manifesto: How to get things right.* Metropolitan Books.

George, B., Sims, P., McLean, A. N., & Mayer, D. (2007, February). Discovering your authentic leadership. *Harvard Business Review.* https://hbr.org/2007/02/discovering-your-authentic-le adership

Gershman, S. (2019, September 23). To overcome your fear of public speaking, stop thinking about yourself. *Harvard Business Review.* https://hbr.org/2019/09/to-overcome-your-fear-of-pub lic-speaking-stop-thinking-about-yourself

Gibbons, S. (2018, December 9). Journey mapping 101. *Nielsen Norman Group*. https://www.nngroup.com/articles/journey-mapping-101/

Glaveski, S. (2019, October 2). Where companies go wrong with learning and development. *Harvard Business Review*. https://hbr.org/2019/10/where-companies-go-wrong-with-learning-and-development

Goleman, D. (1995). *Emotional intelligence: Why it can matter more than IQ*. Bantam Books.

Gollwitzer, P. M. (1999). Implementation intentions: Strong effects of simple plans. *American Psychologist, 54*(7), 493–503. https://doi.org/10.1037/0003-066X.54.7.493

Gottfredson, C., & Mosher, B. (2011). *The 5 moments of learning need*. Apply Synergies.

Gravois, J. (2007, January 19). You're not fooling anyone. *The Chronicle of Higher Education*. https://www.chronicle.com/article/youre-not-fooling-anyone

Greene, R. (2012). *Mastery*. Viking.

Hall, M. J. (2017, February 1). Mapping a journey to inform the future. *TD Magazine*. https://www.td.org/content/td-magazine/mapping-a-journey-to-inform-the-future

Hanson, R., & Mendius, R. (2009). *Buddha's brain: The practical neuroscience of happiness, love & wisdom*. New Harbinger Publications.

Hari, J. (2022). *Stolen focus: Why you can't pay attention—and how to think deeply again*. Crown.

Harvard Catalyst. (2024, March 12). Three rules to express your thoughts so that everyone will understand you. *Harvard Catalyst*. https://catalyst.harvard.edu/news/article/three-rules-to-express-your-thoughts-so-that-everyone-will-understand-you/

Hay, L. L. (1984). *You can heal your life*. Hay House.

Heath, C., & Heath, D. (2007). *Made to stick: Why some ideas survive and others die*. Random House.

Heath, C., & Heath, D. (2010). *Switch: How to change things when change is hard.* Crown Currency.

Hiatt, J. (2006). *ADKAR: A model for change in business, government, and our community.* Prosci Research.

Hibberd, J. (2019). *The imposter cure: How to stop feeling like a fraud and escape the mind-trap of imposter syndrome.* Aster.

Holiday, R. (2014). *The obstacle is the way: The timeless art of turning trials into triumph.* Portfolio.

Holiday, R. (2016). *Ego is the enemy.* Portfolio.

Holiday, R. (2022). *Discipline is destiny: The power of self-control.* Portfolio.

Horsley, K. (2014). *Unlimited memory: How to use advanced learning strategies to learn faster, remember more and be more productive.* TCK Publishing.

IDEO. (2012). *Design thinking for educators toolkit* (2nd ed.). IDEO. https://designthinkingforeducators.com/

International Coaching Federation. (2020). *ICF definition of coaching.* International Coaching Federation.

Kalbach, J. (2021). *Mapping experiences: A complete guide to customer alignment through journeys, blueprints, and diagrams* (2nd ed.). O'Reilly Media.

Kaplan, R. S., & Norton, D. P. (1996). *The balanced scorecard: Translating strategy into action.* Harvard Business Review Press.

Katzenbach, J. R., & Smith, D. K. (1993). The wisdom of teams: Creating the high-performance organization. Harvard Business School Press.

Kaufman, R., & Guerra-López, I. (2013). *Needs assessment for organizational success.* Association for Talent Development.

Kaufman, R. (2015, January 15). How does your needs assessment align to the bottom line? *ATD Blog.* Association for Talent Development.

Keller, G., & Papasan, J. (2013). *The one thing: The surprisingly simple truth behind extraordinary results.* Bard Press.

Khatib, D. (2025, April 18). *The case for storytelling: A tool for influence, engagement, and action.* ATD Blog. Association for Talent Development. https://www.td.org/content/atd-blog/the-case-for-storytelling-a-tool-for-influence-engagement-and-action

Kim, G., Debois, P., Willis, J., & Humble, J. (2016). *The DevOps handbook: How to create world-class agility, reliability, and security in technology organizations.* IT Revolution Press.

Kim, J., & Zitek, E. (2024, November 7). Research: Performance reviews that actually motivate employees. *Harvard Business Review.* https://hbr.org/2024/11/research-performance-reviews-that-actually-motivate-employees

Kim, W. C., & Mauborgne, R. (2003, January). *Fair process: Managing in the knowledge economy. Harvard Business Review.* https://hbr.org/2003/01/fair-process-managing-in-the-knowledge-economy

Kim, W. C., & Mauborgne, R. (2015). *Blue ocean strategy: How to create uncontested market space and make the competition irrelevant* (Expanded ed.). Harvard Business Review Press.

Kimsey-House, H., Kimsey-House, K., Sandahl, P., & Whitworth, L. (2018). *Co-active coaching: The proven framework for transformative conversations at work and in life* (4th ed.). Nicholas Brealey.

Kirkpatrick, D. L., & Kirkpatrick, J. D. (2006). *Evaluating training programs: The four levels* (3rd ed.). Berrett-Koehler.

Knapp, J., & Zeratsky, J. (2018). *Make time: How to focus on what matters every day.* Currency.

Knapp, J., Zeratsky, J., & Kowitz, B. (2016). *Sprint: How to solve big problems and test new ideas in just five days.* Simon & Schuster.

Kolb, D. A. (1984). *Experiential learning: Experience as the source of learning and development.* Prentice Hall.

Kotter, J. P., & Rathgeber, H. (2016). *Our iceberg is melting: Changing and succeeding under any conditions.* Penguin Random House.

Kouzes, J. M., & Posner, B. Z. (2016). *Learning leadership: The five fundamentals of becoming an exemplary leader.* Wiley.

Kouzes, J. M., & Posner, B. Z. (2017). *The leadership challenge: How to make extraordinary things happen in organizations*. Wiley.

Kozyrkov, C. (2018, December 4). What great data analysts do—and why every organization needs them. *Harvard Business Review*. https://hbr.org/2018/12/what-great-data-analysts-do-and -why-every-organization-needs-them

Kriss, P. (2014, August 1). The value of customer experience, quantified. *Harvard Business Review*. https://hbr.org/2014/08/the-value-o f-customer-experience-quantified

Kristensen, I., Liu, L., & Sherman, E. (2025, May). The CEO as chief resilience officer. *McKinsey Insights*. https://www.mckinsey.com/capabilities/strategy-and-corp orate-finance/our-insights/the-ceo-as-chief-resilience-officer

Langer, E. J. (2010). *Counterclockwise: Mindful health and the power of possibility*. Ballantine Books.

Langer, E. J. (2014). *Mindfulness*. Da Capo Lifelong Books.

Lee, T. H., & Duckworth, A. L. (2018, September–October). Organizational grit: Turning passion and perseverance into performance—the view from the health care industry. *Harvard Business Review*. https://hbr.org/2018/09/organizational-grit

Lembke, A. (2021). *Dopamine nation: Finding balance in the age of indulgence*. Dutton.

Lencioni, P. (2000). *The four obsessions of an extraordinary executive: A leadership fable*. Jossey-Bass.

Lencioni, P. (2014). *The five behaviors of a cohesive team*™ [Assessment program]. Wiley Workplace Learning Solutions.

Lencioni, P. (2016). *The ideal team player: How to recognize and cultivate the three essential virtues*. Jossey-Bass.

Lencioni, P. (2022). *The 6 types of working genius: A better way to understand your gifts, your frustrations, and your team*. Matt Holt Books.

Leonard, D., & Martin, J. (2019, December 9). How your organization's experts can share their knowledge. *Harvard Business Re-*

view. https://hbr.org/2019/12/how-your-organizations-experts -can-share-their-knowledge

Leonard, D., & Rayport, J. F. (1997, November–December). Spark innovation through empathic design. *Harvard Business Review.* https://hbr.org/1997/11/spark-innovation-through-empa thic-design

Lieberman, M. D. (2013). *Social: Why our brains are wired to connect.* Crown.

Liedtka, J., & Ogilvie, T. (2011). *Designing for growth: A design thinking tool kit for managers.* Columbia University Press.

Lipmanowicz, H., & McCandless, K. (2013). *The surprising power of liberating structures: Simple rules to unleash a culture of innovation.* Liberating Structures Press.

Lucidchart. (n.d.). How to create a customer journey map. *Lucidchart Blog.* https://lucidchart.com/blog/how-to-build-custome r-journey-maps

Manyika, J., Chui, M., Brown, B., Bughin, J., Dobbs, R., Roxburgh, C., & Hung Byers, A. (2011, October). Straight talk about big data. *McKinsey Insights.* https://www.mckinsey.com/capabiliti es/mckinsey-digital/our-insights/straight-talk-about-big-data

Markman, A. (2018, July 25). How to cure your dread of public speaking. *Harvard Business Review.* https://hbr.org/2018/07/ho w-to-cure-your-dread-of-public-speaking

Maurya, A. (2012). *Running lean: Iterate from plan A to a plan that works* (2nd ed.). O'Reilly Media.

Maxwell, J. C. (2022). *The 21 irrefutable laws of leadership: Follow them and people will follow you* (Rev. & updated ed.; S. R. Covey, Foreword). HarperCollins Leadership.

McChesney, C., Covey, S., & Huling, J. (2022). *The 4 disciplines of execution: Revised and updated: Achieving your wildly important goals.* Simon & Schuster.

McGonigal, K. (2012). *The willpower instinct: How self-control works, why it matters, and what you can do to get more of it.* Avery.

McGonigal, K. (2015). *The upside of stress: Why stress is good for you, and how to get good at it.* Avery.

McGuire, T., Ariker, M., & Roggendorf, M. (2013, March). Making data analytics work: Three key challenges. *McKinsey Insights.* https://www.mckinsey.com/capabilities/quantumblack/our-insights/making-data-analytics-work-three-key-challenges

McKeown, G. (2021). *Effortless: Make it easier to do what matters most.* Crown Currency.

McKinsey & Company. (2021). *The next normal in customer experience.* McKinsey & Company.

Meadows, D. H. (2008). *Thinking in systems: A primer* (D. Wright, Ed.). Chelsea Green Publishing.

Merchant, N. (2011, February 28). The right way to get your ideas heard. *Harvard Business Review.* https://hbr.org/2011/02/the-right-way-to-get-your-ideas-heard

Merrill, M. D. (2002). First principles of instruction. *Educational Technology Research and Development, 50*(3), 43–59. https://doi.org/10.1007/BF02505024

Meyer, E. (2014). *The culture map: Breaking through the invisible boundaries of global business.* PublicAffairs.

Miller, D. (2017). *Building a StoryBrand: Clarify your message so customers will listen.* HarperCollins Leadership.

Minto, B. (2009). *The pyramid principle: Logic in writing and thinking* (3rd ed.). Pearson Education Limited.

Moore, D. A. (2020). *Perfectly confident: How to calibrate your decisions wisely.* Harper Business.

Mortensen, M., & Gardner, H. K. (2017, September–October). The overcommitted organization. *Harvard Business Review.* https://hbr.org/2017/09/the-overcommitted-organization

Muragishi, G., Aguilar, L., Carr, P., & Walton, G. (2024, December 24). The power of small acts of inclusion. *Harvard Business Review.* https://hbr.org/2024/12/the-power-of-small-acts-of-inclusion

Murphy, K. (2020). *You're not listening: What you're missing and why it matters.* Celadon Books.

Nawaz, S. (2018, October 17). How to blow a presentation to the C-suite. *Harvard Business Review.* https://hbr.org/2018/10/how-to-blow-a-presentation-to-the-c-suite

Nestor, J. (2020). *Breath: The new science of a lost art.* Riverhead Books.

Nonaka, I. (2007, July–August). The knowledge-creating company. *Harvard Business Review.* https://hbr.org/2007/07/the-knowledge-creating-company

Nussbaumer Knaflic, C. (2015). *Storytelling with data: A data visualization guide for business professionals.* Wiley.

O'Donoghue, J. (n.d.). How to define in design thinking. *Make Iterate.* https://makeiterate.com/how-to-define-in-design-thinking/

Pasricha, N. (2016). *The happiness equation: Want nothing + do anything = have everything.* G. P. Putnam's Sons.

Pasricha, N. (2019). *You are awesome: How to navigate change, wrestle with failure, and live an intentional life.* Gallery Books

Patterson, K., Grenny, J., McMillan, R., & Switzler, A. (2002). *Crucial conversations: Tools for talking when stakes are high* . McGraw-Hill.

Patterson, K., Grenny, J., McMillan, R., & Switzler, A. (2004). *Crucial confrontations: Tools for resolving broken promises, violated expectations, and bad behavior.* McGraw-Hill.

Praslova, L. N. (2025, February 24). The false dichotomy of merit and inclusion. *Harvard Business Review.* https://hbr.org/2025/02/the-false-dichotomy-of-merit-and-inclusion

Prilepok, M. (2018, September). *Managing conflict effectively in negotiations.* McKinsey & Company. https://www.mckinsey.com/capabilities/operations/our-insights/managing-conflict-effectively-in-negotiations

Product Mindset. (2023, August 20). McKinsey's pyramid framework for storytelling. *Substack.* https://productmindset.substack.com/p/2836-mckinseys-pyramid-framework

Project Management Institute. (2017). *A guide to the project management body of knowledge (PMBOK® guide)*. Project Management Institute.

Rasiel, E. M., & Friga, P. N. (2001). *The McKinsey mind: Understanding and implementing the problem-solving tools and management techniques of the world's top strategic consulting firm*. McGraw-Hill.

Riegel, D. G. (2022, December 9). The best public speakers put the audience first. *Harvard Business Review*. https://hbr.org/2022/12/the-best-public-speakers-put-the-audience-first

Ries, A., & Trout, J. (1993). *The 22 immutable laws of marketing: Violate them at your own risk!*. HarperBusiness.

Ries, E. (2011). *The lean startup: How today's entrepreneurs use continuous innovation to create radically successful businesses*. Crown Business.

Roberts, L. M. (2023, September 14). Where does DEI go from here? *Harvard Business Review*. https://hbr.org/2023/09/where-does-dei-go-from-here

Rock, D., & Grant, H. (2016, November 4). Why diverse teams are smarter. *Harvard Business Review*. https://hbr.org/2016/11/why-diverse-teams-are-smarter

Rohn, J. (1996). *7 strategies for wealth & happiness: Power ideas from America's foremost business philosopher*. Harmony.

Rosenberg, M. B. (2015). *Nonviolent communication: A language of life*. PuddleDancer Press.

Roy, D. (2022, January 13). *The data-driven future of storytelling: MIT's Deb Roy on the message and the medium*. McKinsey & Company. https://www.mckinsey.com/industries/technology-media-and-telecommunications/our-insights/the-data-driven-future-of-storytelling-mits-deb-roy-on-the-message-and-the-medium

Rozovsky, J. (2015, November 17). *The five keys to a successful Google team*. re:Work with Google.

Rumelt, R. (2011). *Good strategy, bad strategy: The difference and why it matters*. Crown Currency.

Sandosham, E. (2024, March 3). What exactly is data storytelling? *Medium.* https://eric-sandosham.medium.com/what-exactly-is-data-storytelling-dc094e61f016

Sargut, G., & McGrath, R. (2011, September). Learning to live with complexity. *Harvard Business Review.* https://hbr.org/2011/09/learning-to-live-with-complexity

Schmidt, E., Rosenberg, J., & Eagle, A. (2019). *Trillion dollar coach: The leadership playbook of Silicon Valley's Bill Campbell.* Harper Business.

Schön, D. A. (1983). *The reflective practitioner: How professionals think in action.* Basic Books.

Schwartz, T., Gomes, J., & McCarthy, C. (2010). *The way we're working isn't working: The four forgotten needs that energize great performance.* Free Press.

Seligman, M. E. P. (2011). *Flourish: A visionary new understanding of happiness and well-being.* Free Press.

Senge, P. M., Kleiner, A., Roberts, C., Ross, R. B., & Smith, B. J. (1994). *The fifth discipline fieldbook: Strategies and tools for building a learning organization.* Doubleday/Currency.

Senge, P. M. (1990). *The fifth discipline: The art and practice of the learning organization.* Doubleday/Currency.

Senge, P. M. (1994). *The fifth discipline fieldbook: Strategies and tools for building a learning organization.* Crown Currency.

Senge, P. M. (2006). *The fifth discipline: The art & practice of the learning organization* (Rev. ed.). Doubleday.

Shank, P. (2015). *Write and organize for deeper learning.* Learning Peaks.

Shapira, A., & Horsager, D. (2022). To win over an audience, focus on building trust. *Harvard Business Review.* https://hbr.org/2022/03/to-win-over-an-audience-focus-on-building-trust

Shapira, A. (2015, June 30). Breathing is the key to persuasive public speaking. *Harvard Business Review.* https://hbr.org/2015/06/breathing-is-the-key-to-persuasive-public-speaking

Shapira, A. (2022). *Speak with impact: How to command the room and influence others.* AMACOM.

Siang, T. Y., & Dam, R. F. (n.d.). 7 simple ways to get better results from ethnographic research. *Interaction Design Foundation.* Retrieved September 9, 2025, from https://www.interaction-design.org/literature/article/7-simple-ways-to-get-better-results-from-ethnographic-research

Sinek, S. (2009). *Start with why: How great leaders inspire everyone to take action.* Portfolio.

Sinek, S. (2014). *Leaders eat last: Why some teams pull together and others don't.* Portfolio.

Six Seconds. (n.d.). *Six Seconds: The emotional intelligence network.* https://www.6seconds.org/

Smart, G., & Street, R. (2008). *Who: The A method for hiring.* Ballantine Books.

Stanier, M. B. (2016). *The coaching habit: Say less, ask more & change the way you lead forever.* Box of Crayons Press.

Stengel, J., Lamberton, C., & Favaro, K. (2023, May–June). How brand building and performance marketing can work together. *Harvard Business Review.* https://hbr.org/2023/05/how-brand-building-and-performance-marketing-can-work-together

Stone, D., & Heen, S. (2014, January). Find the coaching in criticism. *Harvard Business Review.* https://hbr.org/2014/01/find-the-coaching-in-criticism

Stone, D., & Heen, S. (2014). *Thanks for the feedback: The science and art of receiving feedback well.* Viking.

Stone, D., Patton, B., & Heen, S. (2010). *Difficult conversations: How to discuss what matters most* (2nd ed.). Penguin Books.

Suby, S. (2019). *Sell like crazy: How to get as many clients, customers and sales as you can possibly handle.* Sabri Suby.

Sullivan, D., & Hardy, B. (2020). *Who not how: The formula to achieve bigger goals through accelerating teamwork.* Hay House.

Sullivan, D. (2018). *Extraordinary impact filter.* Strategic Coach.

Sutherland, J., & Sutherland, J. J. (2014). *Scrum: The art of doing twice the work in half the time.* Crown Currency.

Sweller, J., Ayres, P., & Kalyuga, S. (2011). *Cognitive load theory.* Springer

Syed, M. (2015). *Black box thinking: The surprising truth about success.* Portfolio.

Takai, J., Hartenberger, L., Ichilcik, P., & Murphy, T. (2024, October 23). Invest in the art of storytelling to raise your return on inspiration. *McKinsey Insights.*

Tan, C. M. (2014). *Search inside yourself: The unexpected path to achieving success, happiness (and world peace).* HarperOne.

The Arbinger Institute. (2015). *The anatomy of peace: Resolving the heart of conflict* (2nd ed.). Berrett-Koehler Publishers.

The Arbinger Institute. (2016). *The outward mindset: Seeing beyond ourselves.* Berrett-Koehler Publishers.

The Myers-Briggs Company. (n.d.). *MBTI® basics.* The Myers-Briggs Company. https://www.myersbriggs.org/my-mbti-personality-type/mbti-basics/

Tipton, S. (2023, December 1). Create drip feeds to revolutionize learning retention. *TD Magazine.* https://www.td.org/content/td-magazine/create-drip-feeds-to-revolutionize-learning-retention

Tolle, E. (1999). *The power of now: A guide to spiritual enlightenment.* New World Library.

Tracy, B. (2011). *No excuses!: The power of self-discipline.* Vanguard Press.

Travis, D. J., & Nielsen, T. C. (2016, December 12). Culture fit is a myth. *Harvard Business Review.* https://hbr.org/2016/12/culture-fit-is-a-myth

Tuckman, B. W., & Jensen, M. A. C. (1977). Stages of small-group development revisited. *Group & Organization Studies, 2*(4), 419–427. https://doi.org/10.1177/105960117700200404

van den Driest, F., Sthanunathan, S., & Weed, K. (2016, September). Building an insights engine: How Unilever got to know its customers. *Harvard Business Review.* https://hbr.org/2016/09/build ing-an-insights-engine

W.K. Kellogg Foundation. (2004). *Logic model development guide.* W.K. Kellogg Foundation.

Wardle, D. (2024, July 25). To make your pitches more engaging, appeal to multiple learning styles. *Harvard Business Review.* https://hbr.org/2024/07/to-make-your-pitches-more-eng aging-appeal-to-multiple-learning-styles

Watkins, M. D. (2013). *The first 90 days: Proven strategies for getting up to speed faster and smarter* (Updated and expanded ed.). Harvard Business Review Press.

Webb, C. (2020, January 24). How to nail the Q&A after your presentation. *Harvard Business Review.* https://hbr.org/2020/01 /how-to-nail-the-qa-after-your-presentation

Weiss, J., & Hughes, J. (2005, March). Want collaboration? Accept and actively manage conflict. *Harvard Business Review.* https://hbr.org/2005/03/want-collaboration-accept-an d-actively-manage-conflict

Williams, D. (2023). *The diligence fix: How striving for more revenue stresses your sales organization and what to do about it.* Function Press.

Willink, J., & Babin, L. (2017). *Extreme ownership: How U.S. Navy SEALs lead and win.* St. Martin's Press.

Willink, J., & Babin, L. (2018). *The dichotomy of leadership: Balancing the challenges of extreme ownership to lead and win.* St. Martin's Press.

Wiseman, L. (2017). *Multipliers: How the best leaders make everyone smarter* (Rev. & updated ed.). Harper Business.

Wiseman, L. (2021). *Impact players: How to take the lead, play bigger, and multiply your impact.* Harper Business.

Wodtke, C. (2016). *Radical focus: Achieving your most important goals with objectives and key results.* Boxes and Arrows.

Yerkes, R. M., & Dodson, J. D. (1908). The relation of strength of stimulus to rapidity of habit formation. *Journal of Comparative Neurology and Psychology, 18*(5), 459–482. https://doi.org/10.1002/cne.920180503

Zander, R. S., & Zander, B. (2000). *The art of possibility: Transforming professional and personal life.* Harvard Business School Press.

www.ingramcontent.com/pod-product-compliance
Lightning Source LLC
Chambersburg PA
CBHW020916140626
46545CB00015B/62